PEOPLE IN OUR LIVES

34 TRUE STORIES BY 34 AUTHORS

COMPILED BY HENRYK HOFFMANN

HIGHER GROUND
BOOKS & MEDIA

Higher Ground Books & Media
Springfield, OH 45504
www.highergroundbooksandmedia.com

ISBN (Paperback): 978-1-955368-91-9

Printed in the United States of America 2025

Cover photo by Betsy Jackson Hoffmann

The pieces "A Path to Spontaneity?" and "A Picasso Dream" were originally published as
Chapters 22 and 27, respectively, of the autobiographical book Chopin and Beyond: My
Extraordinary Life in Music and the Paranormal by Byron Janis (Hoboken, NJ: John Wiley &
Sons, Inc., 2010). Reprinted by permission from Turner Publishing Company LLC (December
2024).

PEOPLE IN OUR LIVES

34 TRUE STORIES BY 34 AUTHORS

COMPILED BY HENRYK HOFFMANN

For our children.

yours

and theirs …

Table of Contents

FOREWORD

or

Invitations Accepted

By Rebecca Benston, Publisher (Springfield, Ohio)

A while back, one of my wonderful authors, Henryk Hoffmann, reached out to ask if I would be interested in publishing his latest project—a book filled with heartfelt stories from a collection of authors called *People in Our Lives*. He submitted an awesome proposal and a very organized plan for structuring the manuscript, so I accepted, having worked with him on another book, *Ironies, Coincidences and Absurdities in My Ordinary Life on Both Sides of the Atlantic*.

Along with this proposal, he extended an invitation for me to add my own story to the mix. I told him I would think about whether or not I had anything valuable to contribute. I then set the project aside until it was time to prepare it for publication. Generally, I work on a couple of books each month in between working another full-time job to support myself and my daughter. These days, I don't get much time to write. Sadly, it's something I truly enjoy but my other obligations often prevent me to being able to sit down with my thoughts long enough to put anything significant on paper. But when God has a plan for us, hiding behind our "obligations" isn't an option.

As the time grew nearer for me to put together my submission for the project, some things happened. My ex-husband, a diabetic amputee who had recently started at-home dialysis, began to have more significant issues with his health. He had been placed on the waiting list for a kidney transplant, but while he was waiting, he had a stroke which sent him back to the hospital for what we thought might be an extended stay with some significant recovery time attached. Of course, we prayed for him and managed to go see him one time (he had gone to a hospital in Columbus a little over an hour away) before things took an even worse turn and before we could make it to the hospital again, he ended up passing away.

He was only 57 years old and our hope had been that he would make at least a partial recovery, however, it was not to be. And so, the man I'd known for over 25 years, the father of my daughter, the only person I'd ever trusted enough to marry and share my life with was gone. And though we had been divorced for over fifteen years, I felt pain like I'd never felt…and I've unfortunately experienced a great deal of it in my 53 years. Thoughts of all of the things we went through together and all of the things that eventually broke us flooded in and I was overwhelmed by grief to which I wasn't sure I was still entitled. Coupled with watching my daughter struggle through the pain of losing her father much too soon, the ensuing days proved to be quite challenging.

The idea that it is in fact, the people in our lives who make it worth living is probably the most profound realization one can reach as they make their journey here on Earth. I can't help but think that this book reached me at a time when God knew I needed to say a few things. And, as always, He knows best. So, here's what I want to say. When someone comes into my life, I am always interested in learning how their presence will impact me. Not selfishly, but out of curiosity. I love to study people and the way they treat each other. How we can learn and heal and grow from our time with one another. Robert was someone whom I loved deeply throughout the time we were together. He gave me the most precious gift I've ever received—our daughter, Mya. Had it not been for him, I wouldn't have been able to experience the life I was meant to live as a mother. For that, I will be forever grateful to him. No matter what negative things we might have gone through, or what problems we may have encountered, I always wanted the best for him. The idea that he isn't here is so difficult for me to accept, but at the same time, I understand it. If his absence now means that his pain has finally subsided, then I'll gladly take on some of that pain in exchange for his relief. He was still very much in our lives after the divorce, and now, is still very much in our hearts.

Had I not met and married Robert when I did, I also might never have followed the path that led me to meet Henryk through our work together on these books. We never know what our impact on someone else will be, but I'm happy that I chose to walk the path that led me here. Thank you for including me in this wonderful project.

Introduction

Dum inter homines sumus, colamus humanitatem.
"As long as we are among humans, let us be humane."
— L. Annaeus Seneca, *Moral Essays*: Volume 1

Esse quam videri.
"To be rather than to seem."
— Marcus Tullius Cicero, *De Amicitia* ("About Friendship")
(the state motto of North Carolina)

I have been admiring Paul Auster's books (e.g., *The New York Trilogy*, *The Music of Chance*, *Sunset Park*) and films (*The Music of Chance*, *Smoke*, *Lulu on the Bridge*) for quite a while now, but it was his novel *The Brooklyn Follies* (2006) that made me include him among my few true favorite authors. I was captivated by the book's enormously perceptive narrator/protagonist (Nathan Glass), a former life insurance salesman, now divorced and diagnosed with cancer, who not only addresses his weaknesses and mistakes of the past, but also looks forward to his relatively short remaining life and does his best to accomplish the ultimate peace of mind. He survives a heart attack towards the end of the book and, afterwards, has some great new ideas that make him happy despite the tragic events that take place on the last day of the tale, September 11, 2001. The book itself is an impressive collection of colorful characters—Nathan's daughter (Rachel), nephew (Tom Wood), niece (Rory) and her daughter (Lucy), and people in their lives (especially ex-convict Harry Brightman, now a used bookstore owner)—all experiencing rich, if occasionally unusual, relations and associations, leading to completely unpredictable events and dramatic plot resolutions.

When in hospital, talking to other seriously sick patients and not hoping to live much longer, Nathan Glass is hit with a realization of how anonymous people really are and how their identity is entirely erased after death except in the minds of those few that have known them and are still alive. It is then that he comes up with the idea of giving ordinary people a chance to become immortal by charitably publishing their biographies. While his idea may appear somewhat farfetched in terms of feasibility, a similar but less ambitious plan—consisting in providing various people a chance to share their most indelible experiences and give credit to those that made a difference in their lives—may not be that hard to execute.

For the last four decades or so, I have been reading books of different genres and by a rich variety of authors, learning a great deal about life and the world and getting a lot of intellectual and emotional satisfaction, but, in many cases, my major goal was to find evidence of the fame of people that were already famous. The message found in the final pages of *The Brooklyn Follies* inspired me to rethink the subject-matter of my writing and, as a result, infer that there are a lot of people in my own life and my wife Betsy's— immediate family, distant relatives, old and new friends, former coworkers, associates and students, neighbors and acquaintances— that, because of their captivating personalities, remarkable talents (frequently not realized by themselves and/or others) and astonishing lives, deserve recognition and fame as much as the celebrities I have written about in my reference books.

In my memoir, titled *Ironies, Coincidences and Absurdities in My Ordinary Life on Both Sides of the Atlantic* (2019), I do write quite extensively about people dear and important to me, but, because the book is focused primarily on anecdotes of a specific type and flavor, not everyone receives the attention and recognition he/she deserves. Consequently, now, five years later, to make up for it, I am giving a chance to others to speak for and about themselves, to voice their own ideas and share their own significant, memorable and precious experiences, preferably with some universal, philosophical and/or inspirational dimensions (if possible, including an ingenious message or a great punchline) and featuring people precious in their eyes for one reason or another.

Thus, the offer has been opened to anyone in our circles willing and ready to contribute a true and ingenious story or a poem of any size. The other guidelines, which should ensure that the general outcome is positive, constructive, uplifting and fairly intellectual, are the following: no politics, no offensive content, no romance (unless as a secondary theme) and no self-promotion. Humor is welcome and nonviolent crime admissible as long as it is followed by redemption and a good lesson learned. The stories should be nothing like romance novels or Hallmark movies; instead, they should strive to resemble mainstream fiction similar to that of Auster's—e.g., by such authors as Ernest Hemingway, John Steinbeck, Sinclair Lewis, Pearl S. Buck, Carson McCullers, Flannery O'Connor, James Jones,

Irwin Shaw, John Updike, Philip Roth, Jerzy Kosinski, Don DeLillo, Larry McMurtry, John Irving, Pat Conroy, Oscar Hijuelos, Fannie Flagg, Anne Tyler, Jill McCorkle and Elizabeth Hay—or films by such directors as Charles Chaplin, Frank Capra, William Wyler, George Cukor, Billy Wilder, Howard Hawks, John Ford (even his westerns), Preston Sturges, Fred Zinnemann, Alfred Hitchcock (at least some of his works, yes!), Stanley Donen, Peter Bogdanovich, Woody Allen, Harold Ramis, the Coen Brothers and the like—just to mention examples from the Western Hemisphere.

It is rather unlikely that the final product will turn out to be a bestseller, but it does not really matter as the premise/prime goal is not to make anyone rich, but to give some people, special in Betsy's and my lives, a dose of excitement, an opportunity to express themselves and an option to honor people they love and/or admire. Besides, the royalties, if any, would go to charity to emphasize the honorable and selfless motivation of all the participants in the project.

According to the self-imposed rule for this publication, I am not supposed to contribute my own story. And I will not. However, I cannot resist the temptation of summarizing here an enormously moving story included in another novel by Paul Auster (after all, the inspiration behind this project), *Oracle Night* (2003). It is a rather unusual book where the reader is told several stories within a couple of other stories told by the narrator/protagonist, a professional novelist and screenwriter named Sidney Orr. The novel he is currently writing (which never gets to be finished for reasons explained later in the book) is inspired by the Flitcraft episode in Dashiell Hammett's *The Maltese Falcon*, a parable shared by Sam Spade with Brigid O'Shaugnessy about a man successful in every respect who suddenly disappears from his current life and starts another as a result of almost losing his life by a beam falling from a construction site. A similar character in the novel being written by Orr, Nick Bowen, leaves New York and his wife after miraculously avoiding death by means of a head of a gargoyle breaking loose and falling down on the street within inches of his head. The most captivating of the stories is told by a man Nick meets in Kansas City, Ed Johnson (also known as Victory), a retired cab driver whose experience in World War II makes it impossible for him to forget what he saw in Dachau. Ed spent two months in the concentration camp as a cook, feeding the malnourished survivors. One of them was a strangely acting woman who did not ask for any food for herself but begged him to give some milk to her baby. After Ed realized that the baby, almost a skeleton, was dead, he poured some milk onto the dead baby's lips anyway, and then watched the woman as she staggered along for several feet and fell down dead. About ten pages later, Nick, the narrator of the novel within the novel, explains in the notes that even though Ed is a fictitious character, the Dachau story is true and was borrowed by him from another book, *The Lid Lifts* by Patrick Gordon-Walker (London, 1945), and recently retold in another nonfiction book.

Ed is also the creator of The Bureau of Historical Preservation, which is a house of memory filled with thousands of telephone books from all over the world and from different periods. Interesting especially to the Polish readers may be the fact that the only telephone book mentioned several times and in different places of the book and even shown in the only illustration of Auster's novel is the Warsaw phone directory from 1937/38, *Spis Abonentów Warszawskiej Sieci Telefonów Polskiej Akcyjnej Spółki Telefonicznej*. Again, the origin of the book and its photo is explained in the notes by narrator Nick, who has received it as a gift from a journalist friend visiting Poland in 1981 to cover the Solidarity movement. The reason behind the gift was the fact (familiar to the friend) that Nick's parental grandparents were born in Warsaw, and their name, listed in the book more than once, was Orłowski (hence the abbreviated version 'Orr').

A brief anecdote that I decided to include in the Introduction at the last minute is a dream I had during the time I was collecting the stories for the book, possibly geared by talking to various people and translating (from Polish) tales created by non-English speakers. It is about my Aunt Sabina, who (at the age of ninety-one) died two years ago, several months after Betsy and I saw her during one of our annual visits to Poland. Sabina was never in America, but in my dream she was sitting in on my Latin class while I was teaching my students about the Roman calendar, explaining the usage of the special names, such as the Kalends, the Nones and the Ides (each, despite its plural form, referring to one specific day in a month). It was not accidental that my aunt was a part of such a dream because I remember often thinking about her when reading with my students the legendary story of how the Sabine women had been abducted by the men of Rome. The dream also reminded me of the coincidence related to the Roman calendar and two of my own special days: my birthday, falling on the Nones, and my nameday (a day that celebrates one's given name usually related to a saint or biblical figure), falling on the Ides, which, additionally, was possible only because the month I was born in is one of the four months when those two special days fall two days later than in the other eight (depending on the moon phase), the Nones on the seventh (rather than the fifth) and the Ides on the fifteenth (rather than on the thirteenth). Maybe it is presumptuous, but I did find such a coincidence to be an omen of my destiny, since my career as a Latin teacher in the second part of my life was something absolutely unthinkable when I was young, something I never even dreamed about or imagined.

A significant asset of the collection is its diversity in several areas, such as the style, the theme, the degree of candidness, the philosophical message about life, the geographical location, the time setting, the focus and general approach to the idea and so on. Moreover, the stories have been written by people of different ages—ranging from teenagers to individuals in their eighties — different social and cultural backgrounds, different professions and different nationalities. Many of the authors belong to the same families, many have moved in the same circles, worked for the same institutions and/or attended the same schools. Consequently, having known each other for a shorter or longer period of time, some of the authors share the same experiences and some even refer to them in a similar or different way, definitely from a different angle. For that reason, the collection can be compared to Akira Kurosawa's brilliant film *Rashomon* (1950; starring Toshiro Mifune, Machiko Kyo and Takashi Shimura) or its somewhat less brilliant remake, *The Outrage* (1964; featuring Paul Newman, Laurence Harvey, Claire Bloom, Edward G. Robinson and William Shatner). With all this said, however, there is one thing that all the stories have in common: they are deeply personal and they are reported (rather than conceived) as a result of some deep and urgent needs to reveal something that has been stored in the author's mind for some time and has never been successfully communicated. The authors of the stories have finally received an opportunity to express themselves without any restrictions; they got a chance to carefully polish and embellish their tales with necessary (at least, in their opinion) details that they would be forced or encouraged to skip while verbally telling them to some impatient interlocutor, whether a close family member or a good friend.

Even though, according to the premise, the project has been open primarily to ordinary people, some of the participating authors, through their significant accomplishments in various fields, have—admittedly and inevitably—come to prominence in a more or less evident way and in smaller or bigger parts of the world, and there are at least two among them who are unquestionably worldwide famous. They are Byron Janis, a renowned classical concert pianist and composer, and his wife, Maria Cooper Janis, whose claim to fame is not as much being legendary actor Gary Cooper's daughter as her distinguished painting career and her active involvement in various major foundations. Having heard some of their stories and having read many of them in the book *Chopin and Beyond: My Extraordinary Life in Music and the Paranormal* (2010), officially authored by Byron but one of its chapters co-written with Maria, I decided to invite Maria to participate in the project (as Byron had passed away several months earlier), and she expressed her enthusiastic interest. Thus, with her authorization and blessing, I have obtained the publisher's permission to reprint two chapters of Byron's autobiographical book. Characterized by originality, depth, insightfulness and amazing facts, the two stories, I believe, add a great deal not only to the project's diversity, but also—by dealing with human relations and matters on several levels—to its intended, or hoped-for, overall or collective message.

I am enormously grateful to all the authors for their participation in the project, as well as to those who have expressed their sincere interest but, for one reason or another, were not able to participate. I strongly believe that writing the stories by you all and reading them by some or many will have made a big difference in one way or another. Thank you!

HH

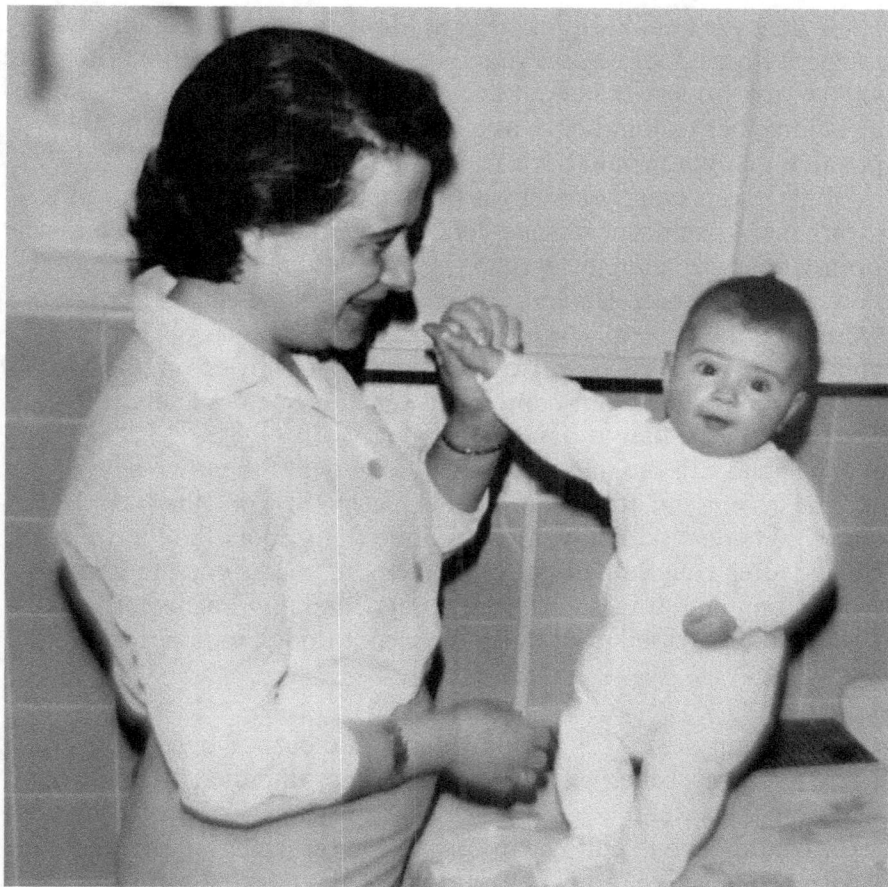

Whenever I Cook I Think of You:
To My Mom

by Martina Badur (Hanover, Germany)

Part 1:

Whenever I cook I think of you, Mom. Now that you are no longer with us, I know how much I have learned from you. There are still so many questions about different things that come to my mind, questions that I should have asked you because I am absolutely positive that you would have known the answers.

I try to represent you here as best as I can, even if I am quite aware that I can never replace you. You were born in a time that was briefly peaceful and gave you a carefree childhood. That happiness, however, was not to last long, because only a few years after you were born the Second World War broke out. It was probably luck, and it perhaps saved your life, that you had to move from the big city to the countryside. Your hometown was almost completely destroyed in the hail of bombs.

One can still see in our town hall a model of the town as it looked before and after the war. It is hard to imagine that people survived here. You know, Mom, I often think about the time when I looked after you. Sometimes I dream about you as you are lying in my nursing bed. It was not that long ago, and my dreams tell me that I have not processed everything we went through together.

Part 2:

It was July 23, 2023, the day that would change everything for us. You had a stroke, but the doctors did not find the clot until four days later. Too late!

I would have liked to have spared you the suffering, but the suffering also gave us a wonderful time. A very intense time, admittedly!

Did I think I would be able to wash my own mother and care of her like you did of me when I was a baby? No! But people do grow when they are forced to step up to the plate. It was always your wish to be able to live at home until the very last day of your life. All I could give back to you was to fulfill that wish. And that unusual opportunity brought us even closer. I started cooking your favorite meals for you; we talked so much; we spent a lot of time together.

I discovered some beautiful things from talking with you: you told me that I was your great love when you saw me for the first time. You were not a cuddly mummy, but you always tried to make me feel safe. You did nice things with me, you tried to make me strong and gave me the support and confidence I needed to pursue my goals. I particularly like to think back to the Advent season. Every evening during Advent, you lit the candles on the Advent wreath, we sang Christmas carols together and you read Christmas stories to me. I still have those two little books from which we sang and from which you read aloud. A great treasure for me!

Part 3:

You encouraged me to be strong, to stand up to injustice. When I stood up to my teacher, and, as a result, sought support from our principal, you were very proud of me, you clearly understood
the whole situation and was my biggest fan at that moment.

You encouraged me to be creative. As a result, even as a child, I came up with a brilliant idea of how to make money on my own by selling my homemade jewelry at flea markets and art bazaars.

You showed me how to cook creatively and healthily. How often did you tell me that you had woken up too early in the morning and then, being forced to think about something, came up with new recipes? Sometimes you got up at five a.m. and cooked.

And when you could not do anything on your own, you put all your trust in me. You told all your visitors how happy you were that I was looking after you.

Part 4:

But, as we very well know, nobody's perfect. You also made mistakes. When the time came that you needed me, it was no problem for me to be there for you. Because I knew one thing for sure: you would have done exactly the same for me. No parenting is all good, we all carry scars from our childhood and adolescence and can only try to do our best when we ourselves become parents.

The biggest scar you had carried with you was the death of your first child. Nothing has ever been able to heal that wound.

I will never forget that moment on December 28, 2024, when I was about to give you pills and you breathed your last. Mom, it meant so much to me to have been with you at that particular moment.

Your death came at a time when we both had no strength left. It was peaceful, nothing scary, nothing strange. It was the last step in your life and, just as you experienced my first breath, I was able to experience your last.

The time we have spent together, Mom, was the most intense time that a person can imagine.

THANK YOU for everything!

Four sisters out to play after the storm of 1949: Shirley, Linda, Marilyn and Joan.

Special Places in My Memory

by Shirley Bayer (Lititz, PA)

The Little House

It is just a tiny little house on the corner of what used to be Curtain Road. There's nothing fancy about its exterior. And inside, it is old and worn with cracks in the plaster and paint that shows the signs of age. But it was young once and in its youth it held the dreams of my father and my mother. I know the walls rang with childish laughter even though I can't say I have a conscious memory of once having lived here. Still I think it's a place where happy memories reside.

My older sister tells the story of the ice storm of '49. The power went out, leaving Mom and Dad with five young children in a cold house with limited options for food or fuel. She tells me that Dad hung a blanket over the doorway into the living room, and all seven of us slept that night with the heat of the fireplace keeping us warm.

The next day my aunt, who lived up the hill, brought over a huge Dutch oven filled with pot roast and vegetables. The sister who said grace that day was so thankful for the warm food that Dad had to cut her blessing short in order that we could all eat before the food got cold. When I look at the tiny dining room, it is hard to imagine a family of seven, plus aunt and uncle, sitting around a table there. But my sister says that is the way it happened and I have no cause to doubt her.

I found a picture the other day. It shows four young girls standing in a row, all dressed up in warm cloths, ready for play. The snow is deep and an outstretched hand reaches to catch the magic of a snowflake. It is a picture taken after the storm. There is another picture of girls dressed in summer clothes, sitting on the curved wall that separates the yard from the driveway. I am the youngest in the picture, and a sister on either side insures that I don't fall. They are happy pictures from happy times at the little house in Minnehaha.

It's a quiet place now, the ring of childish laughter long since gone. Family plans are to put the house up for sale. There is a certain sad resignation in selling the house my father helped to build. I'll miss the tiny corner cabinets where Mom's dishes stayed, and I'll miss the fireplace that kept us warm during the winter storm, and I'll miss the mullion windows that opened to catch the summer breezes. I know I can't stay here forever and there is no way to make time stand still. So, I must be content in having this time to say goodbye to the house that Dad built on the corner of Curtain Road.

(Written in the year 2000)

The Garden

In the quiet of this house, protected from the penetrating dampness of fall, I can recall in minute detail the wonders of my father's garden. From the first sprouting of the seeds to the last autumn leaf on the potato vines it was a wonder. Huge in size, it covered at least half an acre and included every popular vegetable known to the members of his family.

In my father's garden I learned to hop a row without leaving a trace. In my father's garden I could find the first ripe berry of spring. And in my father's garden I could hide under the grape vines and pretend they were my playhouse. If the day was hot and the garden freshly watered, I could escape the heat among the corn stalks, padding down the rows with bare feet. If I was hungry, I could pull up a kohlrabi, peel it on the spot, wash it from the hose and eat it then and there.

There are many lessons on life that I learned in my father's garden. Symmetry and perspective have an aesthetic value of their own. Weeds will always appear in fertile ground, tiny seedlings must be protected and the natural elements kept in harmonious balance. I learned to be honest, knowing that my father had a sixth sense regarding where I had been and what I had done in his garden. I learned that the beauty of a garden had a price when my own little section of flowers withered and went to weeds from my neglect. And I learned that Dad would always be there walking behind the tiller, responding with advice to my questions, chastising my short coming sand entreating me to watch where I was going lest I destroy something of value.

I'm not sure where it comes from, this need to grow things, but my father had it in abundance. And down the genetic line, across generations, spread over time, the need to tend growing things persists. Each of us starts out in life certain that we will never tie ourselves to the work and discipline of a garden and we all sooner or later find ourselves growing something. The enormous gardens of the past have all but disappeared now, and this makes me sad. For the young people growing up this seems like a loss. I can't help but wonder where they learn the lessons that I learned in my father's garden.

(Written in 2000)

Rivers and Boats

For the first sixteen or seventeen years of my existence it was just a ribbon of reflection in the distance. I could see it from a wide variety of vantage points around the town where I grew up. Then one day, a boy I was dating invited me to go out on the river … And thus began my love and fear relationship with the mighty Columbia.

In my memory, I can tap any number of references to rivers: movies I have seen, old Appalachian folk songs, popular melodies, favorite children's poems and, as you might expect, family history. My grandfather was, for a time, a tugboat captain. And when he moved the family west, he tended the buoy light near his home on the river.

My first experience actually being afloat on the water was this first water-skiing trip with my boyfriend. I'll admit that the excitement of the day had to work hard to overcome the thought that, for this non-swimmer, that river represented an enormous amount of water. For everyone else on the boat, these excursions had become routine. For me it was a whole new world.

With the help of the skis, I could fly across the surface of the water and feel the warm air "blow dry" the river from my skin. With the help of the ski belt, I learned to swim. In time I learned not to think about the amount of water beneath me.

In time I married that boyfriend and, when our first baby was just a toddler, we introduced her to a river. We were boat-less then, so it was a smaller river. Its waters were a glossy midnight green along the edge. In the center the waters laughed and tumbled in the sunlight. It was a happy river for a happy time and we swam and snorkeled and drifted our favorite length of it through many summer days.

The big river never stopped calling though, and soon, with a small pull and tug from our friends, we owned our own boat and back out to the big river we went. I think perhaps nothing in life can quite compare to the almost sensual feeling of a boat coming to rest in calm water.

(Written in 2001)

Triple Evidence for the Proverb "There Is Nothing Bad That Does Not Turn out for the Better," or "Every Cloud Has a Silver Lining"

by Izabela Biernacka (Poznań, Poland/Straubenhardt, Germany)

I was born and raised in Poznań, a city in Poland situated about 100 kilometers from the western border, but, when I was less than twenty years old, I emigrated to Germany. At first, I did not want to stay there at all; I went there to visit my parents (Barbara and Włodzimierz), who had managed to defect from our country in the 1980s, motivated by the political situation (Martial Law, etc.) that was not favorable to a happy and prosperous life. My visit, rather unexpectedly, turned into a permanent residence, which has been going on for quite a number of years. At first, I was delighted with everything I saw there, because, after leaving the gray and poor Polish reality at that time, everything encountered or experienced in Germany simply had to be delightful. It was not easy, however, to switch to life in a foreign country, even if there was prosperity there. I missed my relatives, my friends and the place where I had spent my childhood and young adulthood so badly that it took me about a year to stop suffering. By that time, I had also managed to overcome the language barrier, which was a significant factor in the process of adjustment.

Unfortunately, it was not possible to revisit Poland and spend some time there because the communist system would stop you from leaving the country again. There were no mobile phones to call via WhatsApp or Messenger, and reaching anyone in Poland by means of a phone line was almost a miracle. So after about a year I came to terms with life in Germany, and after another year and a half I felt at home there. It coincided with my moving to Stuttgart, where I could work officially, get a regular and satisfactory job and, with a guaranteed income, slowly arrange my life. It was there that I met my first husband, Andreas, with whom I have a son, Dennis. Unfortunately, married life overwhelmed the father of my child and, when Dennis was four years old, our paths diverged. I decided to take care of my own and my child's future by myself.

It was not that easy, especially at the beginning, but there is nothing difficult for those who want to do something and are determined to accomplish their goal. Running from one job to another (there were periods when I had four of them at the same time), I made sure that we did not lack anything. We lived in a three-room apartment, I had a car, and once a year we went on vacation, so our life, although not always easy, was happy. I have to point out here that I would not have been able to work several jobs if it was not for the help from my parents, who often took care of Dennis while I was working, for which, of course, I was always very grateful. For several years I was a busy but happy single mother, and I did not mind the lack of a partner. My dad used to say, "Iza, dress nicely and go to some café, because you won't meet anyone at home." I laughed and, in response, I said that I was not looking for anyone, and if there were someone destined for me somewhere, he would turn up by himself. And so it did happen. In 2003 I met my "other half." His name is Mariusz, and we have been happy with each other ever since that miraculous and unforgettable day.

My mother often says, "There is nothing bad that does not turn out for the better." Referring to the title of my story, here is the first piece of evidence for this saying because, if it was not for the divorce (which, admittedly and obviously, is a bad experience), I would never have met Mariusz, who happens to be the love of my life, and I would not exchange him for anyone and for any treasure. So, when fate connected me with Mariusz, my life changed completely. Of course, it had become happier and happier. First, we met each other, then Mariusz moved from Karlsruhe to my place in Stuttgart, and after three years we rented a house in Weingarten, near Karlsruhe, so that Mariusz would not have to commute so far to work.

We felt very comfortable in our new home in Weingarten, but we had always dreamed of having our own home, so after a while we started looking for a suitable house that we could buy. However, after many house viewings and after calculating the cost of the loan and the time to pay it off, we gave up the idea. Instead, we decided to continue living in a rented place and invest the money we had saved in buying an apartment in Poland, which we would rent out. Unfortunately, after we bought an apartment in Poland and returned home to Germany, the owner of the house we were renting from told us that we would have to move out soon because his daughter was starting a family and wanted to move in there. Needless to say, it was quite a blow.

We were forced to leave the place we were living at and we had no substantial funds at our disposal to resolve this urgent problem. Well, we had to start acting. I thought we would have to rent something again, but my husband said he did not want to rent anymore, so we started looking for a house for sale again. Eventually, we did find a place that suited us, got a loan and bought our dream house. And here is the second piece of evidence for my mother's favorite proverb that "there is nothing bad that would not work out for the better." For, if we had not received the unexpected notice regarding our lease agreement, we would probably never have decided to look for a house of our own.

After we signed the contract for the purchase of the house, we immediately started renovation work. For three weeks, from morning to evening, the so-called "demolition" took place. The house had to be completely emptied, everything knocked off from the walls, the floors and ceilings torn up, the doors and frames removed and thrown away, just like all the bathroom equipment, all the kitchen furniture and everything else. The house was old and the last renovation was carried out in the 1980s. After three weeks of such intensive renovation work, it turned out that, unfortunately, the electrical wires were in terrible condition, and, because the structure of the house was wooden, our newly purchased house caught fire. It was terrible! I was devastated and thought that it was impossible to save it. The damage was estimated at €96,000.00, and the fire brigade's rescue operation, the largest in recent times, was even described in the local newspaper. I was convinced that it would not be possible to renovate this house again. It was black everywhere, and the odor was so intense that it was nauseating. A huge hole, from the basement all the way to the second floor, was created in the spot where the beam in the wall caught fire. It was so large that an elevator could be built in there.

Mariusz, of course, approached everything more "soberly" and convinced me that everything would be fine. There was no way for me to imagine it, but, luckily, my husband (a gifted handyman) coped with the challenge, and ten months later we moved into a renovated house, which almost looked like brand new. Thus, here is the third piece of evidence for my mother's famous aphorism. If this fire had not occurred during the renovation, we would not have replaced the entire electrical installation and a fire would have happened at a later time, perhaps after our move. Who knows what the consequences of that fire would be then; I do not even want to think about it.

I am happy to add that over the next few years we renovated the house step by step from the outside, the roof, the solar panels, the façade, the terrace, etc. And last year my husband installed air conditioning in the house and built a swimming pool outside; so now the house is really what we dreamed of. We feel great and happy in it. So, at the end of my story, I encourage you, with all my heart, to believe that "there is nothing bad that does not eventually turn out to be good," or, as native English speakers would put it, "every cloud has a silver lining."

If anyone wonders what follows from this, I am ready to point out my own conclusion in the form of the following advice: Minor and major failures or misfortunes should never be treated as an excuse to give up one's plans or dreams. Just the opposite. Rather than discourage you, they should make you stronger and more determined to follow your original idea and, without complaining and blaming anyone or anything, find new ways to accomplish your goals in a calm and thoughtful manner, to make the impossible

possible. Your reward will be double. The outcome will turn out to be much better than you expected, and you will learn an amazing life lesson, becoming, as a result, a significantly smarter person, happier and more appreciated by your loved ones!

Translated from Polish by Henryk Hoffmann

Barbara with her husband, Włodek, and their grandson, Dennis.

Light at the End of the Tunnel, or Home(town), Sweet Home(town)

by Barbara Bilitz (Poznań, Poland/Stuttgart, Germany)

As with most people, the closest and dearest people in my life have been (in chronological order) my grandmother, my parents, my siblings, my husband and my children, and then my two aunts, Sabina (my mother's sister) and Franciszka (or Frania, on my father's side), and their children. Grandma Katarzyna (on my father's side), who lived with us for a short time and then (when she moved in with Frania) often visited us, died in 1965 (at the age of eighty) and is very fondly remembered by everyone as a tough person, but at the same time generous, funny and extremely helpful. Our parents, Stefania and Leonard – despite working hard to support a family of six – did not neglect either their children or their cultural needs (appreciating good books, music and films) and led quite an interesting and relatively intense social life. They died prematurely in the mid-1960s, about two and a half years apart, plunging into deep grief many friends, but above all their close family, including four children (two minors), who were forced – each in their own way – to cope with this great loss and the emptiness it caused.

As the eldest of the children, I had the opportunity to watch my siblings grow up, Jerzy (or Jurek, about a year and a half younger), Henryk (Heniu, three years younger) and Danuta (Danusia, eleven years younger than I). Regardless of the significant age discrepancy, from the very beginning we were a fairly close-knit, mutually understanding group with similar (numerous) assets and (few) flaws and almost identical interests, inherited from our parents. Because in different periods of our lives fate threw us in different directions, we did not always maintain close contact, but warm and selfless feelings, care and support were always there, and we never showed the slightest sign of resentment, envy, lack of tolerance or acceptance towards the others. We keep getting together on a regular basis, not only on special holidays, with the exception of Henryk (who has been living in the USA since 1992), whom we see during his and his wife Betsy's annual visits to Poland.

As the eldest of my siblings, I was also the one who got married first (to Włodzimierz, or Włodek, who was three years older than I), and together we enjoyed a pair of children, Krzysztof (Krzyś or Krzysiu) and Izabela (Iza or Izunia). When martial law was imposed in Poland in 1981, which was associated with restrictions on freedom and economic tightening, our children had almost reached the age of maturity and independence, thanks to which Włodek and I were able to make an important decision for the whole family to leave our homeland and seek to improve our lives abroad. It was not easy and required meticulous planning. The opportunity came when we found out about trips to Sweden available to all Poles. Aware of the fact that we may never return to the country, shortly after signing up for such a trip, we distributed our belongings among the children and in full discretion (not including our loved ones) and with the hope of starting a new life, we went to a city in the northern part of the country, from where soon a ship took us across the Baltic Sea to Sweden and … freedom.

Since the saved cash which we managed to smuggle was intended for adapting to life abroad, we wasted neither money nor time on staying in Sweden and immediately initiated actions towards emigration to Germany (which, from a technical point of view, was in our opinion easier because we both had German family names, Bilitz, in Włodek's case, and Hoffmann, my maiden name). Our friends living in Sweden (a Polish lady named Magdalena, a friend of mine from my youth, and her Swedish husband, Göran) bought us ferry tickets and, after a relatively short sea voyage, we finally set foot on German soil. Of course, the lack of a good command of the German language was a serious obstacle in immigration formalities and later in obtaining a job that would suit us. Eventually, however, we mastered the basics of German enough to communicate in some way, thanks to which the range of jobs available to us was significantly expanded. At the beginning, we settled in the north of Germany, in the town of Neumünster, where we spent four years, treated by us as a transitional period on the way to full happiness. Once we had achieved a degree of stability, self-confidence and the necessary financial resources, we moved to Stuttgart, a city that – according to our tastes – should meet all our expectations.

And so it happened. In Stuttgart, we both got a good permanent job, as a result of which we could afford to buy a fairly comfortable apartment in a good district. After we settled satisfactorily in the city, and before the critical political changes in Poland took place in June 1989, we could already think about inviting guests from Poland. We also established good neighborly relations, amongst others with the charming Mrs. Maria, who impressed us with her life wisdom, good advice, cordiality, kindness and even – regardless of her old age – social qualities, including an extraordinary sense of humor (which, according to her example, may seem to be a guarantee of longevity). We proudly introduced Mrs. Maria (who died at the age of ninety-seven) to our guests from Poland, mainly to our family, i.e., brother Jerzy, sister Danusia, her husband, Zdzisław, and brother Henryk, invited to us with Betsy after their wedding in Buk (Poland) as part of their honeymoon.

But the most important thing for us was, of course, to see our own children after too many years. Krzysiu visited us with joy and stayed with us for some time, but in the end he decided that he preferred life in Poland, where he returned and where he later settled down with his devoted wife, Krystyna. Iza was delighted with the opportunity to live in Germany almost from the very beginning and – after starting her own family (her second and current husband is the devoted and resourceful Mariusz) – she was happy to find her new place in life, just like her only son, Dennis, who, after reaching maturity and independence, is settling down for good in the western part of Germany.

So Stuttgart was our family home for twenty-two years and a place where a wealth of marital and family memories were born. I remember the time spent there with tenderness and sentiment. We met many Poles and other wonderful people of different nationalities there. Iza, who also lived there for some time, moved with her husband to another city, eighty kilometers away, in search of better job opportunities. And, at that point, with mixed feelings, we moved – for practical reasons rather than by choice (mainly to be closer to Poznań) – to the eastern part of Germany, the town of Ebersbach, located forty kilometers from the Polish border. We spent four wonderful years there. Then, due to Włodek's illness, we moved back to Poland, to the charming town of Zawidów, located on the Polish-German-Czech border, which my husband unfortunately enjoyed only for half a year, and I enjoyed it for six years. After Włodek's death in June 2016 and, a few years later, the tragic death of Krzysztof's wife, Krystyna, I decided that the best solution for me was to move for good to Poznań, my hometown, and share an apartment with Krzysiu. It also gave me the opportunity to finally spend a lot of quality time with those of my relatives and friends that lived in Poland, especially with Danusia, who was widowed about six months after I lost Włodek.

A person I haven't mentioned yet, but who played a huge role in my and Włodek's lives – especially in our most difficult years, but not only – was Daniela, first an acquaintance, then a colleague, and finally the most devoted friend. Fate made us meet her in Stuttgart in the year 2000. Born in Silesia, she was a widow at that time, raising her son, Nicolas. When he turned seven, she decided to join us in Ebersbach. There, she met an exceptional man, a German named Frank, whom she married and with whom she has a son, Wiktor.

In recent years, because I have found the best doctor for me (of Polish origin, by the way) near the place where Daniela and her family live, I often go there (from Poznań), whether when I get sick, for periodic examinations or for consultations about my general health. I never have to worry about a place to stay. Daniela provides it unconditionally and without the need to "book" it ahead of time, not only for me, but also for my driver (a family member, of course), or even for several people accompanying me. She does not treat it as a favor, but as an opportunity to spend quality time in the company of me and my family members, whom she has gotten to know quite well over the years, on one or more occasions, and count among her relatives. We are always welcome and, contrary to the proverb "a guest is like a fish," not only does she not try to get rid of us after three days, but she always insists that we stay with her as long as possible. Daniela's husband's heart is as big as hers; that's why we love to visit them, which happens on average four times a year. The cordiality, hospitality and sincerity of the Filipps are extremely rare, which we all appreciate and always try to reciprocate.

Now, being close to the finish line of the eighth decade of my life, I spend a lot of time reminiscing about my life, and I realize that it has taken a full circle, literally and metaphorically. I have lived in several cities and towns in two different countries, starting in Poznań and ending up in Poznań, and, almost in each of them, I have tried, with either my husband or my son, to create a place which we could call our home. I would venture to say that I have succeeded in doing so, but I am also ready to admit that it was accomplished as much due to our determination as because of some other forces, which some may call God and others Providence. I agree with both, but, at the same time, I recognize the role of all the People, some mentioned in this brief piece and some probably left out, that have been actively or indirectly involved in this long bumpy road of ours. I am eternally grateful to all of them.

Translated from Polish by Henryk Hoffmann

Heaven Forgive

by Nicholas C. Birosik (Emmaus, PA)

Heaven forgive;
I have misread.
And yet I live;
As a vibration on a thread.
For in this chaos
We find Divine order:
Heaven how I've misread.

It was a desire,
That watered a Heavenly fire.
A calling,
That left me bawling.

But in those tears,
I did find,
What They set behind:
Triumph, Glory — a Story;
Comprised of Heavenly gears.

Fall I not;
Rather I rise.
They said I Ought:

*'Stay you here,
and you will find
your final demise'*

Rise up now,
And you will find
That They have — and *always* endow
The Divine.

Reconcile grief,
For its a petty thief.
Don't you see
That They'll agree:
A Plan, A Path, A Purpose
Has already been set for Thee.

Heaven forgive;
I have misread.
And yet I live;
As a vibration on a thread.
For in this chaos
We find Divine order:
O Heaven, how I've ever misread.

Reflection: The Grace in Misreading

There are moments in life when we look back and realize,
"Heaven, how I've misread." Not in shame, but in awe. In the same
way a seed might misread the dirt as a burial when in fact it's a
planting, so too we often misinterpret endings, redirections or dashed
plans as failure, when they are the genesis of something greater.

The above poem—which I wrote Winter of 2017 (at 16 years of
age)—speaks of misreading a calling, of sorrow, of being brought
low—and yet ultimately of rising up into divine clarity. That
journey, I've come to find, is not unfamiliar. Many of us have faced
similar reckonings.

For instance, consider someone who studies international affairs
with every intention of stepping onto the world stage—perhaps with
the United Nations or a renowned NGO—imagining themselves
changing policy and impacting global relations. But the door doesn't
open. Or maybe it does, but it doesn't feel right. What then?

It would be easy to view that as a detour or even a defeat. But
God's ways are not our ways. That education—the cultural fluency,
the study of diplomacy, history and systems—was never wasted.
Instead, it becomes the foundation for a deeper, quieter revolution.
Maybe that person ends up working in a small town, designing
programs for underserved youth, drawing on that international lens
to bridge ethnic divides and build cohesion. Perhaps they start a
nonprofit that fosters intercultural dialogue at the local level, or
create systems that restore dignity to refugee families. That
seemingly 'misused' degree becomes the very key to weaving
communities together, reflecting God's heartbeat for reconciliation.

What a gift it is to know that God wastes nothing—not
heartbreak, not a shift in direction, not even a dream deferred. In
fact, when we yield our grief to Him, it transforms into grace. The

closed doors were never a denial, but a divine redirection. We were not meant to walk through those doors—we were meant to build new ones.

This is the essence of spiritual growth: not clinging to the shape we thought our life would take, but remaining nimble, open and sensitive to the Spirit's leading. It is in this humility that God can use us most powerfully. Our sorrow becomes soil. Our confusion becomes compost. And out of it grows fruit we never expected to bear.

The poem's closing lines echo: *"As a vibration on a thread. For in this chaos we find Divine order."* That is not just poetic—it is a spiritual truth. God is the master weaver, and even the frayed ends of our lives are being knit into a tapestry of beauty, purpose, and praise.

So we rise. Not always certain, but always called. Called to live with eyes wide open for the new thing God is doing—not just on the world stage, but in the quiet corners, in the margins, in the places we least expected.

And in all of it, Heaven forgives. Heaven guides. Heaven provides.

Thanks be to God.

During a bicycle ride on The Romantic Road (Romantische Straße).

The Fork in the Road

by Bob Block (Warsaw, Poland)

Funny how a simple yes or no can set off a life changing chain of events.

We had a wonderful weekend in the Colorado mountain town of Breckenridge observing the annual Golden autumn change of the aspen groves. The then current girlfriend and I were relaxing in front of a crackling fire in my 1914 brick bungalow in central Denver.

Unbeknownst to me, my life would imminently begin an interesting and unusual turn.

Early that evening my phone rang. On the other end was a recruiter, let us call him Dave, who had reached out to me many times in the past. There were always a variety of opportunities around the country. Each interaction would end similarly with me thanking him for his contact. I would remind him that I was very pleased with my existing senior management roles, my lifestyle in Colorado and my wide variety of friendships. I would typically then give him a few names of other individuals that he might contact with respect to the employment searches he was conducting.

This evening was different. Dave began the call by saying, "Bob I know I've called you often over the years and you were never able to accept any new assignments; however, I have something tonight that may be very compelling, financially rewarding and possibly a very wild ride." We had a friendly chat not relating to this search and then he got into it. "So, Bob, what do you know about Poland?" Well, in a combination of ignorance and jocularity, I said, "Boy, Dave, all I can think of offhand are communists running around in their pseudo-military garb, kielbasa, hairy women, cold & dark and that's about it." After we both finished laughing, Dave said, "I am representing an investment group called Chase international and they are planning on building the first broadband/cable TV network in central Europe. They are looking for a very seasoned marketing/sales/operations individual, and I think you are the right guy. I can tell you that you would at least double your current cash remuneration and the company would pay all your expenses including housing, business class trips back and forth to the US a couple times a year, five weeks of paid vacation and many other perks including a very generous bonus program. I want to put you in front of them as my #1 candidate."

"Well, Dave, thanks for thinking of me, it sounds like an interesting proposition on ..." "Bob before you go any further, if you would indulge me, I would like to set up a meeting between you and the principals in California this week. Would you do that for me?"

Not wanting to burn any bridges, I said sure let us do it. I flew to California later in the week and, as is typical, met the principals in a hotel suite in Santa Monica. For about two hours they outlined the project and very boldly handed me a written offer pre-completed with my name and contact information with the assumption that I would accept it. As Dave had mentioned, it was a very generous offer in all ways. I was intrigued and decided that taking the plunge could be both a risk and an opportunity. 'Poland? Europe? Excellent compensation package. Hey if it does not work out there is no problem coming back to the States and slotting into another domestic position' – I spoke with the recruiter and got him to literally guarantee finding me a great US-based opportunity if the Poland venture fell through.

I told the principals I would like to think this over for twenty-four hours and let us meet tomorrow morning and I will give them a decision. They agreed to that. I then went down wearing my suit and tie to a beach bar and ordered a beer at 11 a.m., an hour which was uncharacteristic for me to have a drink. The bartender was an amiable character, we chatted a bit and I told him of my 'dilemma.' He told me that if I could wait until about 13:00 one of their waitresses, who happens to be Polish, would start her shift. I dutifully waited, had lunch and of course a very attractive young blonde Polish woman appeared. After quite a bit of talking about Poland, politics, quality-of-life, Polish women of course, my mind was made up. (Oh, I did ask her somewhat jokingly "Are there more women like you in Poland?" She told me 'They are everywhere'). I accepted the assignment, gave notice at the company where I was Vice President of Marketing, put all my furniture and most belongings in storage, found a tenant for my Denver home and the adventure began.

I landed in Poland December 9 of 1990 with my two cats, Huckleberry and Jessica, in tow. Spent a month or so at the Marriott in Warsaw with them and they became quite famous on the floor. At that time of year, the Marriott was festooned in all the typical American Christmas decorations – a two-story Christmas tree, a string quartet in the lobby and everyone spoke English. Then, the next day reality hit when I went for a walk in the winter cold and early afternoon twilight of Warsaw. The streets were mainly empty, the shops were basically dark, perhaps lit by no more than a single bulb hanging from the ceiling. Everyone wore dark colors and were tightly bundled against the cold, there were literally no lights on any store fronts – there was grey in more shades of grey than I could imagine in the palates of greyness – a monochromatic scene – coming from the lights and neon of the US it was startling, to say the least. Returning to the Marriott was like entering an oasis.

We started the venture in the Gdansk area. I flew up, was met by a contingent of employees all smiles and was taken to a Baltic seaside hotel.

To say there were differences between Poland and the US would be a gross understatement – there was zero familiarity, no touchstones to gain some sense of balance. Every day was a challenge both in business and in my personal life. Imagine parachuting into the beginnings of a company where of the twenty initial hires three spoke English. No one in shops spoke English, most merchandise and foodstuff were behind counters without branding – just the name of the item – in Polish of course! You had to ask for everything – needless to say I took my trusty personal assistant Gosia with me everywhere – we were joined at the hip.

An interesting anecdote. I was trying to stay in touch with my parents who were in Arizona – an eight-hour time difference. Given that Poland was just breaking the yoke of the USSR system international telephone connections were almost impossible to come by. I had to have my assistant contact the phone company and order a call to be placed to the phone number of my choice from the phone in my flat. That connection could happen at any time that night. Should it be completed, it was full of static and if perchance the number was busy, well, we had to try another day. In order to figure things out I took my assistant and the local director we hired down to the main switching office in the middle of the Gdansk old town to check it out. I was told the ladies there still used old fashioned wired switchboards and I had to see that. Having gained an understanding as to 'how things worked in Poland at the time', I brought an armful of red roses and chocolates and was introduced to the room as an American starting a business in the area – America was the promised land to these folks back then and a Yank was quite a rare animal. Made a huge impression and I was even able to call them to arrange my own calls after that 😊

To bring this full circle, the Poland assignment begat other life adventures living in London and Vienna. Doing business not only in the UK and Poland but in Belarus, Moldova, Latvia, Lithuania and the Republic of Georgia. It is now 2025 as I write this and I have been in Europe for 35 years. I sold my property in Colorado in 2022, bought one near Warsaw in 2001, met a woman in Poland who has been my wife for twenty-seven years, have been to all European countries except for Finland. Who would have known that a simple decision in 1990 would open doors all over Europe?

Had I not taken the road through the wood I chose, who knows where I would be today. No doubt I would not be here.

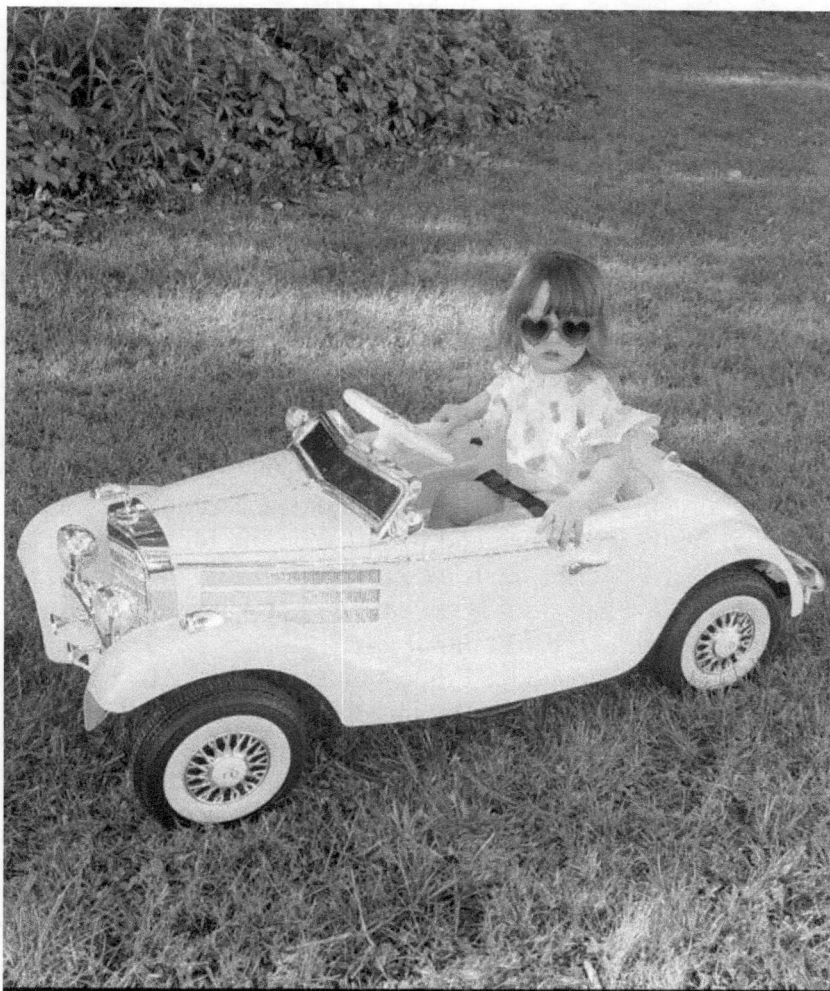

Precious Blessing

by Greg Corrado

As a child growing up and evolving into a young man I struggled deeply with the fact I didn't know my biological father. I grew up in America, but was considered to be a young immigrant. It was strange since I was born in Connecticut to American parents. My father left when I was eighteen months old, that I know of. I don't know anything about him. But little did I know … my real father was soon to be met. I'm not sure of the timeline but I was born in 1986. My mother met my father at some point just before the fall of the Berlin wall. She packed up what she could along with my three older sisters and me, and off we went to Poland as communism fell to join my new father. He took full responsibility, care and love of my family. He selflessly worked so hard from the very beginning to be the absolute best he could for everyone. He was constantly getting better and evolving to such a strong, brilliant teacher, author, friend, inspirational figure, and coach and father. Working for two major private schools in America, he has done so much, and I actually don't even know the half of it. But what I do know is that he is my father. He really is the greatest man.

As a young boy in America I didn't understand why he wasn't like the other kids' dads. Not really into the same things a typical American dad would do with his son. But as I grew older I learned that he was cut from a different cloth. He's better than the other dads. He's extremely intelligent. He didn't teach me how to wrench or play football. He taught me more. He taught me never to give up and how to strive hard to do the right thing. To reflect and grow. He taught me never to stop striving to be better no matter how hard the struggle is. He showed me how to be a professional, how to do what is necessary to excel and how to apply myself and grow. He raised me correctly, and I wouldn't change it for the world. If there is anything I regret most, it's the pain in the ass that I was when I truly just didn't understand. How lost I felt, but I was never let go of by him. I was always guided correctly forward by my father.

As an adult I have faced my own struggles and I have grown into the man I am today. Still, I look to my father for advice and I wish more than anything to have more time to learn to speak Polish again and to have more time with him and my mother.

Now, as the man I am today, I have received the greatest life blessing ever, my beautiful healthy, precious and absolutely brilliant daughter, Charlotte Olive. Born on November 7th, 2023. I am extremely proud and thankful to be the father of my baby girl. I don't want to miss any time with Charlotte ever, and I will forever do everything I can for her, to help her and teach her and guide her in the right direction.

For Charlotte, when you read this:

I want you to know that I love you with my whole heart and soul for all eternity. I want the absolute best for you always. I want to share as many precious memories with you in life as possible. While guiding you in the right direction in life, I want to be there to enjoy being a part of your achievements, to be there to support you, protect you and love you with my whole heart. I'm so proud of you my baby girl you are my whole world. I love you. You're my little tater (like "tater tot"), like so many little pet names we've called you. The way you walk around with a tater tot holding it like a little burrito, you're such a little riot. Full of energy and so adorable, but so wild it's just precious. Thank you, Charlotte, for being literally the greatest blessing. You are so bright and full of humor, always making wild sounds. You're learning how to talk, I'm hearing you say "dadda," daddy, dad. I love waking up in the mornings and hearing you wake up and call me dad! Nothing is more rewarding than getting to see you, picking you up, hugging you and starting the day with a new adventure. Your musical abilities are amazing already. You play the harmonica and you are able to hold drum sticks and play a small drum roll. Amazingly correct at seventeen months. Now, even at nineteen months, saying "oh no" or, while reading your bedtime books, you know to growl when you see a tiger. Or how you buzz when you see a bee in a story. You're so funny and adorable. Full of talent and happiness. I remember when you first came home and I was showing you car races on TV. Now, at nineteen months, you're fully enthusiastic about your little car. You make engine noises and you love cars. It's so cute. I hope to teach you as much as I can.

One of the most precious things is watching you take cheerios or raspberries and, after putting them on your fingers, you make them talk to each other. "Ahdirkadirkadirkadirka," or how you can already make an owl noise with your whistling mouth. It's definitely your spirit animal. When your mother was pregnant with you and we came home from the hospital how there was an owl living outside the house. Now, at seventeen-to-eighteen months, you can make the "whoo" noise of the owl. Your love for animals is very prevalent. I can't wait for more memories to be made.

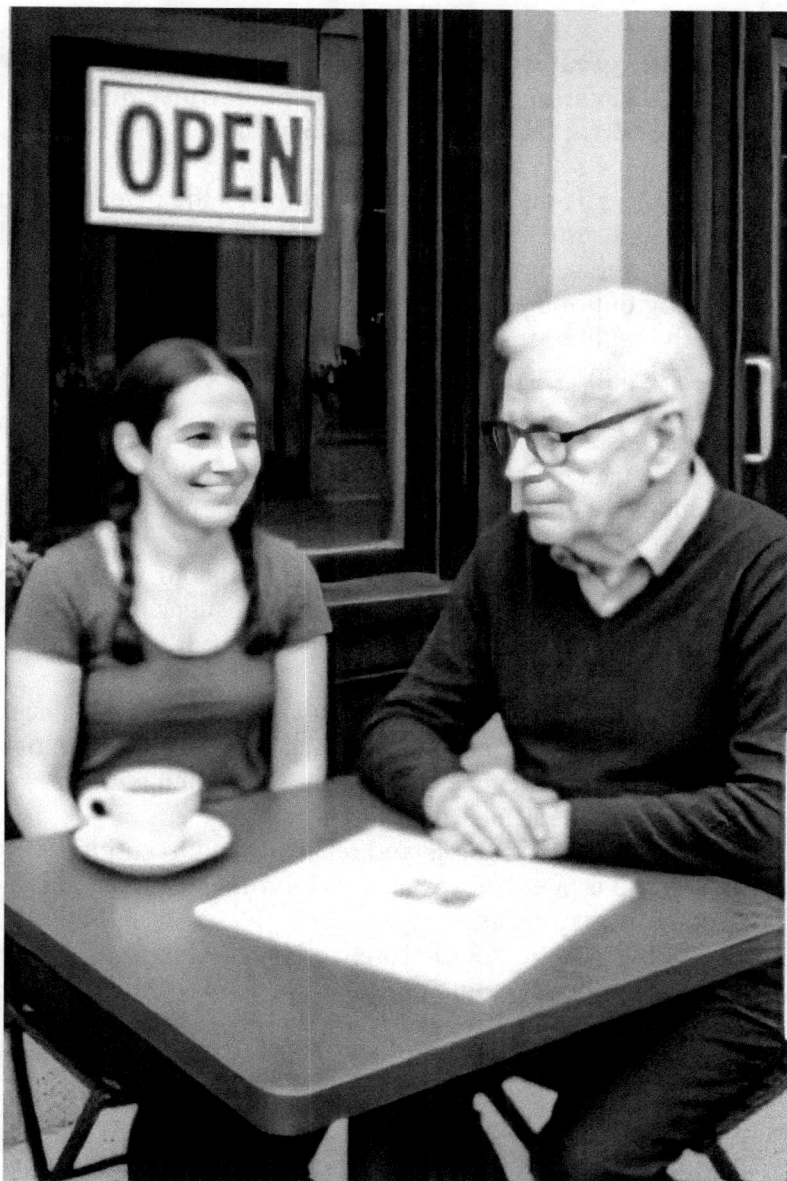

Waiting to Be Understood

by Jenny Corrado (Mount Joy, PA)

Sometimes, the greatest strength lies not in defeating anger with force, but in disarming it with compassion because behind every fury may live a heart waiting to be understood.

It was October 15th, 2008. I was working as the manager of a 1950s-style retail store nestled in a high-end tourist town in South Florida, right on the edge of the Gulf of Mexico. This village was like something out of a postcard—vibrant, sun-soaked and always buzzing with laughter, music and the fresh smell of salt water. Tourists flooded in year-round, but it was the locals who gave the town its soul.

Our store was a cheerful blend of nostalgia and indulgence. The front sold retro trinkets and quirky souvenirs, but the back? That's where the magic happened. We had an old-fashioned ice cream counter that served lusciously creamy, melt-in-your-mouth flavors, dolce de leche being the town favorite. We made our waffle cones in-house, and the warm scent of cinnamon and sugar floated through the air, curling out the doors and down the street. It lured people in like bees to nectar.

Although we offered drip coffee, it was rarely ordered. The town had no shortage of artisan coffee shops with frothy lattes and oat milk cappuccinos. Still, every Monday at exactly ten a.m., as predictable as the tide, Richard would arrive.

Richard was a year-round island resident who lived just over the bridge in a grand estate. He was always the first customer of the day. Always alone. Always grim.

He would wait at the door before we unlocked it, arms crossed, lips tight. The moment the latch clicked open, he'd walk in with a grumble about how the coffee wasn't ready, though it never was, not that early. When it finally finished percolating, he would drown it in cream until it was cold, take one sip and complain that it was terrible. Every single Monday.

"This place has the worst coffee on the island," he'd mutter, barely above a growl. "You'd think a place that smells this sweet could get something as simple as coffee right."

He never smiled. Never said thank you. Week after week, month after month, this ritual repeated itself. The staff grew weary of him. Eventually, they stopped greeting him altogether, just rang up his coffee in silence, eyes down, praying he'd leave quickly.

I'd always coached my team to treat every customer with kindness, no matter what, but even I began to lose patience. Still, something about Richard lingered with me. Maybe it was the way he stared off while reading the paper on our front patio with his adorable dog on his lap. Or how he never missed a single Monday. There was something heavy behind those eyes. Something tired. Something lost.

One slow Monday, I made a quiet decision to change the pattern.

When Richard walked in and launched into his usual complaints, I handed him his coffee with a smile and said, "Good morning, Richard. I hope your weekend was peaceful."

He looked up, surprised. He hesitated, almost unsure of how to respond.

"It was… quiet," he finally said, the edge in his voice duller than usual. He took his coffee and sat at his usual spot outside, flipping open his newspaper.

The next Monday, I waited for him. I had a fresh cup ready, extra hot, extra strong, just how I guessed he liked it before the cream. I brought it to his table myself. "Thought I'd get a head start today," I said with a soft grin.

His eyes met mine, and this time they didn't look angry. Just tired. "Thank you," he muttered. It was the first time he'd ever said it.

Over the weeks that followed, our conversations grew. He started telling me stories of his past.

At first, they came in fragments, tucked between sips of lukewarm coffee. A name here, a place there and languages he spoke like music. Then, one Monday morning, as the fall air finally cooled and the crowds thinned for the season, Richard stayed longer than usual. I brought him a second cup, this time without him asking. He accepted it with a quiet nod.

"You ever heard of a place called Putti?" he asked.

I shook my head.

"That's what they called me when I was a boy," he said. "Putti Henry Eichelbaum. Berlin-born, 1921. I was raised by great parents, educated and thoughtful. They believed in kindness. And they still had to run."

"We left Germany in 1934. Just left everything. We were Jewish."

I sat down across from him, not speaking, just listening.

"We made it to Italy," he continued, "but it wasn't much safer there, not for long. Eventually, we fled to Cuba. That was 1940. I was nineteen. Still a kid."

He looked down at his coffee. "We made it to America just before the doors slammed shut. I wanted to fight, I needed to! I joined the Army in 1942, Infantry in France. The worst of it."

There was silence then. The kind that stretches, not uncomfortably, but like it needs room to breathe.

"They gave me a new name when I enlisted, they said Eichelbaum wouldn't work because it was too German. So, I became Richard Essex, I didn't argue, I never looked back."

Over the next several Mondays, more of his story unfolded, but more on his years after the war, his years in real estate, his love for languages and culture, though he rarely showed it anymore. He had become a man of few smiles, but many layers.

One morning, after he spoke of his childhood in Berlin and the ache of losing a homeland, I told him a little of my own story. How, as a child, I'd moved to Poland when my mother followed her heart across the ocean to marry a man she loved, a Polish man who would become my father for the next thirty-four-plus years. I told him about the small Polish town I lived in, the beautiful countryside and the small, warm kitchen where many languages danced across the air over hot soup and bread with butter. I told him about being raised in a way that wasn't entirely American nor entirely Polish, just … European, blended.

He listened without interrupting. When I finished, he was quiet for a long time. Then he said, "So you know."

I did know, but I did not know the war, or trauma at the scale Richard had endured, but I knew the ache of being between places. The richness and burden of cultural inheritance. The way identity can stretch and split and reform across borders and languages. The longing for a place that only exists in memory.

What started as weekly dread turned into a friendship I now treasure. He still put too much cream in his coffee, but he stopped complaining and started to laugh again.

And every Monday, I'm reminded that beneath the sharpest thorns, there can live a garden of kindness, waiting, just waiting, to be watered.

Sometimes, the greatest strength lies not in defeating anger with

force, but in disarming it with compassion because behind every fury may live a heart waiting to be understood.

R.I.P.
Richard Essex
(June 9, 1921 – May 19, 2015)
You are truly missed.

Costa Rica Before Ziplines

by Robert R. Franklin (Methuen, MA)

The year then was 1978. Anne and I had been married for almost seven years. Family life was shaping up nicely with home ownership outside Boston and two children, Charlie, age five, and Amy, three. Anne's father, Ed, a civil engineer, was globetrotting with projects mostly in Central America and the Caribbean. One such engagement took him and Anne's mother, Claire, to Costa Rica. Ed was working on the infrastructure of a housing development with his former partner, Jim O'Donnell. This presented us the opportunity for a family trip at relatively modest cost.

We flew from the international terminal at Boston's Logan Airport. Our itinerary took us to Miami, where we boarded the Costa Rican national airline for the capital city, San Jose. It was spring. I remember one thing in particular about the flight. Soon after leaving Miami we flew directly over the island of Cuba. It looked huge, lush and somehow foreboding.

Upon landing in San Jose and entering the rather small terminal there, Claire and Ed were present to meet us, but on the other side of the customs area. We had little difficulty navigating that process. Costa Rica welcomed Americans arriving with dollars to spend. But the presence of sober-looking and well-armed soldiers seemed somehow to not disappoint us in our preconceived notions of Central American military security. Jim O'Donnell had rented Ed a middle-aged, two door Toyota station wagon. With four adults in the four-passenger car, and with our luggage and the kids in the tiny way-way back, we were pretty cramped. Fortunately, it was not a long drive into the city. The road from the airport to downtown was probably the only four-lane in the country, with tropical, flowered landscaping left and right. Costa Rica put its best foot forward to visitors to the capital city.

As with most Central American countries, Costa Rica is bisected by a central mountain range running like a spine its entire length north and south. These peaks are high, perhaps 10,000 feet, with San Jose nestled among them a few thousand feet lower. It was modern in many ways, and decidedly third-world in others. The government was the most free and progressive in the region. Certainly, the people were friendly and helpful. Of course, Spanish was the language, with most people in the city speaking some English. Ed told us we needed only two phrases in Spanish. *Dos cervezas por favor* means 'two beers please.' *Dónde esta el baño* translates 'where is the bathroom?' The architecture was a mix of old Spanish and modern American. At that time, the environmental and public safety controls that we take for granted were all but nonexistent in Costa Rica. For example, many vehicles, especially buses and trucks, spewed diesel exhaust so grossly that by mid-afternoon the air pollution was palpable and a blue haze enveloped the city. However, San Jose was blessed. Every night the mountain winds came down through the city and literally washed the air clean of all the filth. By early morning the sky was temporarily pristine until the buses rolled once more. The buses, too, were unique. Most were old American school buses, privately owned by families whose business was one of these bus routes. Buses were graffitied in outlandish colors and designs. (More about the public safety issues later.)

Claire and Ed were staying in an apartment on the second or third floor of a small building in downtown San Jose. It was reasonably modern and clean, it had an elevator and a good location directly across a busy street from a large city park. It had two bedrooms and a maid's quarters with no maid. It also had a teletype machine that Ed's business used to communicate back to the States. It would erupt into loud and clattering action at odd times and intervals. On the floor directly below us, was the Swiss embassy. The Swiss flag flew proudly just below our living room window. Anne and I slept in the second bedroom, the window of which looked out into an air shaft to the roof. The kids slept in the maid's quarters which had only one single bed, used by Charlie. To accommodate Amy, Ed had borrowed a crib-like bed with a straw mattress. It took us a couple of days of complaints by a cranky Amy to realize the straw mattress was infested with fleas and they were chewing the poor child all night. What parenting!

The first couple of days in Costa Rica were spent sightseeing in the San Jose area. One attraction was the central market, or *marcato centrale*. Not far from the apartment, it was lively and crowded, everything under the sun with emphasis on fresh foods and craft products. We also went one day to an open-air fruit market to buy fresh produce. The fresh and tropical fruits were very tempting, and in the first few days I overdid them, resulting in a bout of the green-apple quick-step. At the open market, Amy and I got separated from the rest and, walking back to the car, cute little Amy caught the eye of a rather disreputable-looking fellow. Half drunk, filthy dirty, pants unzipped, and armed with a machete, he, innocently I'm sure, offered Amy some of the papaya he was carrying. I didn't want to offend him and gratefully accepted the proffered fruit. When the guy was out of sight, and Amy about to taste the fruit, I tossed it as far as I could.

The mountains surrounding San Jose included several active volcanos. These were of the type that spew ash rather than lava when they erupt. One day we drove out of town a ways to a national park, the site of the Vulcan (volcano) Irazu. The area around the volcano was devoid of life, being deeply covered by tons of ash from recent eruptions. We drove to within easy walking distance of the top of the volcano. Looking down into the caldera we saw only wisps of smoke to indicate an active rather than dormant volcano. Not as impressive as the lava of Hawaii, but our first volcano experience. The drive to and from the park took us through farming country. Small farms were carved out of the steep mountainsides. One feature of these farms was the fencing. They cut for fenceposts a certain kind of tree that, once driven into the ground took root. They had a living fence which was continually trimmed for firewood kindling. Also seen in the country that day were a number of working farm wagons, drawn by oxen, and painted the colorful designs found in craft and tourist shops.

Another very Costa Rican feature of both city and country areas were the small, family-owned stores, what we would have called convenience stores, known as *pulperias*. Even out in the rural areas those stores were not far from each other. Many had been in the same family for literally hundreds of years. They served the neighborhood as grocery store, package store, gas station, barroom and entertainment center. Each had a name such as *El Pulperia de Santa Maria*. Out in the hinterlands, addresses were stated in terms of distance and direction from the nearest *pulperia*. Each *pulperia* was known for the tiny snack or bite to eat that it served free when customers bought a beer, soda or coffee. These may have been a bite of hot dog, a cracker with cheese, a chicken wing, or the like. They were called *boca*, the Spanish word for mouth.

At that time in Costa Rica a presidential election had been held. Political parties each had a flag. Houses and businesses flew the flag of the party they favored at election time. We saw mostly one flag being displayed, the flag of the winning party. Not so different from our practice of using lawn signs.

It must have been on a weekend when the banks were closed. I needed to trade some traveler check dollars for local currency. Ed figured the best place to do that was the big American hotel in the city, probably a Hilton or the like. Anne, Ed and I went there, and I conducted my financial transaction. In the lobby of the hotel was a kiosk emblazoned with the words *Jungle Adventure*. Anne was curious. We looked over the brochures and talked to the people manning the booth. They offered a three-day tour of the eastern part of Costa Rica. The total cost was only a few hundred dollars. Ed and Claire would mind the kids. Ed convinced us to go for it. A day or two later we were at the San Jose train station for a very early morning departure. The tour company had a private car, the last car on the train. There were perhaps twelve or fifteen people in the car, including a young lady who was our tour guide. The train, made up of six or eight cars total, was diesel powered and the engine belched smoke like all the Costa Rican engines did. We were headed southeast on the narrow-gauge rails for a full-day run to the Caribbean port city of Porta Limor. The train travelled through mountainous territory, crossing deep ravines on seemingly rickety trestles. Rivers, streams and waterfalls were numerous. The eastern half of the country is the wet side of the central mountain range. Vegetation was lush and green. Isolated farms and villages were not uncommon. In fact, the train made over a hundred stops along the way. Some were at tiny towns. One was at a sizeable village where vendors and begging children boarded the train, but were shooed out of our car by the tour guide. Some of the stops were at rural crossroads where an unpaved road or trail intersected the tracks. At some of these stops, passengers would embark or debark from the train, many with goats. At others there would be no people in sight, but the train crew would get off and load milk cans or other produce. At one such stop, there were no people, no cargo, nobody getting off. We just stood there idling for several minutes. Then, down the cart path came a horse with two preteen age boys riding bareback. One piled off and jumped aboard the train. How did the train know they were coming?

Now a word about the railcar. Old. Probably early twentieth century. It did have a restroom at the front end. I took advantage of that, closed the door behind me to find a box-like structure in one corner with a toilet seat in the middle. I lifted the cover and peered in to see the track bed speeding by below. To make matters worse, the train was swaying and lurching a bit, making it a challenge to accomplish the mission. When I got back to my seat I encouraged Anne to experience it for herself. The windows on the train were all wide open. The rear platform was available to those of us on the tour to watch the countryside drop rapidly into the distance. There were frequent tunnels, some of which were long enough to fill the car with diesel exhaust. Lovely. And many of the passengers in cars forward of ours were young Costa Ricans who passed the time hanging off the sides of the train as far out as they could, pulling back only at the last possible moment to avoid being wiped out by signposts or other poles along the rail bed. They seemed to be contesting with each other to see who had the most daring in this dangerous game. No railroad official or other authority even attempted to limit this activity. And that is an example of what I was saying about no public safety controls. It was like what our country must have been 150 years ago. Fascinating! Scary!

Among our fellow passengers and tour members were two schoolteachers from Canada. Very pretty young ladies, and very proper indeed. They were clothed impeccably in starched dresses with high collars and were the absolute picture of decorum. I had to chuckle at the look on her face when one of them first emerged from the railcar's restroom. I laughed out loud when the other, who had been leaning out the window to take pictures of the scenery and the front of the train as we rounded curves, pulled in her head and turned our way with her perfectly made-up face badly smudged with soot from the diesel exhaust.

The lady tour guide was giving a running commentary, mostly in Spanish, from which we benefitted little. She periodically passed out snacks, warm sodas, and, at noon, unrefrigerated sandwiches that we passed on.

As the day went along we descended out of the mountains, passing coffee farms with large racks of coffee beans drying in the sun. The interesting thing about these large square wire mesh racks was they were on tracks which ran out from specially built sheds. If rain threatened, which it obviously did very frequently on the jungle-like east coast of Central America, the racks could be pushed under cover in very short order. When we finally emerged from the mountains the rail line followed the coast southward through tropical, hot forest with occasional glimpses of the blue Caribbean Sea to our left, palm trees and white beaches.

Eventually we arrived at mid-afternoon at the railroad station in Porta Limon. Hot, humid, blazing sunshine. We were met by a tour official in a small jitney bus and we were away for a tour of the city. Porta Limon is a very small city established to provide Costa Rica access to the Caribbean. It was built at the turn of the twentieth century and was populated largely by the descendants of the Jamaican workers who were brought in to build the railroad to and from San Jose that we had just travelled. Therefore, most of Porta Limon's citizens were very black and spoke with a faintly British accent. Spanish seemed to be the second language there. While on the subject of the racial makeup of the Costa Rican people, unlike most other countries of Central America, Costa Rica did not have a significant number of native or Indian people. In the neighboring countries, these descendants of the original native people constituted the lowest rung of social and economic ladders. Since they were mostly absent in Costa Rica, there were fewer truly poor people there than elsewhere in the region. I asked Ed why Costa Rica was different from its neighbors. Ed said that the Spanish who came to Costa Rica killed all the Indians.

Among the sights on our tour of Porta Limon was a central park with outlandish sculptures of welded scrap metal, and trees populated by three-toed sloths. We then went to the airport. It seemed this tour had two options, the three-day option we selected and a one-day option that ended with a flight back to San Jose the same day. To our amazement and mild alarm, it turned out all our companions were on the one-day option, and Anne and I were the only ones left on the bus. Oh, well. The bus dropped us off at our Class A hotel with instructions to be ready for pickup there early the next morning for continuation of our Jungle Adventure. We checked in and moved into our room to change for dinner. If this was a Class A hotel, we were glad we were not in Class B. This room was as threadbare as the linens. However, we had a free evening in a strange and exotic and remote city, and we were off to dinner. We were in Porta Limon at the time of the annual lobster festival, so we were looking for a lobster dinner. The hotel desk recommended a restaurant within walking distance. It turned out to be a disco joint, dark and illuminated with black lights. I was hesitant, but Anne's sense of adventure was strong and she propped up mine. The lobster dinner, which of course was rock lobster without claws, was all right. We glowed from the black lights and even danced briefly to the music. By the time we emerged from the restaurant it was dark out. The warm, humid tropical evening invited us to walk the city streets in exploration. There were many people out and about. All apparently very friendly, although some of the neighborhoods you would not have driven through in a locked car if you were in this country. Eventually we found ourselves in a city park where a religious revival tent meeting was underway. Our curiosity took us to the edges of the crowd, where we listened for a while to a white preacher, sweating profusely in the heat, exhorting his mostly black congregation in fist-pounding Spanish. Of course, we could not understand the words, but somehow the preacher's message was very clear to us. The Gospel says the Apostles were given the same ability.

We found our way back to our hotel, made it through the night, and were up early, packed, checked out, and waiting in the lobby so as to not miss the bus to our continuing adventure. After we waited there for some time, I asked the desk what time the bus was supposed to arrive. I got a shrug. We waited some more. One of the taxi drivers parked in front of the hotel came in to visit with the person behind the desk. They obviously were discussing us in Spanish. Soon the taxi driver came over to us and asked if we would like a tour of the city. We said no, we were on the Jungle Adventure and were waiting for the bus. The taxi guy said the bus wasn't coming. What? He said they never come. Now I was in a panic. He said he would be back in a little while, and by then we would be ready to go for a nice city tour with him. I stomped around for a while longer, in the lobby and out on the sidewalk. Eventually, well over an hour late, the bus showed up. The driver was amused that we were worried and upset. He told us to relax, we were on vacation and having fun.

The bus took us to the waterfront area of Porta Limon, a short ride. Boats were mostly commercial and sport fishing crafts, and small cargo vessels. We then saw our transportation for the day's next leg of our journey. We had an aluminum john-boat affair, maybe seventeen or eighteen feet long, powered by two 25-horse outboards. It was outfitted with plastic seats and a canvas top on a frame. Our guide was a young black fellow who did speak English, but with an accent that made it hard for us to understand him. We were advised to take advantage of the johnnie-on-the-spot at the dock because facilities were few and far between on our route ahead. The bus driver handed us a box lunch each, bid us farewell with a wry grin, and we were on our way.

Today's adventure took us by this boat up the east coast of Costa Rica a distance of 100 kilometers or 60 miles. We travelled along a kind of intercoastal waterway, a series of inlets and lakes connected by rivers, thoroughfares, and sea level canals. From time to time we passed outlets to the Caribbean and got glimpses of breakers and beach. It was hot. It was very tropical with lush vegetation along the shore. To our left we saw ranching operations with brahma cattle occasionally in sight. On the water we saw sport fishermen, some small native cargo boats carrying produce, and even a few dugout canoes. Our guide took time to point out alligators, turtles, orchids and monkeys high up in the trees. We were kind of loafing along all morning, taking in the sights. At about noon the guide pulled over to one shore under a tree for shade and we delved into our box lunches. He wolfed his down with gusto. Anne and I once again passed on the unrefrigerated sandwiches and limited ourselves to the warm sodas and the go-withs. The boat driver told us he lived in the village that was today's destination and that he and his father owned the boat and did transportation services for the tour outfit and for others. He said he was a Jehovah's Witness. Underway again, we began thinking about a restroom call. The guide said we would stop soon. Probably halfway up the coast we came to the village of Tortuguero on our right. It occupied the strip of land between our waterway and the Caribbean. Only a few buildings and people. Upon landing, the first thing we saw was a group of men building a dugout canoe. They did not want their picture taken. We then visited the outhouse, gratefully. It turned out there was a woman there who ran a tiny store which had, to our delight, a kerosene powered refrigerator chock full of ice-cold beer. We each had one and I bought one for the driver. Anne and I then walked the few yards to the beach on the ocean side. It was absolutely beautiful, right out of a travel brochure. The name 'Tortuguero' refers to the green sea turtles that came ashore here to lay their eggs. Meanwhile, our guide was bargaining with the villagers to buy a couple of huge watermelons. Since I had recently become interested in gardening, we asked where the melons were grown, and could we see the fields. The guide acted as our interpreter. The villagers gave evasive answers, but reluctantly led us down a dirt road to see part of their farming operation. The guide looked uncomfortable. The villagers were keeping a close eye on us. We began to realize that these folks were probably growing something other than watermelons, and were wondering why we cared. We backed off as gracefully as possible and headed back for the boat. With the melons loaded we were on our way. We must have been behind schedule because the boat driver, who had been using only one of the outboards, now fired up both and we were flying.

As late afternoon came around we arrived at our destination for the day, the village of Bara del Colorado. It was located at the mouth of the Colorado River, which at this point formed the border between Costa Rica and Nicaragua. It was, of course on the Costa Rican side of the river. We docked the boat at the end of a rather long pier which led to a structure built on pilings. We were met by the tour's guy, our host for the evening. He was about fifty, very thin and lanky, a Canadian who gave every appearance of having gone native. He seemed sociable enough, so we bid goodbye to the boat driver and followed our host to the village. He immediately asked if we drank beer, and when we said 'yes,' he excused himself and headed for the *pulperia* to buy a case. We explored our home for the night. It was rustic but clean, a couple of bedrooms, a dining area, screened porches, small kitchen, and all up on stilts as was every other building in the village. There were no paved streets, a couple of dozen buildings at the most, chickens ranging free throughout the place, a grass airstrip with windsock down at the end of the street. We dumped our bags in our assigned bedroom and decided to take an exploratory walk. We ran into our host returning with the beer, told him we were walking out to the beach, and he cautioned us to keep track of time because darkness comes very quickly here. We walked briefly through the village and then headed cross lots through the airport to the beach. Because of the heat, we were wearing shorts all day. The grass was up to our armpits and there were small lizards in the grass. We were walking single file along an overgrown path that seemed to be heading for the beach when I let out a whoop. Something brushed the back of my bare legs, and I couldn't see what it was because of the grass. We took off running, stopping only when we reached the beach. As we turned to look at whence we just came, a small dog emerged from the grass and ran up to say 'hello.' Sigh of relief. We spent a few minutes enjoying the driftwood-littered beach, the blue Caribbean waters, the setting sun, the pure white sand, and the remoteness of the scene. Then, mindful of our host's admonition, we headed back to the village. Our cottage had electric lights, but power for the village came from a diesel generator which ran only until nine p.m. We had a few beers with the Canadian, talked about life in Bara del Colorado, and about the day ahead tomorrow. Our dinner was prepared by our host's "housekeeper," a woman who was apparently a local. She cooked on a wood fire out in the backyard. The entree for the meal was jack, a locally caught fish. While the meal itself was unremarkable, we enjoyed ourselves sitting around on the porch, drinking a little more beer and watching the village activities until the power went off. It was a long day and we retired early.

During the wee hours of the morning we found out why all the buildings in Bara del Colorado were up on stilts. We were awakened by the most unbelievable downpouring deluge of rain you can imagine. And this place had a tin roof. It was like being on the inside of a bass drum. Sleep was over for the night. We sat up in bed, marveling at the sound of the rain. Finally, I felt my way to the gas-powered refrigerator and retrieved us a couple of beers. As dawn approached, the village roosters began to crow repeatedly. And, where were they? Directly under our cottage to get out of the rain. To this day, heavy rains inevitably prompt comparisons with Bara del Colorado.

I don't remember much about breakfast, but I'm sure we had some. We were too concerned about the weather and the day ahead. You see, it was still pouring. Bara del Colorado was awash. Visibility was very limited in the downpour. The only long pants I brought were the suit pants I wore out to dinner in Porta Limon. I was wearing them now and, for reasons I cannot remember, I wore my wingtip shoes. As protection against the elements for the day's boat ride, we were offered large plastic garbage bags with holes cut out for our heads and arms. There was nothing for it but to go. The tour had a schedule to keep. We donned our garbage bags, grabbed our suitcases, and boarded the same boat as yesterday with the same guide as driver. As we sat at the dock, we tried to hold our feet up out of the inches of rainwater in the boat, but at least the canopy top kept us out of the rain which was coming straight down in the absence of wind.

The other thing about Bara del Colorado that I have left to say until now was that fishermen like Ted Williams came from all over the world to fish at the mouth of the river for tarpon. Over on the Nicaragua side of the river were sportfishing camps where these sportsmen stayed and hired guides to take them out tarpon fishing. Even in the downpouring rain the small open boats were out, and we could see fishermen pulling in amazingly large, shiny silver tarpon.

We were off. As the boat started moving, the rain came in under the canopy. We gave up all hope of keeping our shoes dry and we rested our feet in two inches of water in the bottom of the boat. The garbage bags were marginally effective until the boat swung sharply to follow the river channel and several gallons of rainwater that had collected in the canopy spilled out as the boat heeled and the wind propelled it directly into my lap. I was now thoroughly soaked, cold and miserable. We proceeded up the Colorado River, on the international border. At the confluence of the Colorado and San Juan Rivers, we were to bear left and head into the interior of Costa Rica. Before we did so, however, the driver stopped to pay a courtesy call, I guess, at the Nicaraguan border outpost on the north shore. As we

landed the boat on the riverbank, a couple of soldiers appeared,
uniformed, armed and not looking very friendly. Greetings were
exchanged in Spanish and the guide produced the two large
watermelons he acquired yesterday in Tort Guero. This thawed the
ice. Apparently, the gift was a combination of toll and bribe to keep
the tour welcome to pass freely by the outpost. These were the years
when the Sandinista rebels were creating more and more warlike
conditions in Nicaragua. At this point Anne asked the guide if there
was a restroom at the border station. He asked in Spanish, and the
soldiers conferred. Then they motioned for Anne to step out of the
boat. I was going nowhere. She was on her own. The guide and I
waited in the boat while Anne disappeared with one of the soldiers
and visited the outhouse. All ended well when she returned to the
boat. The rest of the morning was spent boating up the San Juan
river as fast as the twisting channel allowed. The rain continued at
varying intensities. Finally, and I do mean finally, we arrived at
about noon at the town of Porta Viejo. Here there was a dock, but it
was at the foot of a high bank leading to the road level of the town.
There was no staircase or other convenient way to get to the top but
to climb the bank. Ordinarily this would not have been a big deal,
but the rain had made the red clay bank very slippery. By now we
were so cold, wet and miserable, and we wanted out of that boat so
badly that no mere clay bank was going to keep us on the river. We
grabbed our waterlogged suitcases, stepped out of the boat, and
crawled practically on our hands and knees to the top of the bank,
suit pants and wingtips and all. By the time we reached the top of the
bank and the end of the road, we were a sight to behold.

   At the end of the road was a small gas station and at the gas
station there was a VW bus, jacked up with a wheel off, being
serviced. A young guy eyed us amusedly and then came over to talk
to us. He was the tour driver sent to take us by road back to San Jose.
He said he had a flat tire while coming down and that he would be
with us as soon as it was fixed. He told us that in the meantime we
should walk up the road into town to the motel on the right. We
could get some lunch there while we waited. So, there we went,
walking side by side up the unpaved road, suitcases in hand, like a
couple of muddy and drowned rats. Local residents were out on their
front porches, out of the rain. They did not much know what to make
of the spectacle before them. Crazy gringos. As we approached the
motel, there were cafe tables under a roofed open-air dining area. At

the tables were a group of people who turned out to be the tour participants headed in the other direction. They were brought here from San Jose in the VW bus and had been waiting for the boat to arrive. They were eating a lunch of rice and beans. They were very well attired, the ladies in dresses and high heels. They looked doubtfully at us and asked us how we were enjoying the tour. Well, except for this morning. …

The gal behind the counter asked if we wanted something to eat. I said what we really wanted was to change our clothes. Was there a place to change? Oh sure, we could use any of the motel rooms, they were all unlocked. We gratefully headed for the nearest motel room. I opened the door and stepped in. The room was occupied. There was a naked man sprawled out asleep on the bed. I reversed direction quickly, practically knocking over Anne who was right behind me trying to get in out of the rain. Next room, I said. The door to the next room was slightly ajar. I opened it with some trepidation and was confronted with a practically unfurnished room with what appeared to be a dead dog in the middle of the concrete floor. Another quick about face. Our third attempt was the charm. At least the room was unoccupied, but it had obviously been recently used. The bed was torn apart, the ceiling leaked and there were puddles everywhere on the cement floor. And throughout the room the walls were festooned with gobs of toilet paper where bugs had been squashed by the earlier occupant. God, what a place! This was a Class B motel. Regardless, we were so desperate to get into cleaner and drier clothes that we decided to change there. It was hard to find a clean or dry place to stand or to open a suitcase. We had real trouble peeling off our wet garments and no towel to dry off with. Our drier and cleaner clothes from the suitcases did not go on easily. We tried not to touch anything in the room. Instead, we held each other up so we could get changed without losing balance. What an experience!

When we came out of the motel room, we looked and felt a little more human. The rain was stopping. We talked to the people from San Jose and I asked one of the women if she would help me out. In our haste to get out of that boat I neglected to even say goodbye to the guide, much less give him a tip. I asked if she would convey some money to him for me. She agreed to do so and told me sternly that I was too generous when I handed her the equivalent of about 15 dollars. We talked about San Jose and got some raised eyebrows when we mentioned our association with Jim O'Donnell. I guess Jim was a well-known person, not universally admired.

The waitress at the motel asked us again if we wanted something to eat, but all I wanted was a good stiff drink. I ordered scotch for both Anne and me. The VW pulled up and the driver told us he would be back for us as soon as he got the San Jose party on their way. We said goodbye to them and tried to picture the ladies in their Sunday dresses and high heels going down the red clay bank to the boat. If I had been less tired and miserable I would have gone back down there to watch. Instead, I ordered more scotch. Then out of room number one came 'Sleeping Beauty.' He sat at a table, ordered food and proceeded to eat it with his fingers while tossing scraps to a dog that appeared and took up station under the old timer's table. Finally, the driver returned, asked us if we were ready to go, called for the guest check, glanced at us when he saw what we had for lunch, and we were on our way back to the city. What a ride. Three or four hours of gravel road, not well maintained. Neither was the VW bus. If it had any shock absorbers, they had long since given up the ghost. The driver, who turned out to be a Costa Rican descendent but from Long Island, New York, had no mercy on the vehicle or on us. No attempt was made to avoid bumps, driving as fast as possible without killing all of us. About halfway to San Jose the inevitable happened, a flat tire. The driver said we were lucky. Not far down the road was one of the few oases on the entire Porta Viejo road. We drove there on the flat. While the driver changed the tire, Anne and I went into the restaurant. We were the only customers in the place, and we had another round of scotch. After getting underway again we had to stop only once more. Anne needed a pit stop and lacking any facility, the driver stopped on a curve, Anne and I walked back a ways, and the problem was solved.

By the time we got back to San Jose and pulled up in front of Ed and Claire's apartment building, I was desperate to get out of that VW torture chamber. I did not even consider tipping the driver but grabbed our stuff and headed upstairs for a shower. Our Jungle Adventure was over.

The next couple of days were spent in the San Jose area recovering. Then we were away again, this time to see the Pacific coast of Costa Rica. Jim O'Donnell was some kind of partial owner of a cattle ranch up in the northwest corner, and Ed had arranged for a short stay there. Claire decided to stay behind in San Jose, so it was the five of us, kids included, in the Toyota wagon. The western half of the country was the dry part. We were told there had been no substantial rain there for two years. Our drive took us down out of the mountains through very arid areas and steep, winding two-lane roads. No guardrails. On the curves you could frequently see the remains of past accidents where vehicles, mostly trailer trucks, had gone over the edge, probably due to failed brakes. No effort was made to recover or clean up the wreckage. It was left where it landed. Served to sharpen my driving efforts. It was very hot. We stopped for gas, cold drinks and bocas at a small crossroads.

Our next stop was at the Pacific coast resort town of Puntarenas. Cruise ships used this resort as a port of call. Ed was interested most in checking out the casino for future reference. We then headed north on the coastal road. This was brahma cattle country. A certain kind of tree grew in the huge pastures which was shaped like a big umbrella, providing the cattle with maximum shade from the blazing sun. Everything was parched and brown. Ranches were enormous. Nearly north to the Nicaraguan border there is a peninsula west into the ocean. The southern half of this peninsula was the Santa Elena Ranch, our destination. Ed had never been there, but we were following good driving directions. We found the gate to the ranch with no difficulty and, closing the gate behind us, drove a good way down a very dusty trail to the ranch house and buildings. Expecting us was the ranch's hired manager, his girlfriend and her daughter, who was Charlie's age.

There were only a few buildings. The hacienda was one story, cinder block and adobe, tile roof, wide wraparound veranda, very airy and sparsely furnished. The manager and his "family" had moved out to a smaller abode directly behind the hacienda to make room for us. There might have been a couple of minor sheds, but the other important buildings were the bunkhouse for the cowboys (*vaccaros*), their cookshack, and stables for the horses. No barn. Fences kept the cattle out of the dooryard. No lawn, just dirt and dust. No air conditioning.

The manager was a former major in the Costa Rican National Guard, which served as both army and national police force. He was said to have been cashiered due to a drinking problem. He spoke enough English so we could get along. The girlfriend and her daughter spoke only Spanish. Among Jim O'Donnell's partners in this ranch were members of the Samosa family. One of the Samosas was at that time dictator of closely neighboring Nicaragua. We do not know if that was the military connection. Everybody called the major 'Major.' There was also a dog. Mixed breed, mostly German Shepherd, he was named *El Tigre*. The name had been changed from whatever it had been after an encounter with a jaguar. El Tigre limped severely and was covered with facial and other scars from the fight. He was retired to the hacienda from cattle work, and was highly respected for his courage in taking on the "tiger."

Upon arrival it was learned that if we wanted milk for the kids we would have to go to the store to buy some. Anne and Ed got directions to the store and headed for the gate. I had had enough driving and stayed behind. At the store they found a public phone and called Claire back in San Jose to say we arrived safely. They bought me a cowboy hat. They bought milk that was frozen into a solid block. It was the only way milk could be transported over the distances in the heat without spoiling.

That evening we had spaghetti for supper, cooked and served by the girlfriend. We sat on the veranda seeking relief from the heat. There was no proper bed for little Amy so she slept on a cot with dining room chairs placed backwards against it to prevent her from falling on the floor. The *vaccaros* began arriving from their duties out on the range. They were a rag-tag and rough-looking bunch to be sure. All wore leather chaps, and some had chaps for their horses as well. Many of the horses were bleeding from scratches and cuts on their legs and flanks, apparently from encounters with the ubiquitous cactus. We sat on the veranda and watched them pull in, care for the horses, and prepare their evening meal. They all seemed to do their own cooking in the cookshack. A wood fire was started in the building, but there was no chimney, only a smoke hole in the roof. I couldn't understand how they could stay in the smoky building long enough to cook their food.

The next day the Major took all of us to the beach for the day. The beach was part of the ranch along the south side of the peninsula on the Pacific. Our vehicle was the Major's old rattletrap Jeep pickup truck. Anne, Amy and the girlfriend's daughter rode in the cab with the Major driving. The rest of us were in the back holding on for dear life as we drove quite a ways over ranch roads, through desert-like landscapes to the beach. We brought with us a fried chicken picnic prepared by the girlfriend. The beach was beautiful, crescent shaped with pure white sand and warm, pale blue calm ocean water.

Palm trees lined the back of the beach, and it was picture postcard perfect. Not another soul was in sight. We and the kids swam in the Pacific waters. The three kids buried the Major in the sand. Only his head was left showing. We walked a bit behind the beach on an old cart path seeing large lizards on the ground and green parrots in the trees. We ate our picnic in the shade of the palm trees. As the afternoon wore on, Anne and I were wading in the gentle surf, not far out from the beach, when, down in the clear water, we saw a large barracuda cruising casually along parallel to the beach and not far from us. Out of the water. No more swimming. Back in the truck for another bouncing ride to the hacienda. Memorable day.

We spent another evening on the veranda. Charlie was eagerly awaiting the return of the *vaccaros*, and to our consternation insisted on walking across the yard to talk to them. Of course, none spoke English, but they were taken with little Charlie and, while Anne barely dared to look, hoisted him into the saddle of a horse and walked him around, hanging on to the pummel but good. It was quite a thrill for the young boy, heart failure for the parents. He survived. Amy brought with her a picture book designed to start a three-year old on reading. We used it in language lessons with the little girl, telling her in English the word for pictures of elephants, umbrellas, and the like. She taught us the Spanish words in return. Interesting. Charlie and the girl had been playing well together, jabbering back and forth in languages neither understood, which apparently did not pose any problem at all. The girl, however, was a bit bossy prompting Charlie to say in exasperation that he was getting tired of being ordered around in Spanish.

The drive back to San Jose was memorable for only one event. Anne wanted a turn behind the wheel of the Toyota. The problem was that she had inadvertently left her pocketbook containing her driver's license back at the apartment in San Jose. We decided to give her some experience anyway. Bad decision. Murphy's Law. Within a short distance we encountered traffic stopped ahead. A spot check was being conducted by the police. Anne was panicking. I was thinking fast. I told Anne to get out of the car and go back to fuss with the kids through the tailgate. I crawled over the gearshift to get behind the wheel. Then Anne got back in on the passenger side. The young cop saw the whole maneuver. When we got to the head of the line I presented my Massachusetts license, but he was not interested. He asked in Spanish to see Anne's license, and was gesturing about the exchange of positions he observed. I played ignorant saying *no hable Español*. Anne gave him a line of English of which he understood none. Ed tried some pidgin Spanish from the back seat. Quite a scene. Finally, the policeman gave up in utter disgust of this bunch of dumb gringos and waved us on with the word pas. Phew! On the outskirts of San Jose was a large national penitentiary in plain view. It was reputed to not be a nice place. I believed it, and for a minute there I thought I was about to find out firsthand.

That is my true story of 1978 Costa Rica before Costa Rica became a world-renowned eco-tourism destination of all-inclusive luxury resorts and ziplines through the jungle canopy.

This could go on forever. I could wax poetic about a family Sunday dinner at the finest restaurant in San Jose where the baked fish was served whole with the head and eyes intact. And the evening out with Jim O'Donnell and his wife, leaving the kids unhappily in the care of the O'Donnell's' Spanish-speaking housekeeper. Or the day the kids swam at the public baths in San Jose where artesian waters were called Ojo de Agua, the Eye of Water. On the way home, I had a tense but award-winning encounter with U.S. Customs in Miami. And in Miami there was an overnight visit with Anne's college friends, Pam and Wes Warren, and their intolerable children. But I digress.

That is my true story of 1978 Costa Rica before Costa Rica became a world-renowned eco-tourism destination of all-inclusive luxury resorts and ziplines through the jungle canopy.

El Fin

Hurricane Helene left a nearly unrecognizable landscape of fallen trees and debris. This twisted tree trunk is an example of some of the storm's milder damage. Photo by the author.

Helene's Strange Gifts

by Jim Gardner (Asheville, NC)

Maybe because it was the 25th something felt like Christmas. Not the sing-song Christmas of jingle bells and tinsel, but the eerie quiet of things being shut down, Kris Kristofferson's "Sunday Morning Coming Down" on overdrive. But September 25, 2024, a Wednesday, turned uneasily noiseless after sundown as the rains came ahead of the hurricane winds and fury of tropical storm Helene.

Forecasters had predicted historically heavy rain, so my wife and I had braced for the storm by taking our usual preventive measures to keep our basement dry: rolling out tarps along the corner of the house where the gutter system always failed and a steady downstream would pool and eventually seep through the concrete. Knowing this rain would be stronger than usual, I opened four umbrellas and aligned them on the tarps to act as a kind of temporary awning. The wind quickly blew them out of place, so I took some scrap plywood from our garage and improvised a kind of off-ramp for the gushing water, covered it with more tarps, then I went back inside to change into dry clothes. When our dog, sensing something outside, barked at a thump, I peeked out a window and saw an adult black bear back out of an overturned trash container and, now carrying a large white trash bag in his mouth, lumber his way across our neighbor's yard, presumably to find a suitable picnic spot somewhere out of the rain. It's not unusual in our neighborhood in recent years to see a bear in the trash, but this storm bear—black body outlined by the encroaching crepuscular darkness—presented an image that in retrospect foreshadowed something evil, like a biblical prophecy of doom. Like one of the images from Bob Dylan's "A Hard Rain's A-Gonna Fall."

It rained through Friday morning. This was no Gene Kelly rain to dance and sing in; this was something out of a Jack London story, a cruel and indifferent universe shooting arrows of violent rain down from a gloomy sky of dread. Previous floods in 1916 and 2004 had brought destruction after some 22 and 23 inches of rain respectively; Helene sent down 30 inches in about 36 hours. Any more and we would have expected to see two bears walking up a ramp onto an Ark.

As the rain subsided, people were drowning and homes were being washed from their foundations as the French Broad River and its tributaries, including the Swannanoa that runs in a valley between

Black Mountain and south Asheville, became destructive freight trains of watery, muddy death. We didn't know the scale of the destruction yet and had no idea that our fellow citizens just a couple of miles away were dealing with existential threats, some losing their lives. A grandfather and grandmother and their six-year-old grandson perished after taking refuge on a rooftop and being overtaken by the floodwaters.

My family's story is one of the fortunate many whose lives were inconvenienced but not taken by Helene. We had braced ourselves for the power going out, and it did, Friday morning. We wouldn't have power, or water, or internet again for weeks. And it would be days before we had even a cellular connection for calls or text messages.

Neighbor B. had invited a few friends over a couple nights after the storm, when everything was still a question mark and a sense of adventure mixed with apprehension drove our thoughts (and when we were huddling around battery-powered radios or car radios for updates from the County's official broadcast twice a day over the public radio station.) Around a fire pit we sat: R., who during the next weeks would open up his home to us many times—"Come any time!"—as his internet connection remained solid after ours failed; C., who would help our neighbor R. stabilize a huge oak tree that had split almost to the base of the trunk, with the bulk of the tree looming over her house and garage; S., who works with teens in a mental health institute and pondered over the devastating psychological effects of the storm. Our host B. poured vintage bourbon; his wife and children had made it out to family in Georgia on the few highway routes that hadn't been closed. He would volunteer at a local church distributing relief supplies as he awaited news of the public high school where he teaches. School wouldn't open again for a month.

About an hour into our gathering, one of our phones pinged, and then all of us began receiving text messages for the first time in days. My first message was an apparent wrong number. Then there was a message from a student I taught 25 years ago checking to see if I was safe. The news broadcast to the outside world must have been dramatic.

A couple weeks later the same group reconvened and shared stories and information, and compared notes. I observed that the experience brought to mind the Walker Percy character who, while dodging a sniper's bullets, sees the back of his hand as if for the first time, a sense of being alive and in the moment, a feeling of awe having been shook out of mindless everydayness. Something like that was happening to us after the storm as we saw our lives anew, accepted small and large gifts of generosity and kindness from strangers and neighbors, and appreciated the essentials of water, food and shelter that we had so often taken for granted.

If hikers on the Appalachian Trail receive "trail magic"—the unexpected gift of food or water from a stranger, or the welcomed bit of encouragement or gift of support, a rain jacket maybe, that makes all the difference and keeps the hiker moving forward—then we were experiencing "storm magic" and reaping the benefits of countless acts of kindness. A few for which I'll always be grateful:

• Our neighbor R. gave us homegrown cherry tomatoes and a five-gallon bucket of flushing water. And when I was clearing the brush from two fallen trees, she pitched in at the end of a long day and helped me move a small mountain of logs.

• Neighbor P. brought a chainsaw and helped clear the fallen branches in our backyard. Neighbor R. walked up carrying a bow saw like the one I was holding and immediately pitched in; with their help we finished the job in a fraction of the time it would have taken me working alone.

• Our neighbors B. and A. loaned us their camping stove (and showed us how to use the propane tanks to fuel it); they brought paper towels, toilet paper, and other paper goods; they brought us cake, coffee, protein bars, and bananas. And B. appeared one night with a wonderful dinner of grilled chicken and small potatoes, perfectly seasoned.

• Our nieces brought water and snacks and information about the relief supplies available from the Red Cross.

• Our neighbors K. and K. dropped off a container of potable water as they were leaving town. And, on our front steps, they left a huge container of vegetables, cheese, and other food. Mangoes, peppers, bread, half & half. We used what we could that night on a pizza dinner cooked on our little outdoor charcoal grill.

• Our neighbors R. and M. gave us homemade vegan ice cream. After M. and their little boy evacuated to California, R. charged my wife's hearing aids and allowed us to bring our laptops to use the internet at his kitchen "internet cafe."

• Our family J. and L. brought food, water, and offered dog care. When I botched the simple task of pouring gasoline into our car from a gas can that another neighbor had loaned us, J. did it easily by using a funnel. A funnel! How did I forget that, how did it not even occur to me? Storm stress distorted my basic functioning. This was the gasoline can I took out of my car when we found an open gas station in Hendersonville, and experienced a moment of terror when I couldn't get the gas pump handle to stop the flow of gas. Visions of gas pouring out on the ground, catching fire, flames shooting everywhere like a scene from Hitchcock's *The Birds*. Fortunately, the pump handle somehow snapped back into normal and my nightmare didn't continue. But the stress and terror were real. Storm stress.

• One day our neighbor PJ, who had loaned us the gas can, parked a trailer outside and told everyone who hadn't left town to put their trash containers out so he and his brother could load them up and make a landfill trip. As we were cleaning out our refrigerator at the time, this was a timely and heroic bit of storm magic, especially considering that the main road to the landfill was closed and access was only via winding roads of questionable stability.

• Neighbor E. took special interest in our safety, probably thinking that the elderly couple across the way might need extra help. When she found out that we planned to stay, she encouraged us to leave and even arranged for us to stay a few days at her mother's house 30 miles away in Hendersonville, where there was power and water.

These were mostly small acts of neighborly kindness that had a huge impact, from people in our lives who had been acquaintances and neighbors but who we now knew on a deeper, more human and authentic level than before, thanks to storm magic. Another category of storm magic was the acts of kindness, compassion and bravery that we all benefited from collectively. Throughout Western North Carolina, first responders, government workers, firefighters, soldiers, and volunteers were giving their best efforts, and sometimes risking their lives, to help the victims of Helene. At least one first responder died during a rescue attempt.

Thousands came to help, including World Central Kitchen workers and a rescue team from Riverside, California. A mule team from Kentucky took supplies into a remote mountain area.

We developed a routine of going to a local church that had set up a relief station. A huge tanker of potable water sat parked at the entrance to the parking lot. Its driver was D. from bayou country in Louisiana, working as a contractor for FEMA. He would not see his family again before Christmas, but made no complaints and generously helped us fill and carry the five-gallon buckets from and to our car each trip. "I'm here until your water is back," he said.

In the all-of-everything-good-and-bad nature of the storm aftermath, examples of humanity at our worst sometimes compromised the good will and "WNC Strong" bonhomie. Lost tempers, frayed nerves, loud and quiet meltdowns, honking horns, rude shouts—all part of the experience as residents navigated panic and stress. A demagogue came for a photo op, mocked his opponents, and told lies about the government's response, prompting threats against FEMA workers and the temporary shutdown of one of their relief stations. Self-appointed influencers on social media spread disinformation, claiming that "thousands" of people were missing a month after the storm, or that FEMA was confiscating homes. All wrong, false, untrue. And the NC state legislature would later pass a relief bill that included dozens of power-grabs unrelated to the hurricane.

In contrast to the opportunistic exploitations and inaccurate hyperbole, the social media and news outlet posts that offered video footage of the storm aftermath were sobering documents of the magnitude of the unprecedented event.

One of these, an AccuWeather post on Twitter/X, featured aerial video footage of the storm damage, along with audio clips of a couple of residents. An unidentified man summed the situation up poignantly, giving the storm homespun personification:

> It started at Wednesday
> Pouring down rain
> It rained Wednesday, Thursday
> And she came Friday.
> So you can imagine all that rain
> Plus that wind
> I mean, everything that she *could* move,
> She moved.
> That's some powerful water.
> That's some *powerful* water.

We need more help, yeah.
I mean, whoever can come in and help,
Come in,
'Cause we need help.

That vernacular poetry rivaled the best writing I could find on hurricanes. When we had temporarily evacuated and were spending a few days at our neighbor's mother's house, I had some hours to read and reflect. On a bookshelf I found Marjory Stoneman Douglas's 1958 book *Hurricane*, in which she described "swills of white, sheets of white" and "tons and smashing tons of water . . . the tossed hollow of pandemonium." Her quoting Caribbean locals describing the leaning trees of storm aftermath—"drunken forests"—would come to mind frequently in the coming days whenever we would see what Helene had done to our mountain woods.

I sought out other writers, too. Zora Neale Hurston, in *Their Eyes Were Watching God*: "[H]e saw that the wind and water had given life to lots of things that folks think of as dead and given death to so much that had been living things. Water everywhere. Stray fish swimming in the yard . . ." And Asheville's Thomas Wolfe describing the 1916 flood: "It looted the bottomlands of the river; it floated iron and wooden bridges from their piers as it might float a leaf; it brought ruin to the railway flats and all who dwelt therein. The town was cut off from every communication with the world . . ." Another WNC writer, Wilma Dykeman, captured an essence about the river: "For the French Broad is, above all, a region of life, with all the richness and paradox of life."

Musicians also grappled with the enormity of Helene and the "paradox of life" that is the French Broad. In a haunting ballad, songwriter Wesko sang, "There's violence down on Market Street / But we didn't know violence 'till we met Helene." More famous musicians, including Asheville natives Warren Haynes and Luke Combs, along with Eric Church, James Taylor, Dave Matthews, and others, would organize and perform in benefit concerts, and at least two compilation albums appeared on the Bandcamp website to raise relief money.

On October 4, a Friday, electricity returned to our house, seven days after the storm ended. On October 15, 18 days after the storm ended, water flowed through our pipes again; there would be daily notifications from the Water Authority to boil the water before using it for drinking or food preparation. On October 20, 23 days after the storm, our internet connection returned. On October 24, nearly a month after the onset of the storm, an 80-foot tall walnut tree in our backyard leaned dangerously after roots shifted; a tree crew we had already hired to work on another tree promptly included it in their plan for the day and took it down in a powerful fell that shook the ground with a deep boom. "Timber!" On October 28, a month after the storm, schools in the city district reopened, with 24-packs of bottled water stacked in every classroom. On October 30, an AT&T worker came to install internet hardware—we had switched providers after our previous company showed indifference to billing us during the storm for service we didn't receive. On November 18, 52 days after the storm ended, the City of Asheville notified us that the water flowing into our home was now potable, safe to drink. The Army Corps of Engineers had helped restore the main reservoir, which had suffered an almost complete destruction (but a recently added spillway had helped the dam to hold; otherwise, a spokesman for the City's Water Authority said, the flooding water would have destroyed everyone and everything between Black Mountain and Asheville's Biltmore neighborhood.)

Two months after the storm, on a Thanksgiving like all others and like no other, I mull over Marjory Stoneman Douglas's assertion in her book *Hurricane*: "There is only one story, that of the survivor."

We don't know when or how the people in our lives will become new to us, and new people—in the form of hurricanes or other forces of nature—might storm in and change our lives forever.

Four generations of strong women.

New World

by Ewa Grelus (Poznań, Poland)

When I hear the word 'family,' I immediately recall the definition I learned from my high school social studies textbook, which says that "family is the basic social unit of every individual." Many years have passed since high school. I have overcome many milestones, many crises, many upheavals; I have shed seas of tears of both joy and sorrow; I have had a broken heart, a rehabilitated heart, a comforted heart. I have traveled many miles by car, plane, bicycle, rollerblades, on foot; I have drunk a sea of coffee, and, as for family, I fell in love so deeply that I got married and had children. And the definition from social studies still lingers in the back of my mind, constantly reassuring me that family is the basic social unit. Meanwhile, according to psychological studies, most of our traits develop within this very institution called family. Why? Because it is the basic social unit through which any person functions properly. There have been certain moments in my life that I reached for my phone to call my Grandma or my Mom, to send a picture to my cousin, to receive birthday and nameday wishes from aunts, to send a text message that I am here and I do remember.

Sometimes, I felt like stopping for a moment. Those people have always been the compass in my steps, the map I used when I was lost. Now that I am a mom myself, I can see how important we, the parents, are to our children, how much they need us in everyday life to be explained how this world works, why you should not eat ice cream for breakfast or why an apple with ketchup is not a good idea nutritionally. In today's world of 'life facilitators,' where the phone replaces meetings, the vacuum cleaner vacuums by itself, dryers dry clothes and pots cook soup by themselves, we should have more time than ever before to be and live together. Even though we do not always succeed as we would like to, I have always tried to make sure that my children spend time with their cousins, aunts, grandparents and other members of our extended family. I would like them to benefit as much as possible from these visits and encounters – especially from the time spent with their grandparents and aunts, who are not always as young and strong or willing to run too fast.

I do not remember too much of my grandparents from my childhood. They passed away much too soon, certainly too early for me to get a chance to remember them in a real way. Although I used to like to believe that I remember them, I think that these are images so strongly programmed into my mind by the stories of my mother and grandmother that they have been adopted by my brain into the chapter of "memories," but, in fact, they are just representations of my memories. However, my thoughts about my grandparents always began like this: "but they loved you." Very often I say this now to my children when we talk about their beloved grandmothers and grandfathers, whom they have around them. I want to know always that grandma and grandpa love them the most.

When I open the drawer filled with memories about my grandparents, I see two images. The first memory takes me to the park where I feed the ducks. I do not know how many times I actually fed them, but my mind is convinced that it was every day until I was two years old. The second memory of my grandfather takes me to Nowy Świat (New World) Street in Poznań. Although I should point out here that I have no idea if it actually happened there. But in this particular memory, I am in Nowy Świat Street, and my grandfather shouts after me, "but look how she's running." Because it was always emphasized how small, round, plump a little dumpling I was, full of energy, smiles and joy from my surroundings, it was hard to say whether I was running, waddling or escaping from something. But in that simple, prosaic sentence, there was immense pride and joy in what I was doing. Of course, later I repeated that rather uncensored sentence in a childish manner, also expressing pride in my own achievement. Yes, I heard it, because, as I said, a one-and-a-half-year-old child cannot remember this; someone must have helped her to remember it. It was family. It is. Because these stories continue to unfold. And the one about my running has been etched in my memory so strongly that to this day I feel the wind in my hair (if I even had any), I remember every sound of those words and my grandfather's chest rising with admiration. This is the essence of that magical power – Family.

So, we are in New World Street, and I would like to stay there a little longer. That is where I have my memories related to my family. Even though I never lived there, and even though my grandfather was no longer around, and I was old enough to create my own memories, I was quite often in the apartment in New World Street because that is where my grandmother still lived. The strongest person in the world that I had the privilege to know, meaning my grandmother Sabina.

I will not start telling the story about her by saying that she was the most perfect woman in the world, because I think many people would roll their eyes in protest and some of you would put the book down saying, "how boring." Grandma did not have a perfect character; she was not the easiest person to get along with, and she definitely was not someone that agreed with everything and nodded her head. But Grandma had strength. Please remember that what I write comes from my own head, not AI; there is no good story here, it is created by my mind which has adopted someone else's stories as its own and bathed them in a sea of emotions and experiences, giving them a unique character. Apparently, only a cow does not change its mind. I believe that as long as a person is growing, both memories and experienced stories take on a different character.

But going back in time, Grandma is actually a model of the ideal woman. I like to think that way. The grandfather I mentioned earlier was Grandma's second husband. I have always liked to imagine that the other one was waiting for her because she was so special, perfect for him. It probably was not like that, but who am I to stop thinking that way and boost Grandma's profile in the category of uniqueness, who am I to introduce a little Hollywood romance into the otherwise gray reality of those times? Let us deny it, women in the old days needed men.

Grandma had three daughters, so-called "her own," but at some point in her life, she ended up with four additional children. That was an extra bonus. Two boys, two girls, 50/50. So, all in all, she had seven children to manage. No modern woman could handle that. That is for sure. I have never heard grandma complain. She would rather say that one of them was a rascal, one was the sensible one, another loved reading books, someone liked to study, someone was the youngest, someone shared, someone did not share – and that is how the stories began. She never complained how much trouble she had in the new reality.

That is how it was; Grandma was an extremely active person. She lived in Nowy Świat and created this new world for those children. For everyone. Not everyone would have been able to achieve that, but she definitely COULD. I have the impression that she did not worry for a minute; she picked up the phone or went where she needed to go and took care of everything. Action – reaction. Nobody had to tell me about it; I saw it live. Grandma was a woman of action. Somewhere in my mind, I saw her as the lady who stopped streetcars in Gdańsk. She was like Henryka Krzywonos in Poznań, at least for me. If someone had to stop those streetcars in Poznań, she had the power, strength and determination to do so. And still, there were seven children. I do not know how they all lived together, so I will not tell the story of an idyll because it is not even my story; it is the story of those people. But to this day, they all stay in touch; they call, write, meet up, and there are miles and even an ocean separating them sometimes with a six-hour time difference. Being together, being there for each other at difficult moments is really a testament that family sticks together, and everyone in it is for each other. If it were not for the strength of this woman, surely these words would not be in this sheet of paper because the inspiration for this story is family. Mine began with her.

Sometimes I think that maybe I could have talked to her more about some stories, anecdotes, curiosities from the world 'once,' before the transformation, before the era of mobile phones. But, on the other hand, I think that what I have extracted from those stories explained more about "how" than about "what" was done back then. I can translate more of that "how to live" into my behavior now.

When I went to college (I majored in Educational Studies at Adam Mickiewicz University in Poznań), she talked about how she worked on the campus in Szamarzewskiego Street, and although she was a janitor and cleaned the building, I know she was very-well respected by the academic staff. I must admit that my imagination always carried me towards the meetings with professors; I envisioned her as a working woman from a famous Polish sitcom, with an apron and a headband, drinking coffee with a professor of pedagogy, sociology or philosophy. The professor was gray-haired, wore a brownish-gray suit, a wide tie, somewhat in the style of you know who but less flashy, they were sitting at the reception with glasses (in special baskets) full of strong coffee with plenty of grounds at the bottom. To hell with it, it did not happen that way, but who can stop me from thinking that way.

This woman could win people over like no one else, she could talk to anyone, and she was well respected. Do not think that we sat every day sipping coffee in constant sympathy. No, that was not the case. Our conversation could be stormy; after all, I am quite a determined person myself, I wonder where it came from … When I moved out of my family home and lived in Piaskowska Street, she told me about her working for the Germans during the war, picking potatoes. As a young person having pretty much everything one needs – let us be honest – barbies, lego blocks, strollers, dolls, everything, I could not imagine how it must have felt to go to the other end of the city to work in someone's backyard for money. And it is worth pointing out that she was, as my mother says, a young lady, a young girl at that time. Sometimes I felt that many places on the map of our Poznań somehow formed a string of special memories for her. She never complained about how hard it was for her, how hungry she often was, how she was lacking many basic things. My mother always supplemented that part of her story, frequently talking about the more genuine version of her mother, making the story less Hollywood-like, but I prefer the version of a Polish wonder woman.

Grandma often allowed herself to tell me how I should live, intertwining, of course, very reasonable thoughts from the perspective of time. She really disliked how young people (including me) relate to older ones. She said her ears swelled when she heard young people forget to use the words 'mom' or 'grandma' when addressing the adults. At that time, I thought she was exaggerating.

In reality, many times, this aspect triggered arguments between us. But, looking back, I miss her guidance about little or minor things in everyday life. At some point our whole life gets simplified when parents become friends, aunts and uncles become buddies, and that is not the direction the world should be heading. Because family is the most important unit and should not stand out against the backdrop of our entire social and emotional life.

I remember when, after buying my new apartment and being proud of furnishing my thirty square meters with a small budget, I showed my Grandma pictures of how it looked (when she was no longer able to walk and leave her home, and when photographs were her only window to the outside world), she frowned and pointed out that there were no curtains in my apartment (things that, just like tablecloths, were out of fashion now). Another clash. And so I did buy curtains, and she bought a tablecloth for me as a Christmas gift, when I was about to invite my first guests. Red, because – even though she loved white tablecloths as a symbol of purity and elegance – she said she had bought a modern red one. My guess, however, was that white ones were not available. And so, our relationship continued, we sparked up and learned something new from each other, because, let us face it, a red tablecloth was a huge step towards generational compromise on her part.

It did not matter whether I bought a new dress, a vase, a wardrobe or a car; I was proud of everything. Grandma always asked me how my job was going, whether I was making a decent wage, whether I respected my boss, and she proudly admired each of my accomplishments, even though she did not always say it. More often, she would say, "You must remember, child..." and then she would give advice. Apparently, people did not usually want it, because by nature people know better, but her advice somehow became automatic. She always said we should do our own thing, to make ourselves happy, but without hurting others. This was practically her creed: not to hurt others. She always helped everyone, and actually for us, her children and grandchildren, it was natural, and we do help each other in every possible way. If someone in the family has a problem, we always call each other – whether the problem is of advisory, financial, tax or health-related nature – and we look for resources to help, we ask and search. That is what my Grandma did.

Let us agree, Grandma Sabina did not loaf around on any topic, she had a whole network of contacts, and if it was not to get it "through the door," then it was done "through the window," if it was not accomplished by calling this number, she called another number until everything was resolved. I think that if I could not find myself a husband, she would have found one for me. At the same time, she used to say, "You always have to show a man half of your behind," but it was in the context of the spiritual sense, not the physical one, as she emphasized the importance of women's behavior maintaining some mystery. She illustrated that opinion with some funny stories about her own relationships with her husbands.

As I have already mentioned, Grandma was not an ideal, even though I would like to thinks so, and she made her mistakes, some of them in the area of raising her children. While speaking (proudly, of course) about her grandchildren, she often compared them to each other, telling Ola that Ewka did this, telling Piotr that Ewka did that, telling Marcin that Piotrek did that, and so on and so forth. But it stemmed from the fact that she had had so many kids around her and tried to do her best to cash of her observations related to everyone's accomplishments and assets. It is hard to for me to forget the greatest strength my Grandma showed when she had to bury her beloved daughter; it was a moment for which no one is ever ready. Period. We were all there with her, with each other, because the tragedy impacted our entire family. As a mother today, I am unable to comprehend how she was able to function and go on living, to be at that funeral, to be in this world without her daughter. In this story, tears flow freely when I think about it; yet, she did manage. Because she had enormous strength. Then she shared that strength with her two nieces when they lost their beloved husbands. I do not know this story, I can only guess how much support they could offer to each other.

When I look at my daughter, I cannot even put into words how much I see that aura of strength that I have always seen in my grandmother. Grandma had strength and intuition. When she said, "Be careful," you knew you had to be alert. When she said, "It will be fine," you knew it would be fine. Sometimes she would call just to hear if everything was alright because we were on her mind. When she asked about someone too often, it was a signal that we needed to check if anything was wrong. When someone said he would call but did not, she would get worried.

I remember my grandmother's funeral vaguely, as a blur. In fact, I have the impression that I was not even there. Moreover, I am even convinced that she herself was not there. My husband stayed home with my son because he was sick, and I went to the ceremony with my daughter. Tiny, not even six months old, she was in a stroller. My friend pushed the stroller so that I could calmly get through the whole ceremony, but I knew something was wrong. Besides, strange things had been happening since morning, the world was clearer to me – although I think it was Grandma's doing – I could not figure out what was wrong. The ceremony was beautiful, I was one of the organizers, we chose flowers, the music, everything; the priest read my words, but neither of us was there, neither Grandma nor I. After I got home, we had to go to the hospital because it turned out my son needed surgery. Do you know what my first words were when I called my Mom? I asked her if she had called Grandma to ask about her special connections up there, the connections that I felt I needed badly. My Mom did not respond. And then, I already knew that I also had connections up there. Someone who had great power. But it was hard for me to adapt that form of her help. I switched to survival mode, and we overcame all the difficulties, and, after a week, we returned home safe and sound. I was already in a new reality. Without her.

While sorting Grandma's belongings, we came across albums and photos. In the photos, she was always surrounded by people, often wearing beautiful and big beads, a dominating red accent – in the beads, earrings, sweater – and there was always a smile. Many photos were from dancing events, in the embrace of men, during weddings or other parties. I remember that my wedding was a family celebration that, finally, did not require tears or farewells to loved ones. We could all meet in beautiful outfits for an event accompanied by live music by an orchestra (I cannot imagine it any other way), all smiling. After all the storms, we deserved a proper dance party, with all the uncles, aunts and cousins. Unfortunately, Grandma couldn't leave the house at that time, but, of course, she experienced all the preparation and organization with me. There were white tablecloths, full elegance and preordered pieces of cake just for her (that is how it is in our family: wedding cake, her favorite dessert of the night, was always delivered to her home). I remember that I did not really want to have a videographer because I was stressed about being recorded, but, in the end, I agreed for Grandma's sake. The recording was live, lasted for several hours, and there was music from the wedding. She was so happy watching it, seeing close-ups of all of her loved ones having fun, dancing, enjoying themselves in every way. She herself admitted having a great time saying, "My little foot was dancing during the whole wedding."

There is no doubt that Grandma loved life and having fun – as it is best illustrated by her frequent trips to the sanatorium. Legend has it that she was a record holder in terms of the number of times she spent in a sanatorium and that, in her heyday, there would not be anyone, either in Kołobrzeg or Ciechocinek, that would not know her. She loved dancing and adored singing. She sang beautifully and powerfully. I remember when I was ten and my cousin Adam was born. Grandma was smitten. Totally in love with that little man, with his blond curls. I was so jealous of her beautiful singing for little Adaś. I know that when she was home she also sang a lot – to the flowers, to herself, to the neighbors. She loved music, watching concerts on TV. She enjoyed life just as it was. And it was full of people. Although over time it became increasingly difficult for her to go out, people would still bow to her even on the phone.

Her name, Mrs. Trojanowska, triggered smiles among shopkeepers who always asked me and others to send their regards to Grandma. She loved having people around, and the happiness of her loved ones was a priority. She longed for weekly reports from overseas from Henio or for Basia's calls from Germany. It did not matter where someone was; for her, it mattered that she received phone calls which confirmed that people were thinking of her. I smile broadly at this memory because, after all, she called me more often than I called her. Not because I did not think about her, but because I knew she was there. That was enough for me. I also knew that Grandma, while listening to my Mom's daily reports, would ask about me, my school, my exam results, and then about my children, their health and whatever was the topic of the day. On her birthday, she would wait for the last phone call and only then she could sit down on the couch. On the other hand, on my birthday, she was always the one to call me first.

My birthday has always been my day. When I worked, I would take a day off, I would receive her first phone call, then I would join my Mom in Grandma's apartment to have a special cup of coffee together. Now I no longer take time off, the first phone call is not the one I wait for, and, despite the beautiful cards and other forms of celebration, I miss that wonderful phone call around eight a.m. and have to control myself in order to stop the tears from flowing down my cheek. I recall proudly bringing my babies to my Grandma's home as soon as they were ready after being born and, before that, asking my mom if she had shown her the picture yet. I always waited impatiently to hear what she thought about my babies, about their looks, about their yawns and smiles. And then I found out that Grandma was the one to ask about them first.

She was the natural leader in the family. Not because she was the oldest, that was obvious to all of us, but because she had the strongest character. As a matter of fact, I am quite convinced that all women in our family were endowed with this kind of strength. My Mom, Aunt Krysia, Aunt Basia, Aunt Danusia, my cousins Ola, Asia and Iza, and my daughter Gabrysia. I will not modestly deny that I have it too. Every day I try to seek out more situations and moments in my memories from which I could extract something that truly makes sense.

My Gabrysia is now three years old. I remember every moment of her life so far, but, when she was born and we were cuddling, I noticed that her hands and her fingers reminded me a lot of my grandmother's hands. I thought then, "You will be strong, just like her, Gabrysia." I have probably been affirming her since birth that she will be a wise, strong girl, and that the whole world is ahead of her. And I am convinced that it will be so. Gabrysia has my aunt's middle name – Krysia – Grandma's daughter who passed away prematurely. Aunt Krysia was my first guide and my first mentor. And not a day goes by without me missing her and wishing that she were still around. But I have Gabrysia now, and I feel that she is a connection between me, my grandmother and Aunt Krysia. Gabrysia knows how to interact with people despite her age. She knows when I am upset – enough that she needs to apologize or give me a compliment about my nice eyes or dress. If nothing else works, she says that she loves me. However, I remember her strength being demonstrated last year when I had a mole removed as part of a routine procedure. I had a band-aid on my knee, which was enough to draw her attention, and later a tiny scar. Every day Gabrysia looked at that knee, touched it and asked me what it was and if it hurt. Even a second before leaving for daycare, she always touched it. After a few weeks, when I had already forgotten about it but she did not and kept asking the same questions, I decided to ask my husband to get the results. In fact, she kept asking that question for eight weeks until the phone rang and I, reluctantly, answered it getting the bad news: the mole was bad and I had to report to the hospital. The doctors took over my care, and Gabrysia stopped asking those questions. I knew from that day that Grandma's strength, power, intuition and instinct were already in other hands, going into the world, because Gabrysia has my eyes and little nose, Aunt Kasia's smile and Grandma's head, character and strength.

I do not know how the story will continue, what new memories I will manage to collect, what strength I will have to act with, how many more tears I will shed, and how much happiness I will experience, because I still am not able to believe it. But I know that, while living next to my grandmother for thirty-five years, I did not think about the person I was dealing with and what kind of strength I was subjected to. Only when I was ready to accept her into my life as a mantra, a guiding sign, and part of myself, I finally understood who I am and what I am capable of doing. I believe that everything happens thanks to family, because we are strong, powerful and confident, thanks to people we surround ourselves with. I had, and still have, wonderful people around me, especially strong and powerful women, who inspire me and thanks to whom I know that no matter what happens to us we have the strength to keep living and enjoying life.

Even though equality marches for women are being organized nowadays all over the world, I do not have to participate in any. In our family, we have already been walking enough, fighting for our rights and strength, and truly invoking happiness. It is not because we have it easy; we do not. Each of us has our own sorrows, dramas, separations, divorces, chronic illnesses, premature farewells, griefs, traumas and tears behind us. But someone once left us at this point of the map of life, left us herself, her faith and strength, and we know that regardless of what happens we have each other – family and this New World – whether it will be a street name, a point or a call to each other. And when the existing one falls apart, we will create a new world, just like she created it every time it seemed that everything had fallen apart.

Room 262

by Jennifer Lange (Pirri) Hoeper (Phoenixville, PA)

Walking into Room 262 that day felt familiar and different, all at once. I had made this trip countless times over the past several years, through seasonal changes, COVID, happy times, and sad times. The thirty-minute drive would sometimes pass quickly, while other times it felt never-ending. Upon arrival it was always the same song and dance – through the main doors to the check-in station, then down the hall to the left, each time passing clusters of nurses and residents, all going about their day with a sense of routine that felt oddly depressing even to someone like me, who loves a finely tuned schedule. There was a constant feeling of loneliness in that building. Many people coexisted within those walls, yet most were "journeying" alone. Even as a visitor, it was impossible to shut out the thoughts of my own personal guilt… "I only have an hour today. She is so lonely all by herself. I can't leave her to in favor of going do something 'fun.'" The same thoughts that would always flood my mind as I walked down the corridor.

As I approached the door, always slightly ajar, I told myself to put on my best "face," unsure of exactly what I might be walking into. Some days, Room 262 was a happy, goofy place. Most days, however, it was a prison for my grandmother who at age ninety-six felt trapped within those four walls, isolated from the world she once knew. This "assisted living" scenario is not unique to my family, I'm sure, and this idea of the "next phase of life" is often met with resistance from the person impacted the most. For my family, it was clear that many of us carried our own sadness and guilt around my grandmother's living situation. If only there had been another, better option... Regardless, my grandmother was far from shy about her feelings. There were many times where she would express her own disinterest for the place, usually with a snide remark – I'll spare you the language. But how could I blame her? I never liked the place either. There wasn't much to it, really... a bathroom to the right, a small closet to the left, and then an open room filled with a few pieces of old furniture that my grandmother had brought with her from her life before.

Actually – wait – I owe more credit to the closet.

I would most certainly be scolded for not mentioning the stylish wardrobe housed in that tiny closet. If there's one thing my grandmother prided herself on it was her taste in fashion. My mom would tell us stories of my grandmother (her mother) spending most days as a stay-at-home mom to six kids, maintaining a house, preparing dinner, and all the while never missing a chance to don her best set of clothes, a small heel, and a fresh coat of lipstick just before her husband (my grandfather) returned home from work. The classiest of ladies, with wits to go along with it, that's for sure.

So now that you're caught up on the closet... back to Room 262.

It was either the bed or the chair where you'd find my grandmother sitting – usually the chair. The bed was reserved for sleeping or, unfortunately, for days tougher than most. This was a tough day, more so, a tough week. For years we knew this time was coming, but my grandmother was known for her tenacity. She was a true fighter in every sense of the word. Born in Philadelphia (if you've seen the movie *Rocky*, you understand what I mean here), raised six children, grieved the loss of her eldest to cancer, survived the passing of her beloved husband of fifty-four years, and still she kept going. The trials and tribulations of life and heartbreak never stopped her from continuing on, even when the days were difficult. Not only was her strength apparent through her life experiences, but her time in Room 262 posed its own challenges that still proved no match for Mary Lange. To be isolated in a room, during COVID nonetheless, with limited mobility and only a window and telephone as a connection to the outside world, most people in her position would have surely given up – and as we know, many did. It is because of this history, that as a family we never knew when "it's time" was really *time*. As I walked into Room 262 that day, with my mom and aunt sitting by her side, I knew that what my grandmother was experiencing was different *this* time.

Over the course of a few hours, discussions were had about the level of care my grandmother should receive and how to keep her comfortable. All of those "standards of care" that you hear about when someone is entering the final stages of life, and more often than not, the topics you wish you never had to discuss or think about. A priest administering last rights, relatives coordinating travel plans, and the periodic "changing of the guard" to make sure a bedside moment was not missed. The feeling of sadness in Room 262 was heavy, but, as the hours and days trickled on, our family made every effort to bring light to the space.

Six kids, their spouses, nineteen grandchildren, twenty great-grandchildren, friends, even a dog (!), the list goes on. During the last week of her life, Room 262 became a motion picture of my grandmother's life and legacy. Her strength persisted through that week, as visitors held her hand, recounted outrageous family stories, and even had a drink (or several) in her company – a true Irish gal, she was never shy about a good time. Through the pain, her face still lit up during those special last moments. Somehow, someway, although Room 262 had never been my favorite place, I found new comfort in sitting there for hours each day knowing that it was exactly what my grandmother needed and wanted. She continued pushing through all of those moments, some of which I'm sure were a blur to her, but others appeared clear as day. When she was feeling well enough to share a final thought or two, a simple, strained, "I'm going to miss this," told me everything.

My grandmother continued to wow all of us that week. Each day or moment when we thought it might be the end, she found a way to surprise us and keep fighting. Although she was no longer coherent, someone new entering the room would send her pulse shooting upward, letting us know that she was still there and even possibly enjoying the joke or conversation that was happening at the foot of her bed. What amazed me most of all was knowing how much she despised Room 262, how she had been stuck there all of those years, and all of the tears and pain I had witnessed inside of those walls. I thought for sure she would want "out." But as she continued fighting, I started to see the deeper meaning behind it all.

My grandmother's life was full of strength, in more ways than one. So really, her fight itself was no surprise. But as I watched her throughout her final days, I learned that her strength was coming from something deeper. It wasn't medicine, luck, or that crazy Philadelphian spirit keeping her alive; it was love! Her connection to her family was stronger than fear, pain, and even nature's timeline. Witnessing the love in Room 262 taught me something much more meaningful – that a successful life isn't measured by what you've built or owned, but by having someone to live for – and loving them deeply enough to hold on. My grandmother spent her life teaching all of us how to be witty, smart, strong, beautiful, and of course fashionable … but in the end, her quietest, most important lesson was that true human connection – **love** – is what this life is all about.

So, in the end, if it weren't for that dreaded Room 262, a place I never liked, I would have never received my grandmother's greatest lesson about life and love. She taught us all what *she* already knew – that sometimes you have to sit in that discomfort to really learn a thing or two.

This is how we spend winter evenings in Ińsko – with tea, a warm blanket and our beloved series Northern Exposure.

A Red Phone and Green Jeans, or All Roads Lead to Shangri-La

by Beata Hoffmann (Poznań/Ińsko, Poland)

It all started over thirty years ago. In early August 1991, our Dad took my three-year younger sister, Katarzyna (Kasia, or Kaha, as she likes to be called now), and me, seventeen years old at that time, to Ińsko to participate, for the first time, in the relatively unknown (at least to us) Ińsko Film Summer Festival. Since then, Ińsko, a small town situated in Stargard County (in the northwestern part of Poland), has become the destination of our annual vacation. We often took our friends there, who, like us, were delighted with the magic of this fabulous place. It surprised all of us as an extraordinary combination of a unique, irresistibly intimate and friendly atmosphere of the festival and a charming movie theater located next to a picturesque and transparent lake surrounded by the verdant nature of the Ińsko Landscape Park (established in 1981). A place annually populated by dedicated film aficionados and brimming with joy, excitement and intellectual stimulation in an enormously festive atmosphere. We needed nothing more to be happy than to go to Ińsko every summer, where we would enjoy the diverse film repertoire of the festival and the company of old and newly met friends and acquaintances, people of all ages but with the same or similar interests.

For a change, in 1993, I decided to spend my winter vacation in Velké Karlovice, a mountain town full of snow, hills and forests that at that time was already a part of the Czech Republic, because, as of January 1 of that year, the Czech Republic and Slovakia became separate states, in place of the old Czechoslovakia. I went there with my best friend and her friends, who were supposed to teach me how to ski. On the first day it turned out that skiing was absolutely not for me. I had a fall that left me with a twisted leg, a few bruises and a black eye. We spent the rest of the trip in the interiors of the resort, moving between our rooms, the canteen and the bar, where our nightlife consisted of sipping Malibu drinks and having long conversations (in a Czech-Polish combination of a language) with friends we met there until dawn. Time passed lazily but rather quickly for us, as it usually does for those on vacation.

At that time, Kaha was spending the winter in Poznań, our home city with a population of about half-a-million. She was doing an internship in a small stationery store that was owned by our parents' friends. She had to stand behind the counter from 10:00 a.m. to 6:00 p.m. three times a week and sell a variety of stationery products. In the evenings, she would sit at home and listen to the Radio "S," which was our favorite radio station at that time. We passionately listened to it together all day and night, or whenever we had the opportunity. We actively participated in voting for our favorite songs, impacting thus music charts and competitions and often winning prizes in the form of audio cassettes. At one time, on the last Tuesday of the Carnival season, a special day that in Wielkopolska (the area where we lived) is referred to as "Podkoziołek," we even took my car and drove, with some freshly baked pastries, to the radio station, where we had the privilege of meeting our favorite radio celebrities in person.

Another time, around midnight, when my sister was listening to the radio program called "Musical Elevator," some boy called the station and introduced himself as Fragles. He said on the air that he was preparing a neckerchief for his friend who was about to get out of the military service. There used to be a custom for soldiers preparing to end their conscript service to draw symbolic motifs on their neckerchiefs or have a talented friend do it for them, as was the case here. The mysterious Fragles informed the audience about his special task and a little problem resulting from it: he had a major drawing job to do on a neckerchief and needed someone to sharpen his crayons. He also left his phone number in the event someone would get in touch with him to offer a helpful hand. He must have piqued my sister's interest, not just with his original or unusual name, because she wrote down the number and immediately called him, offering to sharpen his crayons. The guy explained to her that he had called the radio station out of boredom, or as a joke, while working alone on the neckerchief, just to talk to someone. Anyway, regardless of that strange misunderstanding, Kaha and the mysterious Fragles did get along quite well, from what I understood, and called each other for several days, extensively chatting about a number of different people and different things as if they had known each other for a quite long time.

I returned from the Czech Republic to the grey and wintery Poznań. Grandma Leontyna, as always, prepared a delicious dinner for me and others. This time it was my favorite beef roulades with dumplings and red cabbage, topped with a sauce that melted in your mouth. Poetry of taste. Our beloved Grandma would prepare something special for us every time we returned from vacation. She knew exactly what each of us liked the most, and we could always count on a culinary feast – a surprise, but not really, for we knew her quite well – when we returned home. In addition, our room and the whole apartment shone and smelled clean. I still remember the smell of polished parquet flooring all over the apartment and the aroma of cake wafting through the kitchen. Grandma was a loving, caring and extremely hardworking person, as well as an excellent cook. After she died she became Kasia's and my Guardian Angel. Her cuisine specialties, in addition to the beef roulades, included chicken broth with homemade macaroni and several other soups, pork cutlets, fried fish, the latter two usually served with mashed potatoes and a variety of cabbage. She was also famous for her desserts: out-of-this-world cheesecake, crumb cake, sweet, braided bread, doughnuts, a variety of pastries and gingerbread cookies (usually baked at Christmas time, along with the traditional poppy-seed cake).

After dinner, my sister and I were sitting in our room. I was lying on the bed, above which on the wall were attached photos and newspaper clippings of Rob Lowe, who was my ideal boyfriend. Handsome, blue-eyed, with an impeccable short haircut, well dressed and cheerful. At one point, I cut out a lot of hearts from paper, which I painted with red paint and used to decorate all the photos on the wall, forming a heart shape. Kaha was sitting at a red and white desk, not far from which a red telephone with a round dial was attached to the wall with its wire plugged into an outlet. I remember that this telephone model was called Pansy (in Polish *Bratek*) and I liked it very much. I did not know about the existence of mobile phones at that time. Kaha told me that she and Fragles had arranged to call each other in the evening after he got back from work. She dialed his number, which I still remember … 4748234.

"Hi, Fragles! This is Kaha. What's up?"

"Hi, Kaha! I just got back from work."

And they kept talking about this and that, about how their day was until, out of the blue, he asked,

"Kaha, how old are you, anyway? Because we've been talking like that for some time now. Well, admittedly, we're having a great time talking, but I don't even know how old you are."

"I'm sixteen," she replied.

There was a moment of silence and, after a few seconds of hesitation, Fragles continued with an unexpected statement/question,

"Well, maybe you have an older sister, because I am twenty-one."

Kaha looked at me, nodded her head in the affirmative manner and answered his question,

"In fact, yes, I do."

Then they both burst out laughing and, in this joyful atmosphere, after a while they said goodbye and hung up the phones.

The next day, during their phone conversation, they arranged a meeting of the three of us on March 8th (which happens to be the International Women's Day, celebrated then much more commonly than nowadays) at the now defunct, but then iconic, pub "Focus" in Paderewski Street, not far from the historical Old Market. Of course, my sister and I had arranged everything in advance. As always, we arrived on time due to my inborn sense of accountability. I was a little nervous because I did not know what to expect. We went inside. On the right side, there was a long, modern black bar; and on the left, along the wall, a long-haired guy was sitting at one of the tables. He wore a dark green sweatshirt, a scarf around his neck and green jeans. He had black sneakers on. He was sipping coffee from a white cup and writing something in a book calendar. As he would later admit, he wanted to make a good impression, and I have to admit that he did succeed. In order to avoid sitting in awkward silence, we had prudently taken with us an album of photos from our last vacation in Ińsko. We were surprised by the interest with which Fragles looked at each photo and how nicely he commented on them. I remember that the meeting was nice, the animated conversation logically switching from one topic to another, and we laughed a lot.

Fragles walked us home all the way to the bottom of the staircase, but we did not want to end the meeting yet, so, instead of taking the stairs up to our apartment (on the second floor), we walked him to the bus stop, which was not far from our home. We still had a moment to enjoy each other. As soon as bus number 82 arrived, we said goodbye with a kiss on the cheek. Fragles got on the bus and the doors closed. And I was standing at the bus stop all excited. On our way home, Kaha and I commented on this unusual experience and concluded that the meeting was full of positive energy and that the guy seemed (at least to me) to be from a completely different world.

From that time on, we kept meeting, partying and going out together. Fragles and I became inseparable. After two years, Fragles organized a small engagement event during which he proposed to me with the traditional beautiful ring while rose petals were falling from the sky. Fragles had many original ideas and a talent for writing amazing poems, which he gave me as gifts without any occasion, and I still keep them to this day. Although he was not Rob Lowe's type, he was handsome. He had lips like Val Kilmer's and he dressed well. He was and still is sensitive, caring and has a big heart. What a guy!

Fragles (whose real name, Maciej, had to be revealed sooner or later, most definitely in this context) and I got married on September 13, 1997, and Kaha and Maciej's sister, Paulina, were our bridesmaids, standing or sitting next to us (on both sides) and officially witnessing the two wedding ceremonies, one taking place in the registry office and one in the church. I can say without any reservations that we have lived happily ever after, enjoying our ups and downs (mostly ups!) at different times in two apartments in Poznań, one small, situated at the very top of a twelve-story building in one of the recently built complexes on the outskirts of the city, and one considerably bigger, where Kasia and I had spent our childhood, in the very center of the city, on a very busy street.

Over thirty-one years ago Fragles called the radio station, and that was the real beginning of our life journey together. A journey full of many amazing stories, the latest of which refers to the film festival town mentioned at the very beginning of this essay. For, enchanted with Ińsko, with its people and its annual event, Kaha, Maciej and I decided that ten days there once a year was not enough for us. Having found out about a nice house for sale there, we decided to buy it together and move in as soon as possible. Even though we all love Poznań, related to which we have plenty of great memories and where we still have many friends, and even though Kaha enjoyed living (with her family) in Warsaw for over two decades, the two cities are too noisy to live in happily and without any reservations. Thus, since June 2022, my sister, Fragles and I have been living in a wonderful place, a beautiful, comfortable and large house on the lake in the town named Ińsko. Yes, it is hard to believe, but we do live here now, and we know that this is where our Shangri-La, or our heaven on earth, is.

Thinking of My Sister, Laura

by Betsy Jackson Hoffmann (Lititz, PA)

She was pretty, I was plain,
Often, though, we were
The same.

Her love abounded for
Those that surrounded.

She was my playmate,
My doll, my kitten.
Many were smitten.

We fought, we loved.
We shared …

Her forgiveness was quiet.
Non-biased –
It made me pious.

Her flare was precise, mine –
Not that nice.
Though we, together, were
Quite concise.

Laura: *te omnes amamus*.
Remembering you with Love …

Jerzy in front of his big idol's residence in Memphis, TN (June, 2000).

My Musical Fascinations et Cetera: A Microstudy in Fandom

by Jerzy Hoffmann (Poznań/Tuchorza, Poland)

I was born in Poznań, a city situated in the western part of
Poland, in 1947; thus, my musical interests and tastes began to
develop in the 1950s, when—along with my siblings, two sisters
(Barbara, elder, and Danuta, younger) and one younger brother
(Henryk)—I was watching from aside (or, rather, from below) our
parents' everyday life, everything they did mostly outside their jobs,
our mother's activities in the kitchen and in the laundry room and
our father's in the mini-workshop in the basement, their family and
social gatherings, as well as their afternoons and evenings spent at
the movie-theater, in front of the TV or with their favorite books.
Like the overwhelming majority of the Polish population, our
parents were both Catholics, but only our mother, Stefania, was a
practicing Catholic and more of a regular church goer than her
husband, Leonard, and it was she that made sure that the children
receive the religious education and go through the necessary process
to receive the first three of the seven sacraments: Christening (or
Baptism), First Communion and Confirmation. It was from our
parents that we had heard for the first time some names of Polish
writers (e.g., Henryk Sienkiewicz and Albert Szklarski) and foreign
(Alexandre Dumas and Ernest Hemingway), Polish actors
(Eugeniusz Bodo, Jerzy Duszyński, Danuta Szaflarska, Halina
Janowska and Zbigniew Cybulski) and foreign (Errol Flynn, Gerard
Philipe, Jean Marais, Sophia Loren and Gina Lollobrigida), and
Polish singers (Mieczysław Fogg, Maria Koterbska and
Sława Przybylska) and foreign (Edith Piaf, Yves Montand, Tino
Rossi). Barbara, Henryk, Danuta and I, along with many relatives
and friends, appreciated everything we had learned from them about
life and the arts, and we somehow managed to remember their
precious advice for many, many years.

When I was born, my family, along with several other families,
lived in a big villa on the outskirts of Poznań, in Wiślana Street,
situated somewhere between the airport and Lake Rusałka. In
December 1955, just before Christmas, we moved to an apartment in
a newly built block situated in the center of Poznań, about a hundred
meters from the spectacular Liberty Square. The reason I am
mentioning it is because the title of this book is *People in Our Lives*,
and there were a lot of people in my parents' lives in both places,
who more than indirectly impacted also the existence of their
children. The doors of our apartments were always open to relatives,

friends and neighbors, who appreciated our parents' hospitality, whether discussing the current events, sharing their joys and problems or simply enjoying a glass (yes, not a cup!) of coffee or tea and some (usually homemade) treats. The relationships developed that way were not limited to a social life; on the contrary, they often included various forms of moral and practical support in a number of areas, such as babysitting, elderly-person care, health, repairs, minor renovations and other services that no one in the post-war communist times could afford to pay for. Thus, it was a big blow for many people when our parents untimely passed away, our mother in November 1964 (a month before her forty-first birthday) and father in April 1967 (at the age of forty-four). While all four of us, as their kids, suffered the most because of the utmost and indescribable loss, Danuta was victimized the most. Not even ten years old yet, she was invited to live with Aunt Sabina, our mother's younger sister, a remarried widow raising three daughters of her own.

Regardless of our age, we shared at least some of our parents' preferences, and, having inherited their film and musical passions, we started, in the late 1950s, regularly going to the movies on our own to see pictures both recommended by our parents and chosen by ourselves. The film that impacted everyone in our family and almost annually added flavor to our celebration of Christmas was *Holiday Inn* (starring Bing Crosby and Fred Astaire), and Irving Berlin's beautiful song "White Christmas" from that movie was even able to compete with the best Polish Christmas carols. While *Holiday Inn* was an old film (released in 1942), shown only on television, the pictures we went to see on the big screen offered a variety of genres, some of them Polish and some made abroad. My sister, being somewhat older, enjoyed some serious Polish films, such as Andrzej Wajda's *Ashes and Diamonds* (1958) and Jerzy Kawalerowicz's *The Train* (1959), both starring Zbigniew Cybulski, an actor frequently compared to James Dean (ironically, Cybulski also died prematurely, at the age of thirty-nine, while trying to board a running train in Wrocław in 1967). Henryk and I never turned down an opportunity to see a new American western. Our favorites were *High Noon* (1952; starring Gary Cooper and Grace Kelly), *Shane* (1953; with Alan Ladd, Jean Arthur and Van Heflin), *3:10 to Yuma* (1957; featuring Glenn Ford and Van Heflin), *Apache* (starring Burt Lancaster and Jean Peters), *Winchester '73* (1950; with James Stewart and Shelley Winters), *Broken Arrow* (1950; featuring James

Stewart, Jeff Chandler and Debra Paget), *Vera Cruz* (1954; starring Gary Cooper and Burt Lancaster) and a few others.

In the early 1960s, my siblings and I were especially thrilled to discover two films that introduced us to the younger generations of singers, musical *The Young Ones* (1961), with more and more popular British singer Cliff Richard and the instrumental band The Shadows, and western *Rio Bravo* (1959), featuring, in addition to western star John Wayne and enormously likeable Walter Brennan (who would become my favorite character actor to such a degree that, some fifty years later, his picture would appear on Facebook Messenger as my profile photo), two superior singers, Dean Martin and Ricky Nelson, together performing on the screen (with some help from Brennan) two unforgettable songs, "My Rifle, My Pony and Me" and "Cindy" (in addition to the over-the-credits song sung by Martin). While Nelson had already won the hearts of the Polish youngsters with his hit "Hello, Mary Lou," Martin would seal his popularity (at least in Poland) as a singer a few years later with the song "Everybody Loves Somebody," which would successfully compete with the greatest hits by some newly created rock bands. Ironically, it was Barbara who had seen *Rio Bravo* first and, as soon as she came home after the show, she could not resist to share her fascination for the western with Henryk and me, telling us the whole plot in detail despite the late hour. Needless to say, Henryk and I went to see it the following day, and we kept revisiting it whenever an opportunity arose, introducing it also to our parents and younger sister, Danusia.

In addition to the British and American singers being discovered by our generation at that time, there were more and more Polish singers, who managed to capture the attention of young people. Quite often they started their careers as vocalists of such bands as Niebiesko-Czarni (The Blue-and-Blacks), Czerwono-Czarni (The Red-and-Blacks), Czerwone Gitary (The Red Guitars), Trubadurzy (The Troubadours), Skaldowie (The Skalds), Blackout, Breakout, Homo Homini (that is a Latin name meaning "Man to Man," possibly a short form of "Homo Homini Lupus," meaning "man is a wolf to man"), Dwa plus Jeden (Two plus One), Budka Suflera (Prompt Box) and a few others. Czesław Niemen, Wojciech Korda, Ada Rusowicz, Stan Borys, Piotr Szczepanik, Maryla Rodowicz, Urszula Sipińska, Tadeusz Woźniak, Grzegorz Grechuta, Seweryn Krajewski and Krzysztof Krawczyk were possibly the most distinguished singers of that time. Some of them did start as band vocalists, but soon became independent. The access to the music of those bands and singers was relatively easy. They performed on the radio and on television, during public shows arranged by state officials for national holidays, three song festivals (in Opole, Sopot and Kołobrzeg) and numerous concerts organized especially in major Polish cities. While their popularity varied depending on the audience's tastes (my favorites were Czerwone Gitary, Skaldowie, Niemen, Szczepanik, Rodowicz i Grechuta), all the bands and all the singers vastly contributed to making people's lives nicer, more meaningful and showing some sense in the otherwise sad existence of the young Polish generation, deprived of democratic freedom and forced to live according to the state-imposed economy.

The access to foreign musicians was not that easy. Even though we could occasionally hear some of them on the Polish Radio, and available in special stores were records amateurly produced on plastic squares the size of single or double postcards, the majority of true fans were dependent on Radio Luxembourg, where they could be exposed to hits by such singers as Chubby Checker, Elvis Presley, Louis Armstrong, Nat King Cole, Frank Sinatra, Dean Martin, Paul Anka, Neil Seda, Connie Francis, Brenda Lee, Petula Clark, Ricky Nelson, Cliff Richard, Roy Orbison and many other British and American singers. (I discovered Presley's enormous talent as early as in the early 1960s, but I developed my true Elvis passion about a decade later, which I described in detail below.)

In the mid-1960s, known all over the world became some British and American rock bands, such as The Tremeloes, The Beatles, The Rolling Stones, The Beach Boys, The Animals, The Turtles, The Byrds, Herman's Hermits, The Monkees and many others. They were all popular in Poland, even though not to the same extent (The Beatles, The Rolling Stones and The Beach Boys were definitely at the very top), and it was a dream of every fan to go to a concert of any of them. Unfortunately, due to the geographic obstacle and/or political barrier, only a few (and rather less prestigious) of the bands visited Poland. Best known among those that did appear in Poland were The Animals (I managed to see their concert with my friend Zdzisław and, needless to say, enjoyed tremendously) and, in the early 1970s, Procol Harum (whose concert I missed for some reason).

I mentioned the last band a little bit too soon because I meant to talk about the seventies after mentioning some significant facts from my personal life. Having reached not only adulthood (eighteen being the official age in Poland), but also some level of maturity, in July 1971, I married Renata, the woman of my life, with whom I raised two sons, Marcin and Jakub (also known as Kuba). A big tragedy in our life was the fact that their elder sister, Agnieszka, was born with a heart failure and passed away before reaching the elementary school age (long before they were born, so they never even had an opportunity to meet her), causing an enormous and long-lasting grief among not only her parents, but also her grandparents and many aunts, uncles and cousins. These biographical data are essential because family has always played an important role in my life, and I have shared my musical passions first with my parents and siblings, then with my wife and eventually with my sons. And, during the 1970s and 1980s, the group included some other people, especially men whom I used to play contract bridge with, including – addition to Henryk – my brother-in-law Zdzisław (Danuta's husband), and my friends Bernard, Leszek, Włodzimierz and Bogdan. Sadly, Zdzisław (a big fan of Led Zeppelin), Bernard (the list of his favorites rather long, from Louis Armstrong and Eric Clapton to Joe Cocker and Van Morrison, plus classical music), Włodzimierz and Bogdan (the last two having an eclectic taste in music), all great guys, loyal friends and exemplary fathers, are not amongst us anymore; they passed away at relatively young age and have been mourned by many.

Having become a husband and father, I continued developing my musical taste, and soon my favorite bands were joined by The Bee Gees, Led Zeppelin and The Electric Light Orchestra. At the top of my personal list were also Simon & Garfunkel, Bob Dylan and Leonard Cohen, all famous for their beautiful folk ballads enriched with poetic flavor and intellectual content. A big event at that time (in 1978, to be exact) was the world premiere of the film *Sgt. Pepper's Lonely Hearts Club Band* (also distributed in Poland), which pleased not only the fans of The Beatles (the band earlier admired in three pictures, *A Hard Day's Night*, *Help*! and *Yellow Submarine*)—the authors and original performers of the songs of the album—but also the buffs of The Bee Gees, the performers of those song in the movie inspired by the record. In the same period of my life, I got also interested in country music—most likely influenced by Korneliusz Pacuda, who had his own radio program called "All roads lead to Nashville" and who was one of the organizers and presenter of the annual country festival in Mrągowo, a resort town in the Masurian Lake District. My favorite country singers include Johnny Cash, whom I also admired as an actor in the western *A Gunfight* (co-starring Kirk Douglas), Kris Kristofferson, also an actor, known for such films as *Pat Garrett and Billy the Kid* (co-starring James Coburn and Bob Dylan), *A Star Is Born* (co-starring Barbra Streisand) and *Convoy* (co-starring Ali MacGraw), Jim Reeves, Willie Nelson, Frankie Laine (who sang the title songs in several movies, including westerns *Gunfight at the O.K. Corral* and *3:10 to Yuma)*, Waylon Jennings, Merle Haggard, Kenny Rogers, Dolly Parton, Marylou Harris, Loretta Lynn and several others.

The whole decade of the 1970s was significant to me because of many highlights (not all positive) in my personal life, but also as the peak of my Elvis passion. Even though Presley was no longer as popular as, say, The Beatles, The Polish TV had for some time been broadcasting several of his movies, including *Love Me Tender*, *Jailhouse Rock*, *King Creole*, *G.I. Blues*, *Flaming Star*, *Blue Hawaii*, *Fun in Acapulco*, *Viva Las Vegas* and *Clambake*. While most of those films, characterized by trite stories and mediocre acting, were just a pretext to show some good songs flawlessly performed by Elvis, some of them—such as *Jailhouse Rock, King Creole* and *Flaming Star*—not only stood out for their conspicuous artistic assets, but also proved Presley to be quite a competent actor. As a result, many Presley songs—"It's Now or Never," "Can't Help Falling in Love," "Heartbreak Hotel," "Are You Lonesome Tonight," "Love Me Tender," "Return to Sender," "Crying in the Chapel," "That's All Right" and others—could now be regularly heard on the radio, and their popularity among at least two generations of fans was confirmed during numerous family and social gatherings (including those with dances).

At the same period, I, as a dedicated music collector, was trying to replace or supplement my cassettes with vinyl albums. Quite excited about the impressive size of my Elvis album collection and looking forward to make the volume even bigger, I experienced an incredible shock when, on August 17, 1977, I heard the news about my idol's death at the age of forty-two. According to the old aphorism, "Art is long, and life (including that of an artist) is short," and there is nothing we can do about it. Thus, with people dearest to me, I celebrated the memory and legacy of the "rock 'n' roll king" on a regular basis, chatting about him and listening to his records during our social meetings. One of the songs that was then added to our usual listening list was "I Remember Elvis Presley (The King Is Dead)," written by Dick Bekker, Eddy Ouwens and Dunhills, and performed by Ouwens under the name of Danny Mirror.

While my other musical preferences were based on/caused by my balanced fascination and manifested themselves strongly in certain periods of my life, my Elvis passion, hard to define, was something else, an intensive and almost metaphysical phenomenon, incessantly lasting till now. Needless to say, my Elvis album record collection kept growing faster (regardless of the exorbitant prices) than those of any other singer or band, both Polish and foreign, belonging to the old or young generation.

A special event in the history of my Elvis fascination was an unforgettable episode that took place during my visit to the USA. It was in the late spring of 2000 when my brother Henryk, then living in the States, and his wife Betsy invited me to spend several weeks in their residence located on the campus of a prep school in Asheville, North Carolina (where Henryk was employed as a Latin teacher and soccer coach). After the graduation (I was one of the numerous family members watching the ceremony as Betsy's third daughter Jennifer concluded then her high school education, following the steps of her elder sisters, Emily and Laura), Betsy, well aware of my passion, not only offered to me and Henryk a trip to Memphis, Tennessee, but also volunteered to be the designated driver. I cannot describe my reaction—it is simply impossible: I remember that period as a series of events watched by me at a distance through dense fog. Based on the information provided subsequently by Betsy and Henryk, I was sitting at the back of the car during the long trip, incessantly humming Elvis's songs and only intermittently looking left or right to admire the beautiful scenery of western North Carolina, Kentucky and Tennessee.

I was not able to recover from the surprise and marvel after we checked in at the Heartbreak Hotel, and the sightseeing of Graceland can be described as an absolutely unlikely dream, never expressed but fulfilled far beyond expectations. The incomprehensible reaction on my part took place as soon as we entered the first of the buildings. My health had not always been perfect, but I had never experienced any form of headache. At that moment, however, the pain I felt at the top of my head and within my skull was absolutely unbearable. I had to stop and tell Henryk I wanted to leave and do something about my strange feeling. Fortunately, after he explained the situation to Betsy, she gave me a tablet which I immediately swallowed without any water and almost instantaneously felt an amazing relief. As a result of that miraculous treatment, I was able to continue the sightseeing and enormously enjoy myself looking at the interiors full of rare furniture, astounding decorations and specially framed collections of golden records, as well as stopping in front of Elvis's grave and taking photos in front of his luxurious cars and two private planes. As far as the unexpected reaction on my part in the form of the headache is concerned, I had no explanation for it then, and I have none now. Even though, after we got back to Asheville, Betsy confessed that what she had given me was not a painkiller but a vitamin C tablet (which would imply that it was used as placebo), it does not explain the cause of the excruciating pain I had before I had taken it. I leave the conclusions to the readers.

My memories of the trip to Memphis and sightseeing of Graceland constitute the peak of my emotional experiences related to music. It would be hard or even unthinkable to expect anything bigger than that. An event almost comparable to it turned out to be, in 2022, the premiere of Baz Luhrmann's film *Elvis*, starring Austin Butler (in the titular role), Tom Hanks (as Colonel Tom Parker) and Olivia DeJonge (as Patricia Presley). The movie not only fulfilled my expectations, both in respect of its plot and the musical illustration of my idol's life, but its artistic qualities allowed me to consider it a perfect and suitable homage paid to the "rock 'n' roll king." My reaction to the final sequence of the film was rather unexpected. While the news of Elvis's death forty-five years earlier resulted in a shock and the visit at Graceland in the year 2000 caused an unbearable headache, the final minutes of Luhrmann's picture squeezed from my eyes an abundant flow of genuine tears.

Translated from Polish by Henryk Hoffmann

The first edition of the Young Hearts Film Festival in Ińsko. Photo by Igor Skawiński.

Where the World Begins
A Story of One Decision That Changed Everything

by Kaha Hoffmann (Poznań/Warsaw/Ińsko, Poland)

I was born in 1977 in Poland, in the Jeżyce district of Poznań — a place where the sound of streetcars rattled in the background, where the smell of fresh bread came from the neighborhood bakery and where the local cinema felt like a second school of life. It was my dad, a passionate moviegoer, who used to take me and my sister Beata to the movies. That's where my love for storytelling began.

That love carried me forward — through film school, through a degree in history at the university, and into the world of editing in television and film. I spent over two decades in Warsaw, working on some of the biggest productions: Idol, Must Be the Music, The Voice of Poland — programs also known outside of Poland — and on some beloved Polish shows, like Kuchenne Rewolucje (our version of Kitchen Nightmares), Nasz Nowy Dom (our Extreme Makeover: Home Edition) and Gliniarze (similar to Cops).

On the one hand — success, momentum, life in the center of it all. On the other — less and less air. Less and less of me. Even though I was surrounded by people, including a few friendships that remain to this day, I felt like something was missing. I needed something real.

In the meantime, I became a mom. Zuzanna and Tymon — two completely different kids, yet both incredibly sensitive and independent. I always had a real connection with them, but more and more often I found myself thinking: I want them to see a different kind of life than what the capital offers. Not the kind that is experienced on autopilot, with sushi deliveries every other day and the sound of work emails pinging at night. I wanted them to see a world that smells like pine forest, where you have to cook your meal before you eat it and where worth isn't measured in brand names, but in meaning.

And then I thought again: Ińsko.

The first time I went to Ińsko was in 1991. I was fourteen. My dad took my sister, Beata, and me to the Ińsko Summer Film Festival. I had no idea then that this tiny town would live in me for the rest of my life. A small lakeside village — quiet, green, calm — that in August would awaken like a spell. Films, conversations, emotions. It was a world completely different from everything I had known until then. I fell in love with this place. That kind of love can't be explained. It just is.

And I kept coming back — year after year. Ińsko became my summer ritual. A place of transitions, crushes, first emotions and the first adult film that stayed with me forever — Pigsty. It wasn't easy. It was shocking. But it was real.

And then life moved on — work, kids, Warsaw. But that thread … it never disappeared.

In 2014, during the festival, the artistic director Przemek Lewandowski screened the feature film How to Beat a Hangover by Bartosz Brzeskot, for which I had served as the editing director and editor. That was the first time I wasn't just sitting in the audience — I stood in front of it as a filmmaker. It was nerve-wracking … and also beautiful.

In 2016, along with a group of festival participants, we proposed making a short film during the festival — just for fun. It turned into something more. A light, funny story came out of it, and we screened it at the closing ceremony. People laughed, clapped, someone said, "This should happen every year." And that's how it started.

Since then, every year we've created these little festival films —
Beata, Fragles (Maciej — Beata's husband) and I, plus festival
participants, organizers, Ińsko locals and even the mayor. That's
how our informal film crew was born — the Ińska Fabryka Snów
(Ińsko Dream Factory).

The films became more polished each year, and my involvement
in the Ińsko Summer Film Festival grew. Eventually, the three of us
— Beata, Fragles, and I — became official members of the festival's
association. That's when the idea came: a bigger project — a
documentary about the festival's fifty-year history.

And that's how Ińsko Summers – Where the Stars Give Up Their
Glamor was born. An intimate, honest portrait of a place that, for
half a century, had attracted people with passion.

And it was while writing that script that I felt it — this wasn't
just a summer romance with Ińsko anymore. This place was calling
me toward something more.

TV work was giving me less and less joy. The pace, the
expectations, the feeling of being just a cog in a machine that no
longer inspired me. Warsaw was wearing me out. My job no longer
brought satisfaction, and the speed of life was becoming unbearable.
At the same time, my private life began to fall apart. A breakup.
Questions about what's next.

One day, Beata and Fragles — my closest friends and creative
partners — came to visit me from Poznań. Not to settle any business.
Just to help me clean out my cluttered apartment. The kind of
cleaning you do when you know something has to change, even if
you don't yet know what.

And right there, between tossing out old junk and taking a coffee
break, I looked at them and asked:

Kaha: What if we all moved to Ińsko?

A moment of silence. Beata put down her tea, looked at me with
a face like she had been waiting her whole life for that question and
said calmly but firmly:

Beata: All right, let's do it.

Fragles froze mid-sip, staring at Beata, then at me, then back at
Beata, as if trying to make sure he heard correctly.

Fragles: Wait, what?!

Beata shrugged like she was casually deciding to repaint the living room, not change their entire lives.

Beata: We all knew it was going to happen eventually.

I burst out laughing. Fragles still looked stunned, trying to process the idea — but there was a spark of excitement in his eyes, even if he didn't want to admit it yet.

Fragles: But how?!

Beata: We pack up. We move.

Fragles ran his hand through his gray beard, sighed, but smiled under his breath.

Fragles: Fine, but we'll need a big house. Everyone needs their space.

Kaha: That's true.

He leaned back like he was already mentally rearranging furniture — and then he remembered something important.

Fragles: You know there's no sushi there, right?

Beata suddenly turned serious, wide-eyed, like the weight of her decision just hit her.

Beata: That's going to be a problem.

Kaha sighed and nodded without hesitation.

Kaha: That's going to be the biggest problem.

A pause. Then all three of us burst out laughing, because deep down we knew — sushi or not — Ińsko was the best decision of our lives.

We already knew it wasn't a joke. This was happening. And it didn't feel crazy — it felt right.

What I feared most was how my kids would react. Zuza had just started at a film-focused high school. Tymon was in the last year of elementary school.

They were not thrilled.

Zuza: Mom, I love Ińsko, but just for vacations. I don't want to live there!

She looked at me like I had betrayed her.
Tymon: We have school here, our friends, everything!

I looked at them both and knew I couldn't convince them with words. I just hoped that someday they'd understand. I was scared too — scared that I was ruining their lives with this decision. But I couldn't back down. I wouldn't.

Kaha: I've made my decision. Maybe you'll hate me now, but I believe, one day, you'll see that this was one of the best things we've ever done.

Silence fell. Heavy, resistant silence. But underneath it, I felt something starting to shift. Not acceptance — not yet — but maybe the first step toward it.

The decision was made.

We bought a house. Big enough for everyone. With space for a small editing studio. With a view of the lake. Moving from the capital, where I had lived for more than two decades, to a town of less than 2,000 people sounded like madness to many. To me, it was completely logical.

Because Ińsko wasn't an impulse. It was a return.

Ińsko, with its 1,800 residents, was about to gain five more —

plus two dogs. And I felt like I was coming home. Back to the girl I was in the '90s, coming to the film festival every summer. Back to the woman who had spent years learning editing, filmmaking, storytelling — all so she could one day pass it on.

This was a new beginning.

In Ińsko, I quickly realized that life could move differently. But after the initial awe came the big question: What now?

I didn't want to go back to editing projects for Warsaw clients. That wasn't why I came here.
I wanted to do something meaningful. Something joyful. Something that gave power to young people. But how?

And then — in true Polish style — I showed up at my neighbors' place with a bottle of vodka and a question:

Kaha: What now?

Asia — an artist, singer, a radiant soul — and Przemek — the artistic director of the Ińsko Film Summer, a charismatic madman who seemed to bend time and space — welcomed me like family. They had moved to Ińsko three years before us. They helped us find the house we live in. They were warm, practical, generous. For me, they became guides. Friends. Chosen family.

Kaha: I'm so done working remotely for "Warszawka." I need to do something here. For the kids. Maybe film workshops in Szczecin?

Asia lit up:
Asia: That's perfect! Do it. Kaha — who else could do it if not you?

Przemek: Teach young people here, in these smaller towns. Szczecin already has access to stuff like that — we don't. I'll give you contacts. I'll talk to people. I'll help.

And just like that — it started.
I'm still grateful that they blew a tornado into my wings.

Film workshops for kids and teens.

And I didn't start small — we launched eight groups spread across the West Pomeranian region.

We wrote scripts. Shot scenes. Learned together. Laughed. Cried sometimes.

We got to know each other — and more importantly, we created.

Watching their focus, passion and pride — I knew this mattered.
This wasn't just a hobby.
It was something that could stay with them. Shape them.
They started to realize they had a voice.
That their stories mattered.
That they had power.
And when I saw how deeply it moved them, one new idea crept in:

What if ... a festival?

A crazy idea.
I mean, who starts an international youth film festiwal ... in a town of 1,800 people?

But if not us — the Ińsko Dream Factory — then who?

Young Hearts Film Festival was meant to be a celebration of young voices.
A space to be seen. To feel. To be proud.

That first edition?
A total leap of faith.

But then ... the submissions started rolling in.
From India. The U.S. France. Germany. Canada. Ukraine. China. Taiwan. The UK. Czech Republic.
And, of course, Poland.
Among them were the films made by our own workshop kids — from Ińsko, Recz, Drawsko Pomorskie, Tuczno, Wałcz, Stargard ...

We were stunned.

And then came the biggest joy —
Watching those kids see their own films ... on the big screen.

There was laughter. Tears. Silence. Cheering.
Parents stared at their children.
Kids stared at themselves — a little in shock.
That's my film.
That's my story.
This counts.

The people of Ińsko fell in love with the festival.
Their reactions, their support — they told me everything I
needed to know:

This matters.

The women at the Ińsko Cultural Center had backed me up from
day one.

I still smile remembering one of our first conversations:

Ola: Jola, remember when Kaha walked in and told us she
wanted to start an international youth film festival?

Jola: Oh, I definitely remember.

Ola: Well, I think we can finally say it to her now.

Jola laughed and glanced at Ola, then at me.
I raised my eyebrows and crossed my arms, smiling.

Kaha: Alright, spill it.

Jola: Ola said you were crazy. That it couldn't be done.

Ola: That's not exactly what I said! I said you were a
madwoman, and only you could come up with such a wild idea.

Jola: But now? We know that kind of madness ... works.

We all burst out laughing.

At first, they had serious doubts — organizing international events isn't exactly common around here.

But they'd already handled tons of big local happenings, and eventually, they threw themselves into this one too.

Kaha: It wouldn't have worked without you.

Jola shook her head, smiling. Ola raised her coffee cup and winked.

Ola: Here's to the madness that works.

I beamed.

Because what we'd created wasn't just an event.

It was a dream come true.

Now I'm in the middle of preparing the second edition of the festival.

Young Hearts Film Festival turned out to be a perfect shot.

But it was more than that — it was the culmination of a path that began way back in 1991,

when I was a teenager watching Pigsty in a dark movie theater in Ińsko.

The circle had closed.

Only now I was the one creating the space, turning on the light, offering the screen.

And I wasn't alone.

From the beginning, it was us — Beata and Fragles and I.

We were the heart of the Dream Factory.

It was alive. It was working. It was inspiring.

And with us were the locals, old friends and new allies — people who believed in what we were building.

Then something unexpected happened:

Three of our workshop films were awarded at Best Off — a national showcase of the best Polish youth cinema.

We traveled to Warsaw with the kids from Ińsko and Recz,

watched their films on a big festival screen, saw them receive
diplomas, give interviews.
They came back different.
Proud.
Stronger.

And so did I.
Because I knew: this wasn't just a local initiative anymore.
It was a new lifeline.
For them.
And for me.

Something that truly worked.

Ińsko had become not just a home —
it had become the center of my life.
A place where we started a film club, workshops, and an
international festival.
People said:
"What you're doing ... it's good."

But with that came something else, something I hadn't expected:
not everyone is ready for change.
Because when you do something from the heart,
without politics, without favors —
for some people ...
you become a problem.
Too independent.
Too visible.
Too liked.

As local leadership changed, so did the atmosphere.
Not among the people — they still came, supported, thanked me.

But from the officials ...
questions started showing up.
About the workshops.
About money.
About whether it was "really needed."

Then came silence. Misunderstandings. A refusal to talk.
But I stayed quiet too —
because I knew what I was doing had value.
And I knew who I was doing it for.

The Director of the Ińsko Culture Center was on my side.
Together, we had plans. Dreams. New ideas.
And then, out of nowhere …
I heard she had resigned.
No conversation.
No warning.
Just … gone.

But I had spoken to her the day before.
We had plans.
She loved her job.
She didn't want to leave.

I knew she had been pressured.
I knew she was told the workshops weren't worth it.
But she had seen the kids come in, seen them light up, seen the
value — and she stood by it.

And that's when I knew:
I can't keep building something beautiful
in a place that doesn't see me the right way.
I'm here to do things that matter
And if I create from the heart —
I won't let anyone walk over that heart.

So I made a choice.
The second edition of the Young Hearts Film Festival would
move.
To a new place.
With new partners.
To somewhere that offered space, collaboration and mutual trust.

And I made this decision in silence.
Not from anger.
Not from being hurt.

But from clarity.
Not against anyone —
but for the young people.
For the energy we needed.
For the truth, which will always matter most.

I believe this change isn't an accident.
It's a call.
To move forward.
And the people who support me —
I know they'll come too.

Today, I'm standing at the edge of something new.
The festival will have a new home —
and it looks like we're joining forces with Kalisz Pomorski and
Drawsko Pomorskie.
It's not just a change of location.
It's the opening of space.
New alliances.
New possibilities.
And new people who — just like I — want to give young voices
a place to be heard.

I feel this is the right path.
And no — it's not always easy.
Sometimes I lie on the couch, unable to move, watching a
meaningless show.
But I allow myself that.
Because I know I'll get back up.
I'll feel the spark again.
I'll meet those who walk this path with me.

After making that decision I could finally breathe.
No need to explain.
No need to be liked.
No fear that someone would twist my words, leave things unsaid
or spin them around.

I could focus on what truly matters —
on the young people who are waiting.

And what about life?
What about my kids?

Well — life came full circle.
Just when I thought my children needed the big cities, that we were growing apart — they … came back.

Zuza was the first to call.

— Mom, I want to come back to Ińsko. I'm tired of Wrocław. I'll commute to school in Stargard — but I want to be home.

A few days later — Tymon.

— Mom, I can't do this in Warsaw. I want to come back. I miss you. I miss Ińsko.

My children whispered the simplest truth:
"We're only happy in Ińsko."

And that was enough.

It was one of the happiest moments in my life.
Because it proved something I now know deep in my bones —
when you do things with love and awareness,
they always come back to you.

Not always how you expect.
Not when you expect.
But they return.
And Ińsko?

Now I know, with all my heart — I am exactly where I'm meant to be.
Because here, in Ińsko, I found the happiness I'd been searching for all my life.
What was supposed to be just a summer adventure turned into my home … and the purpose of my life.
And that — that's the most beautiful twist in my story.

Now I sit on my porch, looking out at the world.
A glass of wine in my hand.
Silence behind me.
Loved ones beside me.
A story I've lived through.
And a deep sense that ...
I still have so much more to do.

Kaha: You know I have this small dream.
Tymon: That they'll finally open a sushi place in Ińsko?
Kaha rolls her eyes, laughing.
Kaha: No. That one day, someone — while accepting an Oscar
— will say that everything started in a small lakeside town, at a
youth film workshop with Kaha Hoffmann.
A pause.
Beata lifts her glass of wine.
Beata: Then here's to the Oscar.
Tymon rolls his eyes — but smiles.
And in the background, the lake at night ...
and the sound of crickets that feels like Ińsko's never-ending
melody.

Ińsko is here — in my heart, in the story, in the old memories
and the new ones.
It is my cradle.
And it will always be.

But now ...
I've gone further.

And just a moment ago,
another impulse came.

If there are workshops ...
If there's a festival ...

Then maybe ...
a summer film camp for youth — the Young Hearts Film Camp?

Well then —
let's get to work.

To conclude my essay with a real punchline ...

After all my struggles, Ińsko's local leadership revealed a change of heart and asked me to move the Young Hearts Film Festival back to its orginal location.

Well, I don't see any reason why I shouldn't do it.

Thus, there is a happy ending to the story after all.

Byron's first unearthing of a version of a Chopin waltz at the Château de Thoiry in France. He discovered this same waltz in yet another version in Chopin's hand at Yale University, the second example of "by accident"/synchronicity (a phenomenon widely discussed by Byron in his book Chopin and Beyond*).*

A Path to Spontaneity?*

by Byron Janis (1928–2024)

SPONTANEITY ISN'T THE SAME AS CREATIVITY, but it's an ambiance in which creativity flourishes—a state some have called being in "high carelessness." It's a feeling of letting go from the bottom of your toes. Some veteran practitioners are said to enter a playground of "passionate indifference," a phrase coined by Teilhard de Chardin, the French Jesuit theologian and paleontologist. If you're feeling "Oh, what the heck" as you toss a splash of Chopin vodka over your poire Hélène, you're approaching the realm of spontaneity. If you're checking on your soufflé every five minutes, you can expect mud pie for dessert.

One of the best songs I wrote for *The Hunchback of Notre Dame* came upon me when Maria and I were strolling after lunch near a little Parisian bistro tucked into the shadow of that beautiful, mysterious cathedral, Notre-Dame. We were walking along one side looking up and pondering the gargoyles, wondering whose faces had inspired the sculptor, when I suddenly said to Maria, "Go on ahead of me, I'll be with you in a minute." I reached into my jacket pocket and found a cocktail napkin from our lunch. The notes spilled out of my head fast and furiously. My only difficulty was preventing the napkin from disintegrating under my fingers as I wrote down all the letters of the melody. I have developed my own musical shorthand, which came about as a result of my arthritis. It is difficult for me to put notes onto a musical staff because of the small space between the lines. I use letters, as Mr. Litow, my old piano teacher back in Pittsburgh, used to do, designating which note is to be struck—A, B, C, and so on. After five minutes the napkin looked like it was covered in hieroglyphs, but a song was born—unpremeditated, spontaneously. I was relaxed—both open and focused—and grateful. But was it good? That I still had to determine.

Speaking of napkins, Maria's uncle, Cedric Gibbons, an art director at MGM for decades, designed the famous "Oscar" statuette on the back of a cocktail napkin in a Hollywood restaurant. Why do you suppose so many sketches and drawings are started on napkins—and used ones at that? Why are so many memorable songs first scribbled on the backs of electric bills? One of the most important currents in the world is Spontaneity, with a capital *S*. If you cherish it too long or start to polish it, watch out. Usually even noticing spontaneity has the same effect as it does in quantum physics: the very act of observing something alters it. In the case of spontaneity, attempting to scrutinize it can eliminate it. As a matter of fact, the existence of even the possibility of observation without it ever having taken place will theoretically alter its position. To ponder that is staggering.

Spontaneity is a charge of imagination that seems to strike out of nowhere. You cannot light a fuse to ignite it. It is not an island you can visit when you're all caught up with your chores. It's more like a floating island that visits you.

So what good is spontaneity if it's so precious you cannot mine it and if you find it you cannot hold onto it? It is definitely a mercurial presence you had best take advantage of and be comfortable with if and when you are lucky enough to have it strike. And at the piano, an artist's ability to spontaneously deviate from exactly what he has practiced so religiously and be creative is walking a fine line—great actors know this feeling in their guts. The words (or the notes) will be the same, but oh, the variety, the range of feeling that can be spontaneously burst forth.

When Cy Coleman, the famous composer of many Broadway shows and songs, and I would play two pianos together, we would have so much fun improvising and enjoying the surprises that only spontaneity can bring. Our collaboration gave birth to the "By and Cy Classic/Jazz Variations" on the famous *Rhapsody on a Theme of Paganini*. Of course, spontaneity by itself is not necessarily a virtue. A person is just as likely to be spontaneously mediocre as spontaneously rare and special.

Spontaneity is also an important precondition for the miraculous. As you pry off the blinders of cynicism, you may find there are miracles occurring tailor-made just for you. You may suppose, for instance, that a man who has spent his entire life immersed in music would be a natural-born dancer. In fact, I have to be gagged and dragged onto the dance floor, I feel very self-conscious, and I'm afraid my balance wouldn't inspire confidence in a penguin. Quite frankly I'll make any excuse to avoid the torture. But for one brief day that changed.

Two women from a body-awareness training program came to teach me some exercises that would help me move my body with more ease. I left the room for a moment to change into workout clothes. I don't understand what happened to me, but when I returned to the living room, I felt I wasn't the same person. I was definitely in some kind of altered state. After bowing deeply to the two women, I amazingly started to dance in a most extraordinary and formal manner, performing a rather complex set of movements as though I had practiced them for months. I must have been following some inner music. It felt like the dance was Southeast Asian, perhaps from Bali or Thailand, and it somehow seemed authentic to the last detail. I had a feeling of intense knowing. It was one of those many events I have never been able to explain. For me to have performed that dance was something of a miracle. The two women for whom I performed seemed mesmerized. They said nothing for what felt like eternity, then got up from the sofa and, bowing deeply, said, "Thank you," with very reverential looks on their faces, and left the apartment. Everything concerning this occurrence still remains a mystery, but spontaneity was the key to it. I felt as though I was being "danced" like the times I felt when the piano was "playing" me.

I once had a student with the most precise command of whatever she played. Notes rolled off her fingers like perfect ball bearings off the line at a Toyota plant. There was an Olympic quality to her playing. But as active and agile as she undeniably was, she was also somehow sadly disengaged. I cajoled, I coaxed, I discussed, I joked, and finally I assessed. "You need to be more a part of the music you play. It sounds like you're more of an onlooker." When she looked at me with grim despair, I offered, "It's not enough to play it, it needs to be felt; and the audience will feel what you feel and won't feel what you don't feel." We were both clearly relieved when our session was over that day. As she was putting on her coat, I asked what route she usually took home. The route she described was the most efficient one from her home to my studio. It happened that she had taken the same route in both directions for the three months we had worked together. I suddenly had a thought. I said, "I want you to find a new route when you go home today. Don't map it out now— just take one block, one building, one tree, one cloud at a time. Just feel yourself drawn along; eventually you'll get home." Her poor eyes were now glazed over with confusion.

The next week, I asked the same young lady to play a Beethoven sonata she had been working on. I hoped I wasn't jumping to conclusions, but it seemed that her change of walking routine might already have had some results because her performance showed a marked improvement. Being a pianist was the means; being an artist was the goal. You never know which of your remarks might make a difference. I could sense the start of a new freedom replacing an old habit—a difficult accomplishment indeed. She was learning the magic of spontaneity.

Every summer while I was touring Europe, Maria and I were invited to visit Pablo Picasso and his wife, Jacqueline. Visiting them was like being plunged into the world of his imagination—and what an imagination! Like all great artists, Picasso remained a child at heart. (At one point, Chopin insisted on seeing a pediatrician, saying, "He will help me most … as there is something of a child in me.")

Picasso often picked up "junk" as he walked, and some of that junk became his whimsical goats and magnificent baboons. His eyes and imagination were constantly triggered and delighted by random things: pieces of metal, a palm frond blown down in a mistral, abandoned bicycle parts, the exquisite patterns of the spine of a filet of sole he had just consumed at dinner. He didn't say, "I'm going out shopping for the materials I need for the baboons I'll make famous six months from now." If you have ever seen photographs of Picasso's studio, you would find altars to spontaneity and labyrinths of his "shopping sprees." His studio seethed with ordered chaos—the artist's credo. Picasso never stopped creating, and he never stopped being spontaneous. He never stopped to create masterpieces—a masterpiece would simply happen.

Did Alexander Calder set out to create a circus, or did a circus emerge out of the telephone booth of Calder's dreams? And what do you suppose Martha Graham's game plan was when she started up with Noguchi's rickrack gowns? Looking back, isn't it inconceivable that the two have shared a common goal? Could she have had any wild notion of how that structured fabric would affect the history of twentieth-century dance? She did not. Do you think Noguchi consciously began his work to influence dance? He did not have a game plan. Spontaneity started the flow, and the creative act followed.

For me, creativity and paranormal also come from somewhat the same place. Think how much more information and inspiration these other realities could give us if only we learned how to tune out some of the daily clutter and static that our mental "radio" picks up. Some of us can do that—our focus and passion are so strong. But others are swept up in the current of the latest trend, and the door is locked for spontaneity to enter. The key ingredient for living, for creativity, and for the ability to experience the paranormal is absent. People with an establishment mind-set tend to retreat to the boundaries of their comfort zone, a death knell for progress. "Don't confuse me with the facts," they seem to be saying. When presented with a piece of reality that is behaving in a new and different way (e.g., psychokinesis), most scientists will retreat to saying, "You can't break the Second Law of Thermodynamics."

Where is the curiosity, where is the joy of discovering something new that breaks through the old ways of thinking? Beethoven became Beethoven by breaking one important musical law—he used the forbidden consecutive fifth, which, in fact, became a major factor in adding to the originality of his works. Cézanne blasted away old rules of perspective, Picasso fragmented form into new possibilities, Seurat created paintings by using millions of dots—did he realize that with pointillism he was inadvertently moving into a scientific visual mode by using the same elements that are the basis of photography?

*The piece was originally published as Chapter 22 of the autobiographical book *Chopin and Beyond: My Extraordinary Life in Music and the Paranormal* by Byron Janis (Hoboken, NJ: John Wiley & Sons, Inc., 2010). Reprinted here by permission from Turner Publishing Company LLC (December 2024).

Picasso sitting in his studio – the black & white charcoal painting on the chair is a painting Maria did in Moscow in 1960.

A Picasso Dream*

by Maria Cooper Janis (New York, NY) and Byron Janis

MARIA'S REMARKABLE FIRST meeting with Pablo Picasso took place in 1957 on the terrace of the famous Hotel du Cap in Antibes. It was all thanks to her mother's friendship with David Douglas Duncan, the internationally renowned prize-winning photojournalist and an intimate friend of the Picassos. He arranged for Maria's parents, Gary and Rocky Cooper, to invite Picasso and his wife, Jacqueline, down to their hotel for a late afternoon drink. It was an impromptu meeting that was to open a wonderful, rich new chapter in the lives of all present.

But I should allow Maria to tell her own story.

"Those two larger-than-life men, Pablo and Coop, seemed instantly enthralled with each other. My father may have been his usual relaxed self, but my mother was a nervous wreck, even losing her impeccable sense of taste by putting on diamond earrings at five in the afternoon.

"I was excited but calm until my wonderful mother, God bless her, said, 'Maria, why don't you show Picasso your sketchbook.' I could have killed her, but now I had no choice. David managed to capture on film the moment of complete horror and embarrassment on my face as I watched one of the greatest painters of the twentieth century turn the pages of my lowly sketchbook. When Picasso commented, 'Oh, she can paint,' I was so flustered I couldn't even speak out a thank-you.

We next saw Picasso and Jacqueline at La Californie, their beautiful bélle epoque villa in the hills above Cannes. We walked up the four stone steps with my father carrying a bag loaded with gifts slung over his shoulder. It was literally a 'loaded bag' as it was filled with a six-shooter, a case's worth of loose bullets wrapped in socks and stuffed inside shoes, and the famous Stetson that he wore in the film *Saratoga Trunk*. Once we arrived and everyone had greeted one another, the 'loaded bag' was eagerly 'unloaded.' With the glee of a teenager, Picasso snatched up his new pistol and led us out into his garden, the one copiously 'planted' with his large, fantastic iron sculptures. I shall never forget the scene that followed.

"The two men began by arranging their targets—several empty paint cans—atop a not-too-distant stone wall. My father shouted, 'Fire away!' and the fun commenced. First Picasso, then Coop blazed away. Unfortunately, the great painter's shots were landing nowhere near the targets, not even the wall. Some were even ricocheting dangerously close to where we were standing. As we ran for cover, Jacqueline scooped up children and dogs, and we all cowered behind one of those conveniently placed sculptures. My father, in true gentlemanly fashion, deliberately missed many of his own shots. Despite our brush with death, everyone had fun. As for 'Dead-Eye' Picasso—well, fortunately for us, his aim with a brush was much better."

Maria and I always looked forward to my concert tours in the south of France—Nice, Menton, Monte Carlo, Cannes. But we looked forward most of all to our visits with Picasso and Jacqueline. I met him in 1967, and his first remark to me was very flattering: "You look like the day you were born." We spent as much time as we could in the blazing creative atmosphere that enveloped Notre-Dame-de-Vie, his home in Mougins, a village overlooking Cannes. "Perhaps home/studio would be a more appropriate description," Jacqueline once said. "He always manages to gradually take over every room in our house—there never is enough room for him," she added with a voice edged with frustration.

Our visit with the Picassos included animated discussions as well as jovial chatter. We'd sit at the dining table, which moments before had been commandeered for use as a work area and was covered with pads, colored marking pens, and paints. Picasso would cavalierly push all of that into a corner to make room for some relaxed moments with as much caviar and vodka as we could eat and drink. The great artist had little patience for the many visitors who came by to greet him. Though occasionally he found them amusing and relaxing, visitors took time away from his passion. He was always polite, but when the creative urge overtook him, off he went, never to be seen.

Picasso had a repertoire of private "tests" for guests and newcomers to see if they could handle the mischievous games he liked to play. On our second visit he presented himself by bursting through a screen door dressed only in his jockey shorts—bare-chested, arms crossed, daring the world to stop him. Jacqueline had just told us he'd been painting all night and that we probably wouldn't have a chance to see him that visit, when—voilà—there he was in a Yul Brynner *King and I* stance, looking completely ageless and ready to work another twenty-four hours. If we'd shown the slightest flicker of shock at his state of undress, we would have failed that test and probably would have been denied entrance to his special charmed circle of close friends.

One day, he challenged me to another test. He asked us to follow him to a room where he kept a huge bronze-colored cowbell on the floor. Standing in front of it, he hoisted the bell as easily as if it were a feather. Turning to me, he said, *"Viens—c'est à toi."* Or, "Now it's your turn." Generally, I like games, and I especially like a good challenge. But I was feeling unsure about this one. That bell looked like it belonged to an elephant, not a cow. I walked over to the cowbell, grippe it by its two handles—and couldn't budge it an inch! It didn't even teeter. Picasso chuckled knowingly. I had obviously not been his first victim. What an enormous strength there was in that five-foot-five, eighty-year-old man. We marveled as he would go to a closet to pull out twenty or so huge canvases backed on very heavy stretchers, moving them around like slips of paper. We sensed a certain pride in him that it wasn't just what was on the canvases that we were admiring.

We left the impeccable cowbell and returned to our sausage, our vodka, and more conversation. At one point, Maria spoke to Picasso of her frequent frustration at attempts to paint me. Picasso said, "Ah, Maria, when that happens, go and paint a flower and then come back to painting Byron." He was right; it worked. He later showed us some recent pictures he'd been working on—a series of pornographic drawings. His face sparkled with the obvious delight he took in showing them off. Another one of his little tests, no doubt.

Jacqueline was the "official" photographer at our gathering and sent us many wonderful photos of our moments together. Some of the mailing envelopes were themselves decorated by Picasso's amusingly playful hand. The postman never realized what was passing through his hands.

Picasso would regale us with amusing stories about people who had tried to curry favor with him. He possessed what Maria's father and Ernest Hemingway called a "numero uno" BS detector.

With a glint of his eye, he told us of the time he admired a vest worn by a famous art collector and museum benefactor who came to visit. The fellow promptly stripped off his vest and, handing it to Picasso, exclaimed, "Oh, here—take it, take it—it's yours." As he thrust the article of clothing into Picasso's hands, the painter was of course delighted. But while thanking his benefactor, Picasso noticed a significant amount of money stashed away in one of the vest pockets. He naturally started to return it but the man protested, with a flurry of "No, no. Keep it. It's yours, it's yours." He pushed Picasso's hand away. At that point Picasso's BS detector kicked in. Perhaps that vest was not such a spontaneous gift after all. Most likely, the man was one of "those people," someone looking for a return favor down the road. Picasso laughed as he told us that he agreed to accept the money anyway, but as they were all saying their good-byes, he stuffed a little of his newly acquired wealth into the collector's jacket pocket, saying, "Just in case you don't have enough for dinner."

Maria told me one day that a fairly well-known actor friend managed to inveigle a meeting with Picasso. En route to Villa La Californie, the actor asked Maria if she thought Picasso might draw him a little *corrida*, or bullfight. "For God's sake. No!" exclaimed Maria. "I would never bring him anyone who would dare ask for something like that!"

But desire overcame manners, and not too long into the meeting the actor asked Picasso, "Maestro, would you please draw for me a little *corrida*?" Poor Maria blanched but was stunned when Picasso promptly sat down with a sketch pad and drew quite a richly colored bullfight scene. Our nameless actor was salivating as Picasso finished the drawing, tore the page out of the pad, and held it up to study it. As the actor's shaking outstretched hands were reaching for the priceless page, Picasso shook his head in disapproval, saying, "*Non, je n'aime pas*," and tore it up into little bits. After dropping the pieces into the wastebasket, he reached down and took out a few crumbled pieces of what looked like a used paper napkin, grabbed a marking pen, and after a few shaking strokes said, "Voila, here's your picture!" Mr. Famous Actor went looking for a bullfight and got gored in the end.

On the morning of April 8, 1973, I awoke, turned to Maria, and said, "I just had the strangest dream about Picasso."

Maria said, "How absolutely incredible. So did I."

She began recounting her dream" "It looked like we were in Villa Californie. The large rooms were full of stacked canvases in various stages—empty to full—of all the fantasies of Picasso's limitless imagination. Picasso was walking away from us, passing from one large room to the other. As he got to the furthest room, he grasped the door handle, opened the door, and stepped through it— but before closing it, he skipped a few jaunty steps backward, and gave us a hearty salute, with a wave of his hand high over his head and a smile that said, 'So long … see you!' All done with a most tremendous joie de vivre. And then—he walked through the door."

I hugged Maria and said, "What an extraordinary dream. Mine was much simpler. The four of us were sitting in that very large, wonderful room that we've been in so many times at Notre-Dame-de-Vie. The walls were hung with the unusual unframed paintings that he had collected, his own as well as others. Many of his white doves were perched on open balconies and windowsills. As there was that table we always sat at with a bottle of vodka, a jar of caviar, and some chorizo, and we were all laughing at the funny stories he was telling. A great feeling of joy seemed to prevail." Maria and I were thunderstruck that we both had dreamt of our good friend at the same time.

As we often did, we turned on the radio at noon that day to listen to the news and heard the shocking bulletin: Pablo Picasso had died at his home in France that morning at 11 a.m. French time. His wife, Jacqueline, was at his bedside. "Maria, that's just about the time we were having our simultaneous dreams about him!" How beautiful that this greatest of artists came to us both in our dreams to say good-bye. What better confirmation is needed that death doesn't stop communication.

In 1980, a number of years after Picasso's death, Jaqueline came to visit us in New York. It was very moving to be with her at the Museum of Modern Art as she gazed upon Picasso's famous *Guernica*, his outpouring of rage against the Spanish Civil War. She had never seen the painting before. Standing there in the empty gallery, a lonely figure silhouetted against this huge, extraordinary work of art, she said nothing, but her face was filled with anguish. Was she reacting to the painting or did seeing it make her feel she was in a now meaningless world? Picasso had been her life. She had lived for him and through him, and the emptiness was too much for her. Not long after, she took her own life.

*The piece was originally published as Chapter 27 of the autobiographical book *Chopin and Beyond: My Extraordinary Life in Music and the Paranormal* by Byron Janis (Hoboken, NJ: John Wiley & Sons, Inc., 2010). Reprinted here by permission from Turner Publishing Company LLC (December 2024).

Posttraumatic Reminiscences from Transatlantic and Transcontinental Air Travels

by Jacek Jaroszyk (Poznań, Poland)

With several decades of my relatively brief life behind me, I have experienced a bundle of various adventures, miracles, revelations and astonishments. I have climbed mountains and crossed seas. I have traveled to many distant places in both hemispheres. Usually with my wife, Katarzyna (or Kasia), occasionally with our son, Mikołaj (Mick), I have flown countless times across the Atlantic Ocean and across the North-American continent, in some cases across both in one flight – primarily to visit my daughter, Natalia, who lives in California with her husband, Peter, and their daughter, Lou Lou.

The overall series of diverse circumstances of those flights, along with all of my sensations, impressions and reflections, have borne fruit in the form of the following two literary pieces, a short story and a poem, both metaphysical, unconventional and fictionalized. While the connotation within the former is rather obvious, the theme of the latter, indirectly inspired by Fred Zinnemann's classic western *High Noon* (1952; starring Gary Cooper and Grace Kelly), is a result of my inflight thoughts preceding a visit of another person, a good friend of mine, Henryk, who, since 1992, has been residing in the USA with his wife, Betsy. Henryk (or Henry), in addition to sharing my genuine interest in film, is a big aficionado of the western genre, and *High Noon* is his number one favorite.

A Rock

He did not really know what made him wake up. Some unidentifiable sound violently interrupted his deep sleep. He opened his eyes and, half-asleep, looked around. Inside the dim-lit plane – a huge transcontinental machine – all the passengers seemed to be in a deep sleep. All he heard was the sound of the methodically working engines of the big jet – some monotonous and partially silenced noise – relaxing and sleep-friendly. He closed his eyes for a moment, falling into a brief nap.

A sense of uneasiness, hard to define, pulled him again out of the half-asleep state. Automatically, he looked at the little round window and froze in terror. He noticed, next to the plane, at the same altitude, a bright object, pulsing with alternating red and green flashes, its round shape emerging from some smoky darkness. He closed his eyes rapidly thinking that maybe it was hallucination, which would disappear as soon as he opened his eyes again. He partially opened his eyes, but the shiny ghost was still visible and only the pulsing flashes were less intense. He concluded that the strange object was slowly and soundlessly pulling away. After a while, the flashes disappeared in the blackness.

The chill that he felt when getting closer to the window made him abruptly come to his senses. The whole sensation was brief and seemed unreal at that moment. He quickly looked ahead and noticed a red glowing sign above the cockpit door: "Don't smoke. Buckle your seatbelts." Suddenly he realized that inside the plane there was no movement and complete silence. despite the conspicuous work of the engines. He felt an animal-kind of trepidation and instinctively grabbed the hand of the female passenger sitting next to him. It was cool and impotent. Her face turned inertly in his direction, revealing wide open and motionless eyes. He screamed in terror, which was enhanced by the fact that he was not able to unbuckle the seatbelt. He seemed imprisoned in the seat. After a brief chaotic struggle, he stood up, turning back. His heart sank when looking around he realized that all the passengers appeared to be overcome by lethargy.

He started to run in the aisle shaking his travel companions, but none of them reacted and moved uncontrollably. He reached the cockpit door and, after forcing it open, he stood as if rooted, completely shocked. The cockpit was empty. The flying and navigational instruments shone in the frightening silence. Some clocks and indicators shone, some lights twinkled. His attention was caught by a small rock-like object, glowing phosphorescently on the floor. After he picked it up, he felt a blinding pain. He lost consciousness.

He was lying with his eyes closed and, slowly, along with the distant sounds, he was regaining consciousness. One of the sounds, which kept regularly recurring, seemed familiar. However, he was not able to identify it. He slightly opened his eyelids and noticed some white silhouette with blurred shapes, which was leaning over him. A tender female voice announced:

"Thank God, he's regaining consciousness."
He blinked a few times and whispered almost incomprehensibly:
"Where am I?"

"Well, finally you're conscious. In the hospital. You've been unconscious for three days and we've been seriously worried – not sure how it's going to end," a tall man in a medical coat explained.

"What happened?" he asked, realizing, at the same time, that the sound he'd heard was the voice of the monitor he was connected to.

"You had a heart attack, but the worst is behind you. Please lie still and don't ask any questions."

He kept waking up and falling asleep, gradually regaining the sense of reality. When he completely recovered, he asked the doctor to explain what had really happened because he hardly remembered anything. The only thing he did remember was boarding the plane and taking a seat by the window.

"We can say," the doctor said, "that you were lucky in an unlucky situation. You experienced the heart attack before the plane took off. The case was rather severe! Because of what happened to you, the flight was delayed by nearly an hour. Both the start and the end of the matter were unlucky. When I say, "the end," we don't really know what to think because the plane has been lost. There is no sign of it anywhere up to this point despite the intensive search. Maybe, due to a malfunction, the plane crashed into the sea. It simply disappeared. You're the only survivor. Admittedly, with a history of a heart attack. So, you can consider yourself lucky. What puzzles me, though, is the nasty burn on your hand – from inside. Extensive and deep. And, it hardy responds to any medication. But it will heal eventually."

The medical round stopped by another patient, and he, suddenly, when looking at his bandaged hand, remembered what had happened on the plane.

The alternative version of the ending:

Overcome by terror, he suddenly ran out of breath and felt a terrible pain in his chest.

When he woke up in the dark, he heard some squeaky continuous sound and evidence of some commotion around him. He understood that the darkness was triggered by his eyelid twitching, and the sound – the signal from the monitor – meant that his heart stopped working. He opened his eyes and saw – from a distance – the commotion around his bed. He was almost naked, and the terrified medical personnel kept chaotically running around the professor, who, time and again, pinched electrodes to his body, which in a funny way – as perceived by him – was bouncing.

"Strange," he grunted to himself, "but I feel completely nothing,"

Instinctively he looked at the window and saw the lights, which had put him in horror on the plane. Now he seemed to expect to see them again, when he woke up dead.

High Noon

High noon –
When cheeks and chin by sweat are bothered.
When breathing makes your lungs ignited,
When no one's body casts a shadow,
 A someone's chill blew out from nowhere
At high noon.

High noon –
I raised my eyes to look at him,
And though the steam of heat was seen,
He cast a shadow, black and tall,
There was no sweat of his at all
At high noon.

High noon –
I was surprised by sudden rain drops
When next to me stood that delinquent.
Asking for guidance, he knew my name,
I realized he's rather "different" –
At high noon.

High noon –
Shocked, I stood still, and he addressed me
"Are you surprised I know your name? –
'Follow Jim', said he, pointing at you,

And we're going the same direction."
At high noon.

High noon –
In deadly silence, just next to him,
My heart stopped beating or almost did,
It echoed strangely;
I saw he heard it
At high noon.

High noon,
After we got to the hotel –
I took a seat in a friendly spot
To stay away from the gloomy hall
And said, "At last you're here,
At high noon."

High noon,
I ask the desk, for obvious reasons,
"What did he want – the guy in black?"
"Your room key, sir, what else d'you think,
Saying he's taking you far to Eden
At high noon."

High noon,
A gun in hand, I run up there,
He's waiting for me, caught in the mirror:

Raises his head, his eyes are shallow.

"Please enter," says he, "Don't be a coward

At high noon."

Translated from Polish by Henryk Hoffmann

Barbara and Dieter at their friend Udo's wedding near Exeter, England.

To Live the Impossible Dream*
OR
The Man Who Made My Dreams Come True

by Barbara Kryk-Kastovsky (Vienna, Austria)

MOTTO:

From Poznan to Vienna and then to DC.
So varied and colorful our life could be!
And then you took me everywhere,
Be it Cape Town or Kobe, we were indeed there.
The Merry Kastovskys we were to many a friend
We thought our life together would never end…

    Is it possible to summarize the twenty-three years with "The Man of My Life" on a few pages? My contribution to this collection of personal stories will be an attempt to answer the question, and it is for the readers to judge if I have succeeded.

It was a "Veni, vidi, vici" scenario. We **came** (to Poznan), we **saw** (each other) and we **won** by having got together after one of the linguistic conferences organized every year at The Department of English, Adam Mickiewicz University, Poznań. Dieter was "everybody's darling," a convivial guy, laughing, joking and playing Viennese waltzes and operettas from, yes! cassettes he brought along. Then I got invited to Vienna as guest professor and my dream of visiting the grandiose city with its rich cultural tradition came true, followed by the fulfillment of my other dreams related to the Austrian reality: waltzing in a ballroom dress at the Hofburg to the music played by The Wiener Philharmonic, not to forget the famous Austrian culinary trimmings: after a ball a Goulash soup at five a.m. is unbeatable! The immersion in the world of classical music ranged from attending numerous performances at the Vienna Opera, like the legendary "Rosenkavallier" conducted by Oskar Kleiber, or the entire "Ring of the Nibelungen" with the unforgettable Hildegard Behrens, almost stumbling down the steep stage in her opulent dress. Our visits to the rich palette of Viennese restaurants included delicious after-opera snacks at the Sirk restaurant opposite or a folksy zither evening at the quaint Piaristenkeller (located indeed in the cellar of the Catholic men's order!).

The number of opera performances we saw in Vienna was soon outnumbered by those we enjoyed at the New York Metropolitan Opera ("Why do you fly to NYC so often?" our friends would ask, "Because we love NYC and The Met where the opera tickets are much cheaper than in Vienna" was Dieter's answer). The wonderful golden ambience full of international guests, the festive atmosphere and the performances, just to mention "Tosca" with Pavarotti (which turned out to be his last appearance!) were then crowned by culinary delights at the nearby restaurant appropriately called "Fiorello".

While in NYC, one can't miss Broadway where we saw many great shows: classics like "Showboat," "Annie Get Your Gun," or "Oklahoma," and more modern musicals like "Mamma Mia!" After the performance we would enjoy a steak dinner at BB King Restaurant where food was served to live jazz music (the only competition would be the jazz bands we heard from every corner during our stay in New Orleans, another of my dreams made come true by Dieter). Another unique musical experience was a visit to Victor Café in Philadelphia where the guests were served by music students singing opera arias to recorded music. When we were served our dinner by a handsome young man, he started singing "Nessun dorma," an aria from "Turandot" and Dieter couldn't resist singing along to the delight of the young tenor and the guests. He just had to give up on the final high C.!

The opportunities to visit the US were plentiful, both thanks to conferences and guest lectures, but also on a private basis, visiting our dear friends Steve and Sara in Conway, S.C. We travelled around together to go to Charleston, Savannah or to relax at the holiday resort Hilton Head. They also got us an invitation for guest lectures at the Linguistic Summer School at Saint Michael's College in Vermont. What a drive it was from NYC to Montpellier, VT where we also took a boat trip across the lake and admired the spectacular Vermont Indian Summer.

But before our US escapades, we spent an unforgettable semester in South Africa where we taught linguistics at University of Cape Town. The trip along The Garden Route with its sea of flowers on the ocean shores was topped up by another of my dreams fulfilled by Dieter: a visit to Kruger Park where everyone had to follow very strict rules: drive slowly and get out of the car only to take a shot and finally reach one of the camps before it gets dark. How many giraffes can one see in a day? We counted 37 graceful giants along with multiple impalas, kudus, wildebeest and birds like vultures or guinea fowl (no parrots, but those we saw later in Australia).

After that adventure we had to face some "conference hopping" which took us to Sweden with its pristine nature and tangibly clean air and Scotland where the waiters sang "The ode to the haggis" while the local specialty was served. When we finally decided to legalize our relationship, it produced additional logistic and professional problems. We managed to squeeze our wedding between a few conferences and the wedding of a dear friend, Arthur, who was also one of our best men (apart from my boss and our wonderful friend Jacek). No time for a honeymoon, but we had our honey year in DC coming up (my guest professorship at AU and Dieter's at Georgetown). We enjoyed our stay tremendously, inaugurated by Bill Clinton's Inauguration Party at the Mall, where the crowd was singing along with Diana Ross and munching on pieces of the gigantic cheesecake. We decided on a honeymoon after all when we saw some offers from the Caribbean: honeymooners' vacation on St. John, one of the US Virgin Islands. It turned out to be the proverbial paradise (another of my dreams came true!) with lush nature, pristine beaches and a multitude of colorful fishes literally swarming around you in the blue waters of the coral reef! So, we swam and snorkeled till dinner offered by one of the restaurants on the premises, or we took a taxi to the spectacular Cinnamon beach. We loved the island so much that we went there 6 more times, and our favorite pelican was still waiting for us on one of the rocks overlooking the Caneel Bay… Sadly, last time we were there, we noticed the dwindling fish population and the coral bleaching caused by the environmental pollution.

Who wouldn`t dream of exploring Mexico? Since we always tried to combine business and pleasure and chose conferences at "sexy" locations, another opportunity presented itself when my paper was accepted by the organizers of The International Pragmatics Association (IPrA) conference in Mexico City (1996). So, having immersed long enough in the intricacies of pragmatic issues, we ticked off the impressive Anthropological Museum in Mexico City and drove south stopping on the way at the most famous pyramid sites: The Sun and The Moon, The Magician, and Palenque in Chiapas which stood up to its reputation of a drug dealing area. During a brief stopover I found a suspicious-looking transparent bag filled with white powder lying by the side of the road, probably a pick-up point, so I turned away and we zoomed off! It was so hot that we stopped to get some water from an old lady standing by the road who offered us … iguana tortillas which we turned down to her dismay! We just could not think of digesting the spectacular lizards we had admired on the bosom of nature before.

Another of my dreams which Dieter made come true was … holding a koala. We visited Australia twice thanks to conferences in Sydney and in Melbourne, but the most spectacular occasion was the visit to The Koala Sanctuary at Tidbinbilla. We also took trips to the Outback and admired the shores of the Coral Sea (no swimming due to the poisonous jelly fish which can kill even an athletic young guy), stopped at "the scruffiest pub in the scrub," and stroked half-tamed kangaroos. A performance of "The Tales of Hoffmann" at the spectacular Sydney Opera House topped it all, also because all the female roles were exceptionally sung by a single artist! We were lucky to be taken on a sailboat trip around Sydney harbor by our old friend Eddie and managed to take some unforgettable shots. That took care of another dream on my list which Dieter managed to fulfill.

What about the more trivial, but still exciting part of travelling, i.e. shopping? We discovered quite early in our mutual life that both of us were shopaholics, so we derived enormous pleasure from buying books, CD's, clothes and, of course, shoes (an Imelda Marcos syndrome?). Our shopping stints at Barnes & Nobles must have been quite entertaining to the shop assistants when we browsed through the stacks (Dieter favored sci-fi and I went for the latest fiction). Then we would go through our acquisitions to make sure we had the same number of volumes in our shopping baskets. The same was true of T-shirts, shoes and other items, after all US prices were always attractive for Europeans. But within EU we also had our favorite shopping destination, which was Spain, not only because of their famous leather goods and competitive prices, but mainly because of the annual conferences of English studies in Spain (ADEAN). We participated in them regularly for many reasons: colleagues and friends invited us to give talks at the conferences held at the sexiest venues (a different city every year, so we had a sightseeing tour of the country from Barcelona to Santiago di Compostella, Leon to Malaga, and many others). The other attraction was the time of the year: conferences were always held in December, with Christmas in the air: the festive shop windows with Christmas carols coming out from every store were just magical! It was in Spain where another of my dreams came true thanks to Dieter. I have always been fascinated by the surrealist movement and the multi-faceted artist Salvador Dali, so when we were at a conference in Lleida, I begged Dieter to drive us to Figueras with its famous *Teatre-Museu Dali* housing his paintings and sculptures. We did go there, and we loved it (buying a few albums and prints was of course a must!). But when I gazed with admiration at an attractive bag/purse/pocketbook – pick one, my Benefactor screamed "Oh, no, not another bolsa!" Thus, my dream did not come true then…

Our complicated life together involved not only travelling between Austria and Poland when I was still teaching both in Vienna and in Poznań but also visiting my parents in as far as Szczecin ("only" 1100 km away!). When we saw them in 2004, we both sang along with Elvis "It's Now or Never!" and decided to move them to Austria, especially since Poland had just joined the EU, which made things legally (but not emotionally or logistically) easier (both parents were in their early eighties). Dieter made my dream come true again and organized the whole trip flawlessly. We put the parents into the car after a removal truck had taken their belongings away and we drove through Germany with a stopover at a hotel near Regensburg. Everything went smoothly and we could let the removal company unload the parents` precious stuff into their brand-new apartment which Dieter managed to get for them in our village with the help of our wonderful neighbor Christa, who happened to be the village mayor then. Thus, another of my dreams came true: all four of us were together and within walking distance!

We gave my Parents a few peaceful years: they could enjoy the beautiful garden outside (designed by Dieter, with its magnificent rose bushes and fragrant lavender) and spend weekends with us enjoying the gourmet meals prepared by Dieter, who was the family cook and could come up with a dish from any cuisine you would wish: Austrian, Italian, Indian or Mexican (Polish dishes remained my specialty, served usually at Christmas).

Our professional life still went on and we did our regular teaching and enjoyed the Austrian conviviality at various parties we attended or threw at home, like our annual garden grill parties (up to thirty participants!) or the obligatory goose party on St. Martin's Day when our department librarian Harald cooked the goose, Dieter made his famous sauerkraut, I contributed a salad and the guests flooded us with delicious deserts. Closer to the professional ambience were the unforgettable fancy dress parties thrown during the carnival season by the Dean's Office for all faculty members. Each year there was a different motto, and the costumes ranged from the circus through the movie world to extra-terrestrial. I loved designing our costumes, which were, accordingly: circus manager + his assistant/Fred Astaire + Ginger Rogers/both of us in space uniforms.

Unfortunately, life has its ups and downs. Dieter had more and more digestive problems on various occasions, like the ESSE conference in Lyon where we were hosted by the university authorities and invited to a sumptuous dinner which he could not fully enjoy. But he wanted to go on with our conference-hopping tradition and for old times' sake decided to participate in an annual MESS conference in Poznan which turned out to be his last... Maybe he wanted another of my dreams come true and take me to my Alma Mater to see our friends? Fortunately, he gave up on the idea of driving, so we flew to Poznań through Düsseldorf (the only connection available) and the flight must have aggravated his condition. Dieter collapsed on the way to the conference venue and made HIS dream come true: he always wanted to die like his mother did: painlessly, of a heart attack. But it was painful for the others: me, his widow and for all his relatives and friends.

Here is where our dear friend Jacek comes up again. He was so shocked by Dieter's demise that he did everything humanely possible to help me. After the official ceremony I was left with the urn to be transported to Austria. Even though the airport authorities assured me I could take the urn on board, I was stopped by the security for lack of the official documents! Jacek suggested contacting the Austrian Consulate in Poznan and the council did find a solution. I brought Dieter's remains home safely and gave him a funeral service he deserved, attended by family, friends and colleagues (Steve and Sara, our wonderful friends from South Carolina flew in to say goodbye to him!). The series of Dieter fulfilling my dreams ended at home where my eighty-year-old Mom survived the morbid news and went on for another 5 years to keep me happy.

But life must go on and I am now together with Chuck, Dieter's predecessor, whom I met in California in 1985, and as the wheel of fortune had it, he became Dieter's successor after all these years …

*A travesty on the theme from the musical "Man of La Mancha."
Second Wind, or a Widow's Lust for Life

by Danuta Krzeszczak (Poznań, Poland)

After thirty-eight years of a happy married life with my charming and caring husband, Zdzisław, with whom I had raised two wonderful children, Piotr and Joanna, and had watched two lovely grandchildren, Damian and Barbara (or Basia, as is the diminutive form of her name) as they were growing up, the most tragic days of my life came in November 2016. The health condition of Zdzisiu, who had been suffering for years from hepatitis C, suddenly, if not entirely unexpectedly, deteriorated to a degree that he had to be transferred from Poznań to a specialist hospital in Warsaw. A few day-long struggle for his life ended up in a failure or defeat not only for the patient, but also for all people close to him, all suffering from an excruciating pain and experiencing an enormous loss for weeks, months and years to go. Zdzisiu passed away at the age of sixty; I was a year younger. His ashes were buried next to those of his grandparents and his father, Teodor, and, during the ceremony, according to his wish, his favorite song, "Stairway to Heaven" by Led Zeppelin, was played in the background.

In my case the mourning time was never over. The interiors of our apartment incessantly reminded me of the important and warmth-filled events in our family, related to holidays, anniversaries, birthdays, namedays, everyday life of parents and children. The relatively boisterous social gatherings, with or without dances, in which Zdzisiu was often the center of attention, fun and humor, suddenly disappeared from my life—not because they were not becoming, but because I had no interest in or desire for such things. My only type of entertainment, or rather a way to forget about the unending sadness, were books, carefully selected films on TV and extremely modest and humble gatherings of not more than two or three closest family members or female friends.

Since I had never had a problem with getting to know new friends, in time the number of people participating in such meetings gradually got bigger and bigger, and soon the range of our group activities also included trips to the seaside (the Polish section of the Baltic Sea coast), either privately to different resorts or within a prescribed treatment at a sanatorium. Besides, in a smaller or bigger group, we started going out to enjoy a concert (my favorite being the ones by Shakin' Stevens, Joe Cocker and André Rieu—the last one filmed and shown on a big screen in a movie theater), a film (Polish or foreign, a comedy or a drama, modern or historical—as long as it dealt with human matters in an artistic and entertaining way), lunch or dinner, swimming, etc. It took a long time before my friends were able to convince me that we should go to a dance, but, when it happened, I did not regret it because, for the first time since I had lost my husband I was starting to feel again that I was alive.

A turning point in my social life was joining a local senior club, which, a few months later, organized its annual New Year's Eve Ball for all the club members and their guests. I was strongly encouraged by my mother-in-law, Monika, her younger sister, Kazimiera, my sister, Barbara, and Grażyna, Barbara's husband's niece, all members of the club, to participate in the event, and I did yield. Even though our company consisted of women only, it posed no problem in the celebratory way we welcomed the New Year. Occasionally, men from other tables did invite us to dance, but, even if they had not, it would not have been a problem since we did not mind dancing with one another (which is absolutely acceptable), and, in my recollection, everyone had a great time. Sometimes with the same company, sometimes with others, I kept enjoying the dances at the senior club, and during one of them, I discovered a surprising fact: the charming one-man orchestra and vocalist, whose musical performance we had been admiring for some time, was a high school friend of my brother Henryk (residing, since 1992, in the USA), and his name was Piotr, the same as my son's. Piotr immediately introduced me to another classmate of his and Henryk's, Jacek, who, seated at a table next to ours, gave me an earful of information, as we sat or danced together, about the past, including some hot stuff, related to their school and classmates.

Meeting those two gentlemen turned out to be just a beginning of an episode of a much bigger caliber. Because Piotr's regular activity in his retired life is playing to dance not only at the events organized by our senior club, but also at a seaside summer resort in Grzybowo, where members of the same class, or, to be exact, those that have stayed in touch some fifty years after graduation, gather annually for about a week at the beginning of August. My female friends and I received a cordial invitation from Piotr and Jacek to participate in their next class reunion, and, I admit, I did not hesitate to accept it. Thus, about seven months later, my good friend Małgosia and I went to Grzybowo to experience a new adventure. Not only were we received very warmly by all (about a dozen people, including at least three married couples) official participants of the reunion, but soon, I, as Henryk's sister, was announced to be an honorary member of the class. Needless to say, after such a promising start, I became a regular participant in the event, visiting Grzybowo in the same or somewhat different company. At the same time, I became a new strong connection between my brother and his classmates. For, traditionally, during those reunions, there was a long-distance contact made between Henryk and his friends, either in the form of me reading a message sent by my brother earlier to me but addressed to them, or Messenger calls, which gave Henryk an opportunity to chat with all of them and, occasionally, also watch some of them in action, i.e., while dancing or, in Piotr's case, beautifully performing some unforgettable hits mainly from the period when we were all young.

My accidental admission to my brother's class also made his own relations with all or some of his classmates much tighter, even though still at a distance. His regular Messenger call with Little Tadziu (nicknamed this way because of another Tadeusz, or Tadziu, significantly taller, with his last name beginning with the same letter also being in the class), who, as a widower with children and grandchildren and one great-grandchild living away from Poznań (where he himself still resides), turned out to be the best and most conscientious go-between, allowed Henryk to share news in his life from afar and, at the same time, find out about everything significant in the lives of all classmates being still in touch. Because of that, in 2019, during one of the annual visits to Poland by Henryk and his wife Betsy, my brother was able to see and spend some precious time with four of his classmates, Little Tadziu, Wojtek, Andrzej and Marian. All of them enjoyed an emotionally fulfilling and interesting afternoon, filled with reminiscing about the good old times, with some typically Polish treats, in a special room of the hotel where Henryk and Betsy were staying at that time. It was just the beginning of their newborn relations and an announcement of further meetings in the near future.

Little Tadziu, who lives in an apartment building not far from mine, where he stays alone except for the times when he visits his daughter's family in Gorzów, in addition to playing a special role in Henryk's life, has become an important friend in mine. He seems to understand my feelings as a widow better than any other member of his class, and, being a cordial, sensitive and compassionate person, he keeps inviting me to his place, where, with a cup of coffee and some sweet treats, we discuss the news in the lives of our families and his high-school classmates, as well as the sad consequences of being single and how to cope with a loss of one's dearest person. A perfect gentleman, he never forgets, despite his relatively serious health problems demanding constant attention, to give me a call and wish me a happy birthday (or nameday), a merry Christmas or a happy Easter, and I do my best to reciprocate his kind thoughtfulness.

Despite my limited income, I have never turned down an opportunity to travel to interesting places, both domestically and abroad, especially when I knew that I would be accompanied by some of my dear and loyal family members or friends. Thus, since I became a widow, I managed to go abroad and enjoy a brief or not-so-brief vacation at a number of places. Both with Zdzisiu and by myself, I have repeatedly traveled to different locations in Germany, whether to visit my sister, Barbara, and her husband, Włodzimierz (Włodek), when they still lived there, my niece Izabela (Iza) and her family or our dear friend Daniela, who, living close to the Polish border, offers her unparalleled hospitality to all of us whenever we are going in that direction, either to visit her family or stop by when passing by. I had loved traveling with Zdzisiu, and our vacations at the Canary Islands almost became a tradition in our life. Having enjoyed different places of the archipelago, we kept going back there to discover more and more amazing sights and experience more and more unforgettable adventures. Going there without my husband was, however, out of the question; it would be too painful.

Instead, the destinations of my foreign trips as a widow ended up being closer to home: Croatia, Greece and Bulgaria. About a year after my husband's death, my sister and I were invited to Croatia for a two-week long stay. It was possible only because our friend Daniela (living in Germany) introduced us to Ewa, a good friend of hers who lived in Petrčane, a village near Zadar, and who needed someone to take care of her three beautiful little dogs during her trip to Poland. During our pet-sitting period, we enjoyed ourselves at the nearby beach and walking in the spectacular area. Once our thoughtful hostess returned, she offered us some additional attractions: she brought us to Zadar, a historically interesting town at the Adriatic Sea, and even to some health muds (from which experience we have some rare photographs of our bodies covered in black slime).

About two years later, Barbara and I spent a week in Greece and

Crete. Not only did we enjoy a stunning view of the seacoast from our terrace, but each evening, after the last meal, we were entertained by a performance of a regional ensemble consisting of singing and dancing. We came back home absolutely fulfilled. As a result, in 2024, I decided to head in the same, more or less, direction once again. Accompanied by friends Grażynka and Małgosia, I went to Obzor, a town in Bulgaria. The week we spent there was an absolute delight. Once again, a room with a terrace offering a magnificent sea view, excellent weather, warm sea water and a wonderful atmosphere. All three of us got back home happy despite a four-hour delay of our return flight.

Even though Zdzisiu was not with me at any of those places abroad, I was still able to reminisce about my special moments experienced with him at the Canary Islands, whether reliving some romantic situations or hearing some insightful comments, positive or negative, that my husband had made about one thing or another. Because of the precious memories that were triggered by the mere fact of being abroad, I fully enjoyed myself in all of those places and never experienced any regrets.

Quite a lot of my good memories are related to the time I have spent with one of my dearest friends, Kasia, who was my coworker when I was employed by the clothing warehouse "Shark," and her relatives. At one of Kasia's nameday parties, I met two of her aunts, Ewa and Lucyna, and we immediately became friendly. Ewa runs her own summer sea resort at Gąski, where, after meeting her, I go every year and rent one of the small houses, which I usually share with my mother-in-law, Monika, my sister, Basia, plus two friends, Krysia and Ania. Needless to say, Kasia, not only because of being related to Ewa, goes there as well, usually at the same time as we do, so that together we can enjoy the gifts of the seacoast, great company and the worldwide famous pierogi served with either goose or fried halibut.

I have been receiving a lot of support during the long period of my mourning from my children, my mother-in-law (who bravely coped with numerous losses of her own, including her husband's, her son's and, recently, her significantly younger sister's), and my elder brother Jerzy, who not only happens to be the only male at our family celebrations and friends' meeting-ups but, as a skilled handyman, keeps helping me with the maintenance of my apartment. Furthermore, I cannot imagine my life during that time without my elder sister, Barbara, who, about half a year before Zdzisiu's death, lost her own husband, Włodek (at the age of seventy), with whom she had shared about fifty years of life, including a challenging period of emigration in Germany after defecting from Poland during the Martial Law. Together they returned to Poland, a small town near the German border, shortly before Włodek's death, and, sometime after he passed away in June 2016, their son Krzysztof lost his wife in a tragic accident, which made Barbara decide to return to Poznań for good and share an apartment with her single and childless son.

Ever since the day of Barbara's return to her hometown, the relations between the two sisters became regular, precious and fruitful in the area of our mutual support and help in every imaginable respect. Basia and I have been spending a lot of time together, whether helping out our cousin Ala with the care of her mother and our Aunt Sabina (who had become my surrogate mother after my parents' untimely death and who passed away in the fall of 2022 at the age of ninety-one), going shopping or to the movies and preparing food for family gatherings. Needless to say, Basia also joined the group of my close and loyal friends, with whom we continue our regular meetings, trips, vacations and dances, not only at the senior club, but also in some other places, such as the restaurant "Beneath the Parrots" near the fabulous Old Market of Poznań. A person that deserves a special mention in the context of the dances in all of the places is the only man that usually accompanies our group. He wants to be called 'Jasiu,' a diminutive form of 'Jan' (John), which means that its best transition into English is 'Jack.' In addition to bending over backwards to make sure that all of the ladies from our table get enough attention, which includes inviting each to a dance at least once, Jasiu also eagerly participates in our traditional meetings at our favorite indoor/outdoor restaurant "Under the Pine Tree" (not far from Lake Rusałka), where we usually enjoy a cup of coffee or tea, sometimes a meal and, occasionally, a small cocktail.

I cannot imagine my life as a widow without the overwhelming support from my close family and the group of devoted friends. My sister has always been very close to me, but she became especially important after my big loss, which so strangely coincided with hers. In fact, our sisterhood turned out to be precious over the years in more than one way. The sadness caused by the loss of our dearest ones, our parents in the 1960s, our husbands in 2016 and, recently, our aunt, the last member of our parents' generation in our family, is still in our hearts, but life – on many levels – goes on, mainly because of the people in our lives. And, as for my husband, I always feel him watching over me, often sense his presence and his incessant attempt to express his strong approval of the way I chose to spend my life after his death. If I had ever had any doubts about it, all of them were dispelled when I was leaving the plane after landing at Burgas Airport in Bulgaria and I heard one of the passengers listen to music on his phone. I recognized the song immediately: it was Led Zeppelin singing "Stairway to Heaven." As much as I was shocked and surprised, it also reminded me of Zdzisiu's favorite advice that he had repeatedly given to me during our life together: "Don't believe in coincidences!"

People. People in our lives and others'. People that we are surrounded by and deal with throughout our lives not by choice but because they are our immediate family, distant relatives, friends, acquaintances, classmates, coworkers and a multitude of others that we encounter when taking care of our needs—whether shopping, using public transportation, going to the doctor's or other offices, having meals in a restaurant, going to the movies or other forms of entertainment, and so on and so forth. All of them, to a varying degree, impact our lives in one way or another, and, even if we do not realize it, we do impact their lives as well. I consider myself blessed because most of the people in my life (the exceptions have been few and far between) have been wonderful in every respect: sensitive, kind, loving, honest, supportive, understanding and compassionate, and I can only hope that they have perceived me in the same way. I cannot blame anyone for the biggest tragedy in my life, losing my husband at a relatively young age, not even the healthcare system in Poland, the quality of which—frankly speaking—leaves a great deal to be desired, nonetheless. I lost my husband because of a serious disease that he was so unfortunate to contract while conscientiously, without expecting anything bad, doing his job.

Until the scientists find cure for all possible diseases, tragedies like mine will be inevitable, just like traffic crashes or similar kinds of accidents—all out of people's control unless caused by human error or intentionally. However, there are many other kinds of tragedies that are definitely related to the weaknesses of human character. They include serious crimes (murder, manslaughter, rape, assault), wars and other forms of political violence. Those phenomena usually result from greed, selfishness, power hunger, vanity, fear, arrogance and narcissism. I have to say that I have been fortunate because, except for enduring life under communism for over thirty years (which did reduce my happiness in ways that I was not completely aware of), I have not experienced, unlike my parents' generation, any tragedies related to war or any extreme cases of political violence. While all my contemporaries in Poland treasure that fact, we are also quite aware that life in peace is not guaranteed to any nation at any time. Thus, let us keep that in mind, pray and do everything else in our power to make sure that people (understood as both 'nations' and 'individuals') throughout the world tolerate and appreciate each other (if 'love' is asking too much) and enjoy life without preventable and absolutely undesired disasters.

Translated from Polish by Henryk Hoffmann

The Warmth You Can't Buy

by Zuzanna Rakowska (Warsaw/Ińsko, Poland)

A few days ago, I just turned twenty. I do not consider myself a super mature person, and I do realize that I have not lived long enough to have acquired a lot of precious experiences that would endow me with a special kind of wisdom. Consequently, I am not trying to teach anyone anything, especially not anyone who is old or older than I, but I believe I have something to offer at least to my peers or people younger than I. Why? Because, just like most youngsters, I have made my share of mistakes; however, unlike most of them, I have drawn my conclusions and have recently started to do my best in order to live according to the lessons I have learned.

I was born in Warsaw, where my mother had moved from Poznań to accept a fascinating job as a film editor for some TV stations. I grew up in a home where there was money – not a lot, but enough to prevent me from ever worrying about it. I was never hungry, I had clothes to wear, I went to school, I could afford what I needed. Money shortage was not a problem in my family unless there was something extremely expensive that I desired to own (more due to peer pressure than because I really needed it) and tried to persuade my parents to buy it for me. I did not feel rich as a child, but I never felt poor either. Everything was in balance – simple, sufficient, relaxed, peaceful – just the way I expected it to be, without realizing that not everyone was that lucky.

I enjoyed living in Warsaw. It was my city, I was quite familiar with most of it, especially with the areas where we lived at two different times. Life for me and my family was fast-paced and intense. But sometimes something you never expect happens, and you are taken by surprise. All of a sudden, life takes you in completely different directions. In my case, it was a move, with my mother, Katarzyna (or Kaha, as she likes to be called) and my younger brother, Tymon, far from Warsaw to a small town in the northwestern part of Poland. Admittedly, I have been familiar with Ińsko because my mother had taken me there a few times to participate in the famous film festival. But it was not easy for me to leave behind almost everyone and everything I cared for. Fortunately, I was able to stay in touch with someone who, at that hard moment of my life, gave me a sense of continuity – a boy with whom I still maintained a special bond, or, maybe, a little more than that.

After a year of living in Ińsko, I moved to another city – to Wrocław, hoping to become an independent person. Wrocław, situated in the southwestern part of Poland, is a beautiful and historical place. A big city, full of people, life, opportunities. Everything was different – faster, bigger, more open. I renewed my relationship with the guy I had known for a long time; it seemed to me (in fact, I was almost convinced) that we were together out of love.

Unfortunately (some may argue about the suitability of that adverb in this context), he had a very rich father who gave him money for everything. He did not work, he did not look for a job, he had no desire to do anything. I, on the other hand, wanted to be active and employed. I did not always have a job, but when I did, it annoyed me that he did not to do anything productive or creative. He just wasted his life. I felt like everything was one-sided, as if I were taking responsibility for adulthood and he was still living like a child, only in an adult body.

There were times when we went out with friends. And friends, as friends are – sometimes there, sometimes not. I had quite a few of them in Wrocław, we socialized a lot and were never bored. But when my boyfriend and I were by ourselves, there was complete emptiness – no more conversation, no more laughter, no tenderness between us. I realized that the only time I had fun was when we were with others. I was bored whenever I was just with him, I simply felt lonely. And, after a while, I understood that this was no longer love.

It took me a long time to say out loud how I felt about him and about our situation. I tried to talk, explain, save this relationship, but I knew I did not want to live like that. In the end, we ended this relationship. It was not easy. I was young, but I knew then that I did not want to waste my time on something that did not give me warmth, did not fulfill any of my emotional and intellectual expectations, did not mean anything to me anymore and, certainly, did not make me happy.

I returned to my family home, to the small town I had so many objections about but have learned to treasure more and more. I made sure that I had no contact with my previous boyfriend. I tried to put everything behind and bring my life back together.

And then – completely unexpectedly – a young man I used to know in the relatively recent past (and believed had something in common with) reappeared in my life. It was a very short acquaintance, but there was a spark between us. It ended quickly, before anything really started. And yet – when he spoke again –

everything came back. At once and in a larger degree.

We definitely fell in love with each other this time. There was a lot of tenderness, love, gestures of care, taking care of each other – in addition to honesty, sincerity and loyalty. It was exactly what you expect from a relationship, what makes you want to get up in the morning and look forward to spending time with the other person. It was promising. It was beautiful.

After a while, we were ready to show our happiness to others. So sometimes we included others when we went out. It was nice, cheerful, sociable. I always needed people, I could not stand being alone. But, sooner than expected, it turned out that these friends were not good for us. More and more people were against us. They made things difficult for us. They said various things that were detrimental to our relationship. They tried hard to separate us, to destroy our mutual love.

And those were not only people that lived in the same town – there were also people from our previous lives (in different places) that tried to interfere. Despite all of this, against all odds – nothing destroyed our relationship, our love turned out to be much stronger than they expected. All of this only strengthened us. We have not been together for a long time, but our relationship was strong, true, sincere, built on love and mutual respect.

We did not make a lot of money and were not able to afford a lot of things that most young people desire and have no patience waiting for. But it did not matter. For the first time, I felt like I had everything I needed – because I had him and he had me. We have built a solid relationship foundation, and there were no more people trying to ruin our lives. We were just there for each other. And that was beautiful.

Then, I understood really deeply that you do not have to be rich to live well. In fact, it was money, or too much of it, that had spoiled my previous boyfriend and ruined our relationship. I realized that you can be happy with very little – as long as you have love and security with another person. When you can trust and depend on each other. When the fulfillment of your primary needs does not depend on your financial resources because being together and nothing else is, most of the time, all that you crave.

I understood that people come and go. Sometimes they disappoint. Sometimes they turn away without a word. It is the same with money – today it is here, tomorrow it is gone. But, as long as we have each other, then we really have everything, or – to be absolutely honest – almost everything.

You have to fight – for yourself, for your happiness, for the person you love. Because it is in those simplest moments, when you are drinking tea with someone who holds your hand, that the greatest wealth lies.

I am twenty years old now. I have been through more than many people twice my age. I have seen that not everything that looks good on the outside makes you happy on the inside.

And I learned something important: true happiness is not the numbers in your bank account. True happiness is warmth that you cannot buy, the special kind of companionship that comes only with true love.

Translated from Polish by Henryk Hoffmann

A Christmas Story

by Abbie Rutherford (From Newcastle, England, living in Berlin)

This poem is dedicated to my family. With living abroad and visiting my partner's family, I can't make it home for Christmas every year now, which is such a shame because we always have the most fun and play the most ridiculous games. I miss you all and love you lots – I hope you don't mind me sharing this story with the world.

Family. Christmas. The table. Noon.
Empty dessert bowls and cream-crusted spoons.
"Thank you!" "Delicious!" "Great!" echo around,
satisfied exhales now the only sound.

Mam takes out the dishes and asks for our help
until my Auntie Sarah lets out a great yelp!
"Oh fuck!" she exclaims, "Oh fuck!" and "Oh Shit!"
"Bastard, wank, bollocks, ass, twat, fuck, and tit!"

Us kiddies, we giggle and widen our eyes,
turning to see what had evoked the cries.
Her color had drained and her face looked much thinner:
"We forgot to make Joyce's! Shit! She's got no dinner!"

—now, let me quickly step aside from the tale;
Joyce was their neighbor (and so old and frail).
No family around, and sat all by herself,
looking forward to dinner from her good Christmas elf—

Now, back to the story: "Shit, what do we do?!"
My mam said, "Mind your language, you've got guests here too."
She was right. At the table sat a friend from Down Under
at his first English Christmas, his eyes filled with wonder.

My Mam, sensibly, said, "We'll just have to tell her,
apologize lots, send round one of the fellas."
"No, we can't do that!" Auntie Sarah protested—
She's never been someone who this could have bested—

"We'll make her a meal from our leftover plates!"
But it was scraped in a binbag straight after we'd ate.
My Mam and her sister shared a hesitant glance.
"We can't," said my Mam, "but it's our only chance…"

Then what to my wondering eyes did appear?
They opened the binbag and grabbed with no fear!
—another aside, yes, the binbag was clean!
My resourceful family isn't THAT mean—

They rummaged and scrounged, digging through peas and mash
to try and find whole bits not looking like trash.
"A whole sausage in bacon!" They squealed with surprise
as Grandad wheezed laughing with tears in his eyes.

"A whole slice of turkey!" "Some stuffing!" "A sprout!"
They cleaned off the items as they pulled them out.
Everybody chipped in, Nana grabbing some food,
Sarah plating it up… and somehow… it looked good!

"But what about gravy?" they all mused as they stared.
"Don't worry," said Peter, "because I came prepared!"
He went to his pocket, his knife was whipped out,
and he pierced the bag's corner—"use that as a spout!"

The gravy flowed well and everyone cheered!
Now the dinner was ready, but their smiles disappeared…
"I'm not taking it round, all I'll do is laugh!"
"Well don't look at me." "I can't, that'd be daft!"

It was Nana and Alan who donned poker face
and delivered the dinner to Joyce in our place.
We waited in silence with all our hands clutched…
Until Alan came in… "She said thanks very much!"

The story had ended, we let out a sigh,
sat down on the sofa, and had a mince pie.
Our Australian guest just stared at us in horror—
no wonder he wasn't at the Christmas that followed!

But…

Here's the real kicker, the real hard gut punch:
Joyce died the next year. That was her last Christmas lunch.
But when she gave the plate back, we didn't feel bad…
She said it was the best one that she'd ever had!

Note: This poem is written about a Christmas that my family had when I was young, somewhere between 9 and 12 years old. Joyce loved the dinner, and she never found out where it came from. I would like to reiterate that the binbag was totally fresh and only contained Christmas dinner food!!! We are good people, really!

The Most Important Day of My Life

by Les Sekut (Smithfield, VA)

What is the most important day in anyone's life? It seems to be an easy question, but it is actually difficult to address it in some kind of coherent fashion and in a way that would make most of the readers agree with your answer. Sure, there are other various milestones in everyone's life, like graduating from high school and grad school, getting married, starting a promising professional career or even paying taxes. Some people will definitely say that the most important days are when we are born and when we die. And, we often believe that our opinion about most of our important days is rather obvious and justified; but, in many cases, what we think is important is not, since we are not completely aware of all the circumstances and consequences of certain events. This can be a very complicated topic. However, I will try to address this question according to my personal beliefs and, hopefully, this will get your attention. I certainly hope that, once you've read my story, you will agree with me, and that the days I am about to describe are, indeed, the most important days of my life or, at least, one of them qualifies to be classified that way.

I have asked around a number of my friends and acquaintances which day they'd pick to be the most important day of their lives, and I was met with confused expressions. They struggled to come up with something personal or fast enough. In my case the choice is rather obvious. I am going to focus on March 14, 1997. It was my important day. I was anticipating that day for nearly nine months – ever since the day my wife told me she was expecting a child. I was excited from the first day, asking myself a lot of questions. Will the child be healthy? What gender? What name? So many questions coming to mind, questions that most young parents ask themselves when they get this wonderful news. And, what was both important and shocking to me, I found out I was going to be present at the delivery of my baby daughter, witnessing her birth. Initially, I was not too happy about it, maybe even scared. Seeing my wife in pain and distress wasn't something I was looking forward to. There were some complications at the initial stage of the delivery on the ambulance ride, but – fortunately – an obstetrician was with us. It was quite traumatic to observe, though. Admittedly, I had second thoughts about witnessing my wife's delivery.

But, eventually, I decided to be present anyway, primarily to support my wife – especially because we had no family here, in this country, and she was basically on her own. Regardless of how I felt about it, I had to be there for her. The hospital was very high tech and with very wonderful staff and doctors at the time. It was the Brigham Women's Hospital. Initially, not much was going on. It was an induced labor; everything was so controlled. The whole process was nothing I would have expected in terms of my wife being in pain or distress. However, there were no complications, it went smooth and fast – without any drama. Admittedly, my biggest surprise was the first split-second, the brief moment when I could see my daughter for the first time. It was like a dream; basically, it was a surrealistic experience. It is so hard to describe what went through my heart and mind when I laid my eyes on my baby for the first time.

The best way to describe what I felt at that moment is by comparing it to time travel. I certainly experienced the biggest "déjà vu" of my life. It is hard to explain why? I didn't think in that moment that it was my daughter; I thought for a second that the baby being born was me, and I was witnessing myself come into the world. My child looked so much like the pictures of me when I was an infant – in fact, she was identical. This made me breathless and really confused, I didn't know what to think about it. And then that overwhelming feeling of exceptional love filled up my heart. I was so bonded to my daughter, and it was such an instant process it absolutely amazed me. I thought it would take me weeks and months to grow accustomed to her or even develop some sort of emotions, but the very instant I saw her I loved her. A new that a screaming infant would be draining and exhausting, so I assumed that, when she was two or three or five, I would develop emotionally with her gradually. But, in my real case, it was an instant process.

My God, now I am a big supporter of the idea that both parents should be present during the delivery of a child, because I am hoping both parents will feel as strongly towards their child as I did. That way fewer children would come to the world with broken families, and both the parents and the children would benefit from it. So, if fewer and fewer children in the nation were to be affected by attachment disorder RAD, children would not suffer as much and grow into more active members of the society, being, at the same time, less prone to crime and other issues. Additionally, once those children become adults they would pass that kind of love and attention on to their own offspring. This way, there would be fewer and fewer broken families, which would improve us all as a society. This would also translate into happier and healthier people, and that, in turn, would lead to less crime based on the profound effect – in the same way as my daughter's birth impacted me. I would assume that it can have a similar effect on more and more people, and this would make them commit more to each other as parents to raise a happy and healthy child. I understand it is not easy, but life is full of obstacles that we have to anticipate and accept ahead of time. All we can do is try to be our best through, among other things, supporting ourselves with good emotional support groups. This could help young people who are trying to start a family with a complete commitment to each other. Children cannot be raised just by remote interaction and child support – it is unrealistic. I strongly believe only a full family with committed parents can help the child have the best opportunity at life.

I am trying to compare by experience as a father to my old experience as a child. Maybe it was not the most important day in my life. But it certainly was the most important period for me when two of my grandmas, both named Helena, were taking care of me. They were so wonderful that even now I am profoundly grateful for all their commitment, energy and unconditional love they passed on to me. I would definitely call this the most important period of my life – especially when I think of the time they were looking after me every day and, no matter what, I could always feel their love. I understand that many grandparents all over the world are looking after their grandchildren, trying to substitute for the parents, but I believe this unwelcome situation – that of so many broken or abandoned families – can and needs to be minimized in the society.

And I would expect not only religious organizations but also state organizations to look into this situation and provide more support for this idea with special programs. They could start with consulting families and bringing financial and emotional support to young parents. They can do everything they can to try to keep families together, and yes, admittedly, it is a very exhausting process. Quite frankly, it can be even scary and intimidating. I think that more organizations should focus on the prevention of broken families. I am confident that everyone would benefit from such an approach. If I have to talk about the most important day of my long life, there are a lot of different situations which I could probably refer to as the highlights. But I truly think that seeing my daughter for the first time and raising her was unquestionably the most important day/period of my life.

This is something that millions of people experience, generation after generation, bringing new life to this world. They sacrifice their own life to raise children and give them everything they need. And, based on my own experience, I strongly believe that we should be grateful to our ancestors who have been doing this for millions of years. They were all doing this because of the unconditional love of their child, above all – at least in most of the cases.

Renata and Beniu in Hamedan, Iran (2000).

Travels with Beniu

by Renata Sołtysiak (Mühltal, Germany)

I met Bernard in East Berlin in 1972. Although we both studied German (or German Philology, as the major used to be called at that time) at Adam Mickiewicz University in Poznań, Poland (where Bernard met and befriended Henryk, the originator and designer of this book project), we used our semester break to work in Berlin for a glassworks company that produced beer and champagne bottles. Bernard, after graduating in 1974, was employed by the University as a research and teaching associate. I, having graduated two years later, got a job as a lecturer at the College of Engineering in Zielona Góra (Bernard's hometown), where we also settled together after the wedding. Since Bernard (or Beniu, as I started to call him after we got closer to each other) worked in Poznań Monday through Thursday, our married life took place mostly during weekends. Fortunately, soon two of our children were born, Tomasz (or Tomek) and Kornelia (Nelka), who added a lot of joy to my days without Beniu and kept me quite busy most of the time. We had no reason to complain; we both had good jobs, a nice apartment and a couple of lovely and healthy children.

However, with Martial War in effect since December 1981, the political situation in Poland was changing very quickly, and the tension was felt by most of the population on a daily basis. In 1983, Beniu accepted an offer from Universität Bamberg for a semester-long guest professorship. During his stay there, he re-established contact with a woman he had known back in Poland and who had moved to Germany with her husband. She described life in Germany to him in such beautiful colors that Beniu began to talk more and more often about us moving there. In 1986, he got another opportunity to teach in Germany for a semester, this time at Universität Kiel. We saw it as a sign to act fast. The Polish authorities allowed both me and Nelka to accompany Beniu, but they insisted that our son stay behind (under the care of his grandparents) as a pledge of our return. Fortunately, everything ended well because eight months later Tomek was able to join us in Germany and make our family complete again.

The start of our life in a new country went quite smoothly because there was no language barrier. I got a job at the University of Darmstadt as a secretary at the Institute for Language and Literature after six months and, after less than a year, we got a large apartment. At the beginning of 1997, Beniu started a job in Wiesbaden (the capital of Hesse) as a clerk for media and communications in the private sector, a job that required of him to drive sixty kilometers each way every day. But, because the job was well paid, he did not mind taking this effort upon himself; however, after a while, these trips to work, mostly on a busy highway with frequent traffic jams, became more and more burdensome especially in winter. Thus, he considered himself lucky when he got a two-year job as a teacher at the University of Darmstadt and then at a private language school. And that was what he always wanted for himself –

to be a teacher. He taught adults, mainly refugees and people whose language courses were financed by the government.

Our life was going well, but Beniu was always curious about the world and keen on traveling. Because we could afford to do so, over the years we visited much of the world. Here are just some examples, which do not include Europe: Singapore, Hong Kong (it was still a colony of England at that time), Indonesia, Bali, Lebanon, Syria, Jordan, Israel, Mexico, Guatemala, Honduras, Egypt, Tunisia, Morocco, Libya, Iran, Galapagos Islands, Ecuador, Bolivia, Brazil, Argentina, China, India, Nepal, USA (including Hawaii). There have been some events during our travels that you cannot forget, like the one in Egypt in 1994. While we were walking down one of the streets of Cairo, we noticed a woman and two men sitting together in front of a house. For no reason, the woman came up to me, hit me on the cheek and ran away. After that the two guys came up to us and said, "She is crazy," and invited us for tea, which we refused. At dinner, we told about the event to our guide, who immediately wanted to call the police.

Another time we were in Bolivia at Lake Titicaca and we experienced samples of incredible poverty and begging of the Indian tribe Urus. We were quite surprised to find out that members of that tribe did not want money from us but, instead, begged for aspirin. During our stay in India, we were in Varanasi and we could watch the burning of corpses on the Ganges bank from a distance. When we were in Nepal, we had a flight over Mount Everest booked, but because the weather was bad that day, we had to give it up. While visiting Patan (Nepal), Beniu suddenly said to me, "Turn around," and I turned around and saw the Himalayas with full majesty and I just lost words seeing this mountain massif so close. In Chitwan National Park, we traveled on elephants' backs through the jungle and experienced rafting on the Trishuli River. During our stay in Libya, we saw in Sabratha one of the most beautiful theaters from Roman times, and Leptis Magna was for us one of the most beautiful Roman cities we had seen so far. We saw a lot and experienced many intense days. But Beniu always said that he did not want to be in the same place in the world twice, and I agreed with him. However, we were both of the same opinion that we should go to Jerusalem one more time because what we experienced in 1997, where all religions with equal rights, Jews, Christianity and Islam could exist side by side, was very touching for us. And what is happening there now is amazing and sad at the same time.

Bernard always had an open mind and was deeply interested in local history, culture and religion; he deepened his knowledge of Buddhism when traveling to China, of Hinduism when in India, of Judaism in Israel, and Islam when we went to Lebanon, Syria and Jordan. And it was not a superficial interest; he just delved into these religions and looked for parallel connections.

I do not know if I mentioned all the trips, but probably the most important ones that allowed us to take a look at what was happening in the world, not only culturally and religiously, but also politically. Apart from traveling, Beniu had a lot of interests some of which could be described as passion. He was a fan of American film (through Henryk's influence) and he loved music – the range of his favorites very large: Eric Clapton, Tom Wats, John Lee Hooker, Chris Rea, Van Morrison, Leonard Cohen, Rod Stewart, Joe Cocker, Robbie Williams, Nora Jones, Bee Gees, Louis Armstrong, Eruption, Chris de Burgh, Red Hot Chili Peppers and many more. I certainly did not list all his favorite musicians, but he listened to music with such delight and spent a lot of money on this hobby. He also loved classical music and, as a child, learned how to play the piano (occasionally he would perform for the family, playing pieces like Beethoven's "Für Elise").

But as it is in life, you cannot always live without worries and problems, and so this fate did not pass us by. In the year 2016, we were in London, staying in the Westminster Hotel directly on the River Thames with a view of the Parliament and Westminster from the hotel. At some point, Beniu tells me that it is amazing that he can experience London in the fog, such typical weather here that we know from the movies. But it was not like that, the wind was blowing, but there was no fog. In the morning we were in Windsor, and in the afternoon he did not feel well. Because we still had tickets for the Underground, I went alone to see St. Paul's Cathedral and walked by the river doing a lot of thinking. After returning home, Beniu complained about his eyes, that he was constantly seeing poorly and only recognizing shapes. After returning to Germany, we visited four doctors and only the last one expressed a suspicion of brain tumor. A few weeks later, Beniu had the first operation, which lasted ten hours because the tumor was pressing on the optic nerve. After minor and major surgeries (in the meantime they removed one third of his lungs and two ribs), he recovered quite quickly, but we both realized that life was short and we would like to use it a little more.

A year later, he felt so good that he suggested a trip to Paris, where he had spent three months a few years before, and wanted to show me Paris so badly. We went there full of joy and plans, but as it is, it does not always work out as we would like. We could not enter the Louvre or take a boat ride on the Seine because the water level was too high and there was a risk of flooding. We stayed in a nice hotel in Montmartre on Place Pigalle and had a view of the Sacré-Coeur from the window. We visited the Arc de Triomphe, the Eiffel Tower, Notre-Dame, Napoleon's Hornbeam and the beautiful Versailles. There were a lot of people and plenty of noise during the tour of Versailles, and Beniu, unable to endure it, wanted us to leave. On his way out, he fell down the stairs; fortunately, nothing happened to him, except for shock and loss of balance. Help came immediately and we took a taxi to the hotel. We had two days left until our return, but he did not want us to rebook the flight hoping that he would be better the following day. He stayed two days in bed, and I went hiking around Paris on my own, but I did not have any fun. I walked on the Champs-Elysees from top to bottom almost twice, I stood for a second on the Pont Neuf Bridge looking sadly at the river and thinking what would happen next. Beniu began to try to read or listen to music, but it was no longer possible because his eyesight was deteriorating very quickly. Listening to music annoyed him because he could not concentrate and then he became aggressive, asking what was wrong with me. Once at home, where we arrived on October 6, 2018 at two a.m., he fell returning from the toilet, and it took a few minutes before he resumed consciousness.

In the morning an ambulance arrived and took him to the hospital, a few hours later he was diagnosed with a bleeding cerebral hemorrhage, and surgery was necessary. That is when the odyssey began, which I will make short. Two and a half months in the intensive care unit, during which time he was connected to the heart-lung machine because he could neither breathe on his own nor eat. In the meantime, he was resuscitated twice. In March, I was able to take him home, but I had to learn how to deal with his epilepsy. After the removal of Tracheostoma and the PEG-Probe, he started to eat a little on his own. I was more and more hopeful that it would get better since I went out with him in a wheelchair for walks. He could not walk on his own for long, but at home he moved without problems. He was very lively at the time, he told jokes, he was cheerful and witty, and communication with him was almost normal. Beniu tried very hard to help me around the house and so, for example, he dried the dishes after breakfast, but he put the plates and cups in wrong place, and when I pointed it out to him, he said that the new way was also nice. Another problem at the beginning was related to diapers; he did not want me to change them for him and, being ashamed, tried to do it himself. But then I only had more work to do and I had to keep a close eye on him because he threw the diapers into the toilet or hid them in some corner of the apartment.

Over time, he accepted that he would not dress himself and put his shame aside. Unfortunately, his brain was working worse and worse and so, for example, he took the car key in his hand and wanted to leave. I went out with him to the car and wondered how he would deal with it. He opened the car and got in, and at that moment I saw that he would not be able to do it because he did not know how to start; it was an incredible sight, his disappointment that he did not know what to do and looking at me sadly he said, "I don't know what to do now. What happened to me that I can't do anything anymore?" and he started crying. During this time, he cried a lot and always asked me to tell him what had happened to him and why and if there would ever be any change and things would get better. I patiently told him his story of illness, but after an hour he was asking me the same questions.

Some situations were very sad and strange. When, for example, I was sitting at the computer and he came to me and said very seriously, "You have to put me in this PC." I asked, "How should I do it, the PC is small and you are too big." And he said, "Very easily, with my head down." Then I sent him to the terrace and he sat a little outdoors, but not for long, because he started sleeping right away. In general, he slept a lot and once I wanted to take advantage of his long sleep and went shopping for two hours. (Of course, the doors and windows were so closed that he would not be able to go out on his own.) When I came back, he was standing dressed in the hall, and when I asked him where he wanted to go, he said, "I have to look for you." I had help three times a week; the person did his toilet and tried to take care of him a bit, trying small games, a bit of reading, but he was so bored that he fell asleep right away. Beniu was not able to recognize people around him, especially if they were strangers. He always got to know Nelka and Tomek and tried to talk to them a bit, but he was getting worse and worse or he was also aware that he did not know what to say, so he kept quiet a lot. Overall, he was doing well in the apartment, but there were situations when he turned on all the lights during the day and said that it was dark as hell. Or one night he made a piece of toast and I woke up because of the alarm activated by the smoke in the kitchen. In response to my question about the smoke and the alarm, he answered, "I don't hear anything and I don't see the smoke either."

It was the first sign for me that his eyesight was disappearing, and the doctor said that the pressure on the optic nerve was so big that Beniu would go blind over time. Sometimes he was so confused that he did not know where he was, and then he said, "We have to go upstairs because that's where our apartment is." Another time, he did not know where the toilet was and peed on a cabinet in the room.

Some other time, I woke up when he was dressed chaotically, socks on his hands, a shirt on his feet, etc. When I asked him what he wanted to do about it, he answered, "I'm going to the street because the weather is nice." I explained to him that it was night and we would go for a walk together the following morning. He did not answer anything and started crying, saying, "What happened to me, why don't I understand anything?" It was a miserable experience when at five a.m. a paramedic rang the doorbell and said, "We have your husband, but nothing dangerous happened, he only had his head a little smashed." He was found by a gentleman who was delivering newspapers in the morning and called an ambulance. From then on, I had to close all the doors day and night. For some time, he had been talking less and less, i.e., he wanted to say something but he had no words, so he just started saying, "Where is he …," or "What can I do…," or "Who…," and did not finish the sentence.

One day, at the beginning of January 2021, a nurse came and said that she did not like the way he looked, a very short breath and strange sounds in his lungs. We called an ambulance, which immediately took him to the hospital for suspected pneumonia. Because of the Corona pandemic, it was impossible to visit the hospital, but, after many attempts, I received a special permission to see him there and the first thing he said when he saw me was, "Where have you been for so long?" After a week I was able to take him home but his mental state was getting worse and worse, he was confused and still wanted to run away from home. Despite the help of nurses, who now came four times a week, I got exhausted because of this constant care and control over what he would do now, because he sometimes stripped naked and sat on the sofa or stood naked in a dark room in front of a bookcase and looked for something. When I found him like that I did not know how long he was standing there, but his body was cold. These last months were more and more difficult because he slept during the day and walked around the apartment at night. These were very difficult days and months, but I felt so sorry for him that such a healthy mind turned, in such a short time, into something that was not life, but vegetation. On top of that, there was this Corona pandemic, which made it impossible, or next to impossible, to contact doctors. Phone calls for medical help or advice took a very long time. Once a doctor I was talking with on the phone told me that Bernard's brain functionality was so limited that there was no help for it. I still had a lot of strength and I would have persevered for a long time if only I could take care of him. On March 24 after breakfast, he felt very weak and almost fell off the chair (maybe it was also an epileptic seizure). I had to call an ambulance and they took him back to the hospital. After two days of waiting to talk to the doctor, I was told that they could not reach him and could not wake him up. Beniu died on March 30, 2021, two months before his 70th birthday.

I was left alone and, despite the repeatedly expressed reassurance from my friends and acquaintances that they were always available to me and would help me day and night, the reality was different. After a few weeks no one called me anymore, and I felt more and more lonely and suffered from the lack of the person with whom I had spent almost fifty years. He was not only a partner for me, but also a dearest friend. To distance myself from this sadness a bit, I tried to travel, i.e., to resume activities that had united us for so many years. I will never forget what a privilege I had as Beniu's traveling companion, getting to know new countries, new customs and history of all those countries we have visited together. Sometimes I thought, and I did share these thoughts with my husband assuming that he would also like it, that I would continue to achieve his travel goals. But, unfortunately, it was not the same because there was no one to share my impressions with during the trip, I was just lonely and without spiritual support and the special person who was ready to talk to me about it.

Two years later, during a trip to Monaco, I met Harry, who had been a widower for eight years, who owns a nice house and is financially well-positioned. Thus, we have an opportunity to achieve something else in whatever is left of our lives. We travel and wander around, but it is not the same as before because life with Beniu was different; we just grew in our friendship and partnership, we knew each other so well that we could communicate without words. At the moment I need to get to know Harry a little better, but, on the other hand, we do not have time, because we are both getting older and you never know what will happen next. I will never forget Beniu because he was and will always be my soulmate and irreplaceable friend – in both good and bad times.

Translated from Polish by Henryk Hoffmann

Kofi's Story

by Tymon Stajkowski (Warsaw, Poland)

It all started in February 2020, less than two weeks before my tenth birthday. A big animal lover, I had long dreamed of having a small dog living with me. I did not know exactly what kind (or breed) of dog I wanted, but my mother, Katarzyna (Kasia or Kaha), while browsing the internet, came across a tiny puppy – a Maltese. As soon as she showed it to me, I knew immediately that this was the dog I was looking for.

At first, clueless as I was, I thought we would get the dog within a few days, but sometime later, in the evening of the same day, around nine p.m., it turned out that we were leaving at once. My sister, Zuzia (five year older than I), did not know anything about what our mother and I were up to, nothing about our plans to purchase a dog. So, we just told her we were going to see some of my mother's friends and I was accompanying her to play with a good friend of mine, the people's son, while my mother would talk to the adults about some urgent matters. Zuzia was suspicious, but she did not ask many questions, so we set off.

The journey was long – we drove from Warsaw (where I was born and where we lived at that time) to Radom, a town over 100 kilometers (about seventy miles) southeast of Warsaw. It was raining heavily, and the wind was so strong that the car was dancing on the road. The one-way trip took over an hour and a half. During that time, I was thinking intensively about what name the new member of our family should be given. I wanted something original. Finally, I came up with 'Kofi' – from the English word 'coffee,' but altered in my own way, to make it sound foreign and be spelled in an absolutely unique way.

When we arrived, we were greeted by a nice lady and a whole family of Maltese dogs. When I saw the one that I was supposed to take with me, I felt as if I were watching a movie – the joy I experienced at that moment is impossible to describe. When I took her (the dog turned out to be female) in my arms, it was probably the happiest moment of my life. The lady offered us some food and gave us the basic information regarding our purchase, and then we set off to bring Kofi to the car.

I already knew then that this dog would be the cutest and biggest troublemaker in the world. And yes, I did name her Kofi, spelled in the Polish (or phonetic way) of an English word for the adults' morning-time beverage.

On our way back home, the weather was even worse. Kofi was scared, shaking with fear, so I held her close, petted her and tried to give her some food – and, yes, she was hungry. She ate out of my hand like nothing else mattered.

At one point, my mom said that there were fallen trees on the road and some cars were skidding. It scared me a little, but all I could think about was getting home safely and introducing Kofi to the rest of the family.

When we finally got there, I went straight to Zuzia so that she could meet the dog. Needless to say, she was delighted and very happy. I also called my dad – he had no idea about Kofi, so he was totally surprised – but the moment he saw her on the camera, he was also moved.

The next day I went with Kofi to see my dad so that he could see her in person. It was obvious from the start that he loved her too – he played with her for so long that they fell asleep together. To this day, Kofi likes to play with him the most.

We also had to introduce her to our first she-dog – Milka. At first, Milka was happy, but over time, a slight jealousy on her part was visible. Kofi, on the other hand, immediately felt at home – she started playing with the toys we had bought for her earlier and chased them like crazy. We also found it funny how she hid in various nooks and crannies – under the wardrobe, the armchair, behind the couch – wherever she could fit. And she literally tore the cuddly toy we had given her to shreds. We did not expect that, but we all had a good laugh about it. The same when she slipped on the panels and sometimes landed on her butt – she looked like a white torpedo dumpling.

We soon realized the unusual coincidental irony resulting from our dogs' looks and names. Milka, mostly brown, was named after the white beverage given to all babies, and Kofi, predominantly white, received a name that implies the drink that, unless diluted with cream, is clearly brown.

After a few days, it was time for her to visit the vet – deworming, vaccinations, check-up. After everything, the doctor said she could go for walks right away – she ran around the grass like a madwoman and rolled around in it like crazy.

After a while, it was time for her first haircut, and since my mom and I had no idea that it was not easy, we decided to do it ourselves, which we later regretted, because it came out terribly crooked as if a one-eyed pirate had done it, and we knew that this job should be left to people who know how to do it.

Kofi always had a problem getting on the couch, so when she got a little older, I decided to teach her to jump on the couch on her own, which was helped by treats. And it looked like this: I would take a treat, hold it over the couch and encourage Kofi to jump on in order to get it, and, after a while, she took a big run-up and jumped on, and, ever since that, she kept jumping on without help and without a problem. I also wanted her to be able to do basic tricks, such as "sit," "paw" and "lie down." At first, she learned the command "paw," then "sit," and finally "lie down."

Over the following years Kofi grew like a weed and got to know more and more places and people, among others thanks to our moving from Warsaw to Ińsko and traveling to our relatives in Poznań.

And it all started with a simple click on a photo on the internet. …Now I know that it was not a coincidence. Because no matter how you look at it, Kofi is the best thing that could have happened to me in my life.

Translated from Polish by Henryk Hoffmann

Tim Turners, First and Second

Flux – The Dynamics of Authenticity and Facing the Hurt

by Timothy J. Turner II (Boyertown, PA)

If you don't vocalize and only internalize, you rot. That is one phrase I have kept close to heart while going on my own journey through this crazy thing called life. It is a lesson that was bred out of tragedy. On January 24th, 2019, my father, Tim Turner the 1st decided to make the choice to leave us. The fallout from that decision left an ecosystem of people in flux. The ship still had its rudder for steering, but the navigator was left questioning where to go next. Even when the navigator doesn't have the next destination, the wind will still blow, and you can't drop an anchor in the middle of an empty ocean. The sounds of the birds chirping, the breeze flowing, and all the other sounds feel off, like they don't understand the gravity of the situation. It is jarring. Though, once again, life continues.

Through this initial period, I crammed it all down. Stuffed it into a box where no one would be able to get to. At the time I felt that I had better things to do. I had to take care of my mom and sister, take over some of the jobs my father did, and, most importantly, ignore all my own grief. This was done through pursuit of solving everyone's problems or minor inconveniences. Whether that be in engineering or in my personal life. To reflect on my opening statement, I was prioritizing rotting over doing anything to take care of myself. Believe it or not, this grand plan did not benefit me at all. In fact, it led to a bigger breakdown where I questioned everything about who I was and wanted to be. I lost all motivation and excitement; I lashed out at friends and became a shell of myself. The cracks that I thought were hidden were only getting more apparent with each passing day.

The cracks themselves arose in different ways, some through memories of my father. How he showed up to every theater performance, multiple nights of the same show—even though he would have preferred that it had been a sport. How I could make him laugh with jokes, push it to the point of being annoying, then break him into laughter again. How he had a habit of never admitting he was wrong, but when he was, his apologies came in the form of gifts rather than words. The future hurt to look at too: the milestones that would never come. No bonding before a wedding. No meeting his grandkids. No guidance during career changes. Each realization hit like a brick, small at first but together weighing the ship down one pound at a time.

After months of staving off the fallout, a single thought crossed my mind "what if I just disappear." That thought may have been the one to change it all around. When that came, I realized something for myself. That I am past the point of being able to wade through this alone. From there I sat with my mom and informed her that I needed to go away, to get help and to face what I had been putting off for so long. I went to a mental health retreat to understand my feelings and forcibly focus on myself.

Getting help was one of the single greatest things I have done. While away I was able to dedicate all helping efforts towards myself. I was able to focus on what had been pushed down and reevaluate its role in my life. This track allowed me to realize a few key things. One: that I was unfulfilled with my job at the time. I felt that I needed to dedicate my current time towards helping others. Two: that the standards I was comparing myself to were never going to make me happy. They were suffocating, based off what the general public considered to be "success." Three: I was stronger than I even realized, I was just too busy putting myself down to see it. Additionally, that strength helped me realize that I was not alone.

Facing these realizations was difficult. It was acknowledging that the identity that I had curated up until this point was more of a façade than it was my authentic self. Built off the "shoulda," "coulda," "woulda"s of the world. I was lucky to have had time to confront these beliefs. Luckier still that the people I was with helped me see the bad that I was holding onto, as well as see the good I was suppressing. One of the good things came about through what is called an amethyst ceremony. The long short of it is that when you are ready to return to your daily life, you pick out a chunk of amethyst. From there, those who you've recovered with pass it around and provide you with one word that they think of when they think of the person moving on. One stuck out in particular. There was a man in the treatment with me, an ex-con, who was always in the gym and marching to the beat of his own drum. He took a pause and looked at me. The word he gave me was "leader." Leading not by force, not by demand, but by the true nature of leadership. He explained that without an agenda, I took command. I made sure everyone got to where they needed to be, understood, and looked out for those who were new and old alike. How, in the exercise where we needed to overcome climbing up a rope course, I opted to pause at each transition and hoist others up before completing it on my own. He let me know that what I did was true leadership, not the false way people pitch it to be. The words he spoke that day still echo within me. They give me reassurance during the turbulent times and bolster the calmer moments.

To this day, that word, 'leader,' stays with me, not just in the way I carried myself in the program, but in how I came to understand a new possibility: the role of a therapist. A therapist is a quiet leader, someone who walks beside you through your pain, guiding without overtaking. From the outside, the work can seem passive, but internally, it demands strength, discipline and emotional fluency. These were muscles I had been unknowingly training. Sitting with others in their most vulnerable states taught me what I needed to bring into my own work: the power of presence, patience and non-judgment.

Through this program, the next steps unveiled new pathways. I saw a different option, one where I felt I could be more of service.

Once I left, I contacted a close friend of mine to go through options of how I could transition into becoming a therapist. We went through different pathways and, at the conclusion, I had the next leg of my journey planned. The first step focused on confirming that I had my own house in order. Being a therapist is not a job that comes lightly. While we cannot control all our triggers or when they happen, we can control our emotional responses to them and the level we show. As a therapist, you do not get warnings when someone is about to offload the tragedies and traumas that they may have faced. They are seeking a professional with the assumption that they are equipped to maintain their composure and help them explore and process. If the therapist cannot respond in an appropriate manner and instead opts to make the session about their own trauma, it is going to do more harm to someone who needs the help. Before even stepping into the arena, I had to know that I could maintain that level of composure. That I would not transfer my own traumas onto the client. To that end, I buckled down and went through the gambit of self-discovery and self-healing. This included individual therapy, group therapy, grief exposure, acupuncture and reiki healing. Each component helped me face and accept what had happened. This prepared me to be able to face whatever was brought to me.

Going through graduate school made everything real. It put an actual timeframe on when the change was going to happen. I had three years, three years to learn all I could within my master's course to prepare before going into the mental health field officially. This timeframe was not without challenges, one which: saying goodbye to the engineering field that I was in for so long. It had its ups and downs: good and bad managers alike, but it was the only professional world I knew. I had started there only about a week after graduating from my undergraduate college. Five years of my adult life, and almost all my professional life, were spent here. Towards the end of my time, I had trusted colleagues, ones I would rather label friends, that it was unsure if I would see again.

You never know the world you are walking into, and fear was doing its best to make me second guess each choice I was making. The funny thing about fear is that it seldom is based off factual evidence. Often, it is stuck on the assumption that a situation may happen, and you will just accept the poor result. For the people I cared about, the only way not seeing them again would turn to fact, was if I allowed it to. Fear is a powerful emotion, but if properly approached, it can be a warning light showing you a path that you do not have to take. Changing careers from engineering to counseling is a huge jump, but I utilized fear to inspire, over detract. I feared not taking the chance more than I feared remaining in comfort.

Engineering itself had also proved to be more of a strength during this transition than I could have realized. The information that I had learned through work was invaluable when relating to clients. There was a greater ability to empathize and relate to those struggling with work and identity. There was the ability to create metaphors from my experiences and translate them into actionable directions. Lastly, it gave me an edge that I was not just spewing things learned out of textbooks. The information came from real life. The tool I thought was incompatible with this change ended up making it easier. Life experiences can show up and help shape something that would otherwise be inconceivable.

During my time in graduate school, I took on many new roles. I went back to my high school and became a substitute teacher and ended up coteaching my own class. I coached rock climbing and took on new responsibilities handling different events. The program also added the responsibility of taking an internship as a counselor while finishing out the program. Each giving new insight into what the future could look like, the different pathways that could be explored. Things that, at the beginning of the journey, I would never have thought about as possibilities. Before the loss, I was so focused on the track I was on that I did not realize that there were splits and turns at each junction. Even more so, being on this train at all was my choice, just as what cart I was in, who I was sitting with, and the mood I was in through it all. There is a tendency to be so focused on the goal that we miss so much passing by. Having the time to stop and see, put so much more into perspective.

We need that time. Where we are, where we've been and where we want to go, each of these bring valuable insight. Another saying that I bring into my life and work to impart in sessions is "curiosity not criticism." When we are processing difficult moments, we are hoping to "move on" from them. Though that is rarely going to happen, we may move farther away in time, but the scars of the past remain. We cannot ever get away from the past. This may seem like a scary thought, but instead it is a blessing in disguise. I tell many people that the actions they take are based off the information that they have in that exact moment of time. We all "know better" in hindsight, but in the moment, we made do with the facts we had. The thing to remember is that knowing the result now enables us to have more foresight into not repeating the same action again. We grow and improve because we cannot move on from the past. Instead, we digest it and turn it into energy that will serve us better. That digestion does not come from repeated beat downs and criticisms over the action. That approach created a whirlpool of negativity whereas all we can see is a storm. We do not see those possibilities that were on the other side. Curiosity is what allows that to take form. Being curious as to why we made the decision, curious as to what decision we would make now, knowing what we know. Instead of vilifying ourselves, we give way to character development, to forgiveness of past actions and to the higher chance of self-actualization.

Now, a year into being a therapist, I have further shaped my approach to life in addition to aiding others in discovering theirs. The field of mental health opens the eyes of so many who come to experience it. One of the first things you realize is that many people are holding more than they let on. This includes not only their own baggage but often trying to take on the baggage of others. They are fighting to stay afloat but ultimately getting lost in the waves. These individuals who come to us are facing the hardest thing: realizing that they cannot get through it alone. Mortality, even just the mortality of mental health, is a tough pill to swallow. The realization that you cannot just push your way through alone can be crushing. I tell many people that "help" is the hardest word to say. The fact that they come into a session shows that they are willing to address that challenge and move forward. In my own journey, I had to be at rock bottom before confronting that hard word. Even then, it was difficult to get out. At times it felt lodged in my throat. There, but not willing to materialize. I needed to be ready to face it, and when I was, change was right around the corner.

The second is the importance of silence. We are in a world where people tend to want to fill space. This can be filled through things, words, people, or any myriads of different things. This is where avoidance thrives. It lives off the idea that if we keep throwing more in, then we can move past it. Struggles have a way of sticking around, even in a filled room. The more we push against them, the stronger they become, just waiting for a falter in your apparent strength. These result in complex patterns: grief masquerading as anger, anxiety as over-preparedness, shame as silence. One lesson that continues to return is this: most people aren't truly looking for someone to solve their problems; they're looking for someone who can sit with them in the dark without trying to turn on a light too soon. Up at college, one of my best friends sat with me during one of my worst moments. I hid myself in the basement sitting in both figurative and literal darkness. She came down, pushed things away and sat down beside me. She didn't say anything or try to figure out what was happening, just was present. That profound silence, and the physical representation told me that she wasn't going to pry or force me to talk, but she was going to make sure that I knew I wasn't alone. Sometimes, that is what we need, just the validation of our human experiences.

Third is the willingness to face the darkness. This brings the beginning two and morphs them into executable practice. The hardest part of the healing process is facing what you need to heal from. Ignoring the wound only lets it fester. To improve, you must look at it directly and honestly. We need to find the root of the problem, not just the symptoms. Nothing just pops into being with no connection to other facets of your life. Everything is interlaced, intertwined and knotted beyond all recognition. I tell whoever I help that I am going to be there for them, but that includes helping them confront what they may not want to. When going through the program, one of my roots was how I truly valued myself. It wasn't highly, in fact, it was a rather low valuation. It fed into my need to take care of everyone but myself. I thought they all deserved the help, but I didn't. I was going to wallow and then hopefully figure it out, but either way the result wasn't important if everyone else was sailing fine. There is a reason you need to put your mask on first before helping others. It is so you don't panic and make the wrong steps. It is also because if you do not help yourself, you won't be able to help people for long. By self-supporting, you are giving yourself the chance to be better equipped to deal with difficulties and help more people in the long run.

The last falls into one word, authenticity. Authenticity is not simply being honest; it is about being congruent. Being steadfast in your beliefs and ensuring that your actions, your thoughts and your emotions align as closely as they can, even when doing so is uncomfortable. I changed throughout life. Starting as the problem-solver who met everyone's needs and fixed the issues. Then the steady one, the rock that people relied on when life was stormy. The one who kept going no matter what, who was praised for his strength but was lacking the internal foundation. Those layers were stitched together by fear, expectation and the illusion of stability. Stripping those away was terrifying, but necessary. It revealed someone more real, more vulnerable and, paradoxically, more capable. To sum it up, it was more authentic. The therapeutic process, and an actualized life, hinges on authenticity. People don't need perfection; they need presence. They need to feel that they are grounded in their own truth. That their thoughts, feelings and sense of self is valid and seen. That is the person I've worked to become for both myself and all those I interact with.

So, what is important about this story, what is it teaching? That it is up to the reader and their takeaways. My own takeaway is that nothing is set in stone, everything is constantly in flux. Additionally, it is crucial for everyone to be authentic and earnest in who they are. This includes accepting the negatives and growing from them as well as cherishing and celebrating all the positives you bring to the table. All of this started through an unfortunate act, and while I am grateful for where I am now, this could not have been done without active and intentional effort. There are many who may try to console through the idea that things happen for a reason. This phrase may be meant as support, but ultimately, things can happen with no grand plan. An action may not be the linchpin to start the next phase or the evolution of an individual's life.

My dad's suicide at the time felt like an end, which, through hard work, turned into a pivotal and positive change in my life. While grateful for where I am today, it would be insensitive to label an action such as that as right or wrong. Right or wrong are in the same boat as the "shoulda," "coulda," "woulda"s of the world. They keep us guessing about our actions over simply living our life. They undermine our efforts and force them into a binary categorization to either reassure or keep ourselves down. We do not know if what we are doing is right until we get all the results down the line. Even then, things may change that can turn a right to a wrong, a yes to a no, or a definitely to an uncertainty. We have our experiences, our thoughts and our actions as tools to create the best possible future in the present. It may not turn out perfect, but it will be ours.

Overall, there is no final version of who we are. We are drafts, constantly being edited by time, challenge, failure and discovery.

Complacency or acceptance of what is happening is just a cop out. It is letting someone else decide the track your life follows. My story is still being written, as all of ours are The goal is not perfection, nor even clarity at all times, but intentionality. If we meet ourselves where we are, hold space for others to do the same and walk forward with curiosity and compassion, we are already doing something extraordinary. It is even more extraordinary if we can find those in this life that enrich our lives and celebrate who we are. I am grateful that I have found these people in all facets of my life from my connections in college, my graduate cohort, my friends, coworkers, family and my wife. The journey continues, and I walk it now not just for myself, but for those still learning that they don't have to walk alone, and those who have supported me along the way.

West Clay Street

by Elaine Walmer (Lititz, PA)

September 30, 1970

My parents, Jim and Pauline, purchased 1026 West Clay Street for $16K. The monthly mortgage of $100.66 was more than they thought they could afford in 1970. Our family of four relocated from a rental in the little nearby town of Leola. Brother John was three and I was a shiny new baby from the summer of '69. Brother James would come along two years later, about the time I started forming actual memories of the house.

The Hood

West Clay Street consists of 14 semi-detached brick homes in Lancaster's 9th ward, all with modest front and back yards. Ours was smack dab in the middle of the 1000 block. Built in 1925, it is one of the oldest. One hundred years old! Every home on our side of the street featured rear balconies and charming front porches with wooden railings. Only our house had a portico, which sounds fancier than it is. (We called it the entryway.)

The neighborhood has always had a lot of appeal, with its treelined streets, private alleyways and proximity to both Franklin & Marshall College and Buchanan Park. It was a great place to be a kid in the 1970s and 1980s, and it still is! A walk around the block will take you past some beautiful single Tudor style homes on Race Avenue and State Street. Expanding a block or two in any direction, you will find more exquisite homes and a few mansions.

At some point I came to realize there was also an *East* Clay Street. It seemed like a different galaxy. The two Clays were separated by Lancaster's busiest pike and acres of industrial mystery. Now known as the "Warehouse District," the chunk of land that once divided East and West Clay is a pedestrian friendly corridor of trendy restaurants, retailers, off-campus college housing and Lancaster's minor league baseball stadium. In conclusion, East Clay Street played no part in my childhood. But I'm sure it's lovely over there!

Friends and Neighbors

We knew all of our neighbors and preferred some more than others. Being a duplex, 1026 was attached to 1024, and our first attached neighbor was Mrs. Blue, a widow who was rarely seen. On the other side of Mrs. Blue was Mrs. Reed, another widow. On the other side of us, at the next duplex, were the Coopers. Mrs. Cooper was a soon-to-be widow. The Coopers were attached to the Shenks, empty nesters who were about the age of my grandparents. In fact, they had a grandson my age who came up from Maryland to visit them for long weekends in the summer.

Obviously, we lived near an older age demographic, but neighborhood relations were warm and harmonious on our side of the street.

The most fabulous widow of all was Mrs. Johnson, who preferred to be called "Fern" and lived on the odd side of West Clay Street. She took vigorous walks every day, maintained a beautiful yard and worked at an office job into her 70s looking like Audrey Hepburn from *Breakfast at Tiffany's*.

I admired Fern, but the Shenks were my favorite adult neighbors on the block. I could rely on them to order at least two boxes of Girl Scout cookies or whatever I was peddling. It was during those cold calls that I was invited into their immaculate home, which matched their pristine lawn. Mrs. Shenk always answered the door with a delighted smile and her checkbook, as though she was expecting me. Mr. Shenk was usually outside tending to the lawn doing other important business. He was a history professor at F&M College in the days when professors wore suits and ties to class every day.

One day in the mid-1970s, Mrs. Blue was gone forever. Soon we had new attached neighbors, Clint and Cindy, a couple with matching long brown hair. They were about my parents' age and didn't have kids. At first, I think we liked them, but that would change. Clint may have suffered from hallucinations from a tour in Vietnam. My brothers and I were advised to keep our distance from him. In overheard conversations, I learned that Clint tripped and fell on a paver that was half on our property, half on theirs. Clint and Cindy were going to "sue" my parents, which sounded very bad. It was because of this strained relationship that my dad honed his carpentry skills and installed a wooden picket fence along the backyard property line of 1024 and 1026.

This Old House

Upgrades occurred slowly and as needed in the 1970s. The home improvement rat race of today just wasn't a thing back then. I'm pretty sure "home improvement" was not even part of the vernacular. People occasionally "redecorated" or "remodeled." *Other* people, that is.

My parents embraced what they inherited from the previous owners. Specifically, the wallpaper. Though outdated and peeling in a few places, the French countryside wall covering on the stairway wall stayed for many years. The green wallpaper of the dining room – damask above the chair rail and textured below – was absolutely adequate. I recall tasteful wallpaper in the master bedroom with a blue and green design. The back bedroom was adorned with pink and gold speckled wallpaper, and that became my room by default. There was more distressed gold wallpaper in the upstairs hallway, much of which was concealed by the bassinette and crib that James would inherit from me.

When James was old enough to move out of the hallway and into the middle bedroom with John, my parents splurged on the first 1026 total room makeover. It was only 1974, but Bicentennial fever was simmering. The boys' room became decked out in so much spirit-of-76 swag you could almost hear the fife and drums on entry. My parents went all out! Blue carpet. Red, white & blue bedspreads. A Bicentennial drum ceiling light. And, of course, wallpaper featuring all the patriotic symbols. Nothing says "sweet dreams" like drums, soldiers, bald eagles and canons.

The living room wallpaper was the next to go, only to be replaced by striped wallpaper in the muted earthtones of the day. My dad, along with a little help from my mom, accomplished this over the course of several cuss-filled days using a ladder, sawhorses and wallpaper glue. As part of our "redecorating," they also hung a wood paneling accent wall on either side of the fireplace and mantel.

My bedroom underwent gradual changes and maintained status as the premier bedroom. Besides having a pink shag carpet and canopy bed, it was one of the two rooms with a window unit air conditioner (my parents had the other one). And it was the balcony room!

While I had the balcony, my brothers had access to the attic through their bedroom. When it came to deciding the creepiest part of 1026, the competition was stiff. It was either the attic or the basement. As kids, we liked hanging out in both places, but never wanted to be in either place alone. The attic is where our family hosted epic Halloween parties, and some of that ghoulish décor was always waiting for you at the top of the attic stairs. Similarly, the unfinished basement was a cool place to hang out and race slot cars or host "meetings" with the neighborhood kids. James and I were doing our own version of podcasting in the 1980s in a makeshift studio in the basement. But being downstairs in that cold, dark concrete space alone was unsettling.

For two decades, our family of five shared one very small bathroom and abided by two simple rules: do what you need to do;

get out. Several porcelain tiles were missing and the door didn't lock or even latch easily. At no time while I lived at 1026 could one take a shower in the bathroom. The faucet worked but the metal pipe sticking out of the wall above was not connected to any water source. Allegedly, there was no way to fix this. So, it was tub baths only from 1970 to 1988 (when I moved out).

We had an eat-in kitchen and gathered at the table most weeknights enjoying BLTs, spaghetti, tuna melts and Hamburger Helper. It's where we met each morning to find a whatever cereal we had to choose from and, on weekends, for pancakes, waffles or eggs.

And then one day my dad became very sick.

End of An Era

On March 25, 1985, my mom became the next widow of West Clay Street. The ambulance was sitting in front of our house when I got off the school bus at the corner of Clay and State. Paramedics were standing on the porch waiting for my arrival.

"Do you live here?" they asked.

Inside, John and James were sitting beside each other on the couch with their heads down. They had arrived home from school a bit earlier than I and already received the news. Someone led me to the kitchen where my mom tearfully informed me that my dad was gone. I believe her words were "there's nothing they can do."

John and I finished high school, started college and moved out of 1026 West Clay Street. It was still our family home for a few years – and maybe we hoped it would be forever. But my mom was already planning her next chapter and sold the house in 1993. She bought a condo in the nearby town of Millersville where James was attending college.

Since then my brothers and I reminisce about so many things. The large coat closet under the stairs where James and I would hide our wrapped Christmas presents. The fireplace. The basement. The attic. The tree fort. The balcony. The concrete parking slab out back that doubled as a 1:1 basketball court. The dilapidated row of garages where our dad kept his motorcycle and the lawnmower. How wonderful it would be to go back.

June 8, 2025

I've been trying to tell this story for months, if not years. I needed one last visit to 1026 West Clay Street.

Yesterday I drove past my wonderful childhood home. It was only my fourth or fifth intentional drive-by despite having lived within ten miles since my mom sold the house in 1993. Noticeably absent were the front yard conifers which served as the backdrop for many a family photo. I was comforted so see that the black light post and portico were still there, unchanged.

But something else was different. For the first time in over three decades, I found someone standing in front of the house where I lived longer than in any other home. A young man was on the sidewalk edging the lawn before the rain rolled in.

I parked the car and walked up to him. "Do you live here?" I asked.

He smiled and said, "I do."

"I used to live here," I said. "This was my house."

Without hesitation, he put down the string trimmer and invited me in for a tour. The moment I had fantasized about for so many years was finally happening. I waited outside on the porch while the new owner went inside to tell his wife about their unexpected company. The porch and the entryway were unchanged, including the individual glass panes. The couple greeted me at the door with their dog, something our family never had.

Everything was so different but so familiar. Though 1026 has changed ownership at least four times since 1993, I was relieved to discover so much original detail, including the vents and returns, and the large coat closet, which the new owners affectionately refer to as the "Harry Potter closet." The original shelves in the dining room, once lined with our distinguished set of leather-bound World Book Encyclopedia, were now adorned with new treasures.

The swing door between the dining room and kitchen was no longer there, but the kitchen itself was basically a very, very refreshed and modern version with the same original cabinetry and trim.

What used to be our pantry was now a lovely powder room.

I declined to see the basement, although I'm told it's now finished, which made me very happy. Upstairs, we turned into the middle bedroom, once the Bicentennial room, now a guest room and the only access to the attic. The top floor was also a finished living space and home office. It was the first time I could look up and not see daylight through the rafters and the roof, which was still original slate the new owners told me.

We made our way back down to the hallway and over to my old bedroom – the balcony room. This was being used as another home office. It seemed so much smaller than I remember. I wasn't sure if I should ask to step out on the balcony, as I recall it not being considered structurally sound in the later years of my childhood. The owners then informed me that all of the balconies on the block had been retrofitted with reinforcements. We stood there gazing down into the backyard where a magnificent curly willow had grown taller than the house.

Aware of interrupting their Sunday afternoon, I thanked the young couple and made my way downstairs to the front door. The nice young man followed me out on the porch where we discovered rain was already falling before he had a chance to finish the yardwork. He said it was ok.

Then he laughed and told me about having dug up an unopened bottle of Dr. Pepper in the front yard where the trees once stood, and said that the bottle was from the 1980s. While I don't remember burying such a thing, it certainly seems like something my brothers or I would have done.

Finally, the young man handed me another treasure that he had unearthed while gardening recently: a rusted skeleton key. Who knows what it once unlocked. To me, it is the key to my old house on West Clay Street.

My Grandpa

by Ella Watson (Mount Joy, PA)

I strongly believe that one person's love, presence and wisdom can influence the way you think, especially if you are young. For me, that person is my Grandpa.

When asked by my mother to write something for this unusual book project, I struggled, at first, to come up with an idea for the most appropriate or captivating topic. Being just sixteen years old, I felt as though I hadn't lived long enough and haven't experienced enough good or bad things to have anything truly meaningful to share. My first instinct was to write about how the absence of my father shaped me, but the more I reflected, the more I realized that the presence of my Grandpa had a far greater impact on my life.

He is truly a blessing. He is someone I admire deeply, someone I look up to the most. Even in his silence, there is wisdom, his quiet presence fills the room with calmness and understanding. I look forward to the peaceful moments we share, whether we're talking about school – usually in response to his questions about my favorite courses, my biggest successes or my possible struggles – or he's asking me random intellectual questions. I have always cherished those conversations, especially when I got the answer right, because his validation means so much to me.

He has been such a powerful influence on the way I think and who I am becoming. Even though my father was not around I still have always had an amazing male role model in my life. I now know what I want in a future husband because of the example my Grandpa set. Watching his patience and gentleness with my Grandma – even in moments when her she is unwavering – has taught me more about love and strength than words ever could. He is consistently patient, always kind and endlessly understanding.

He may be quiet, but his presence in my life is louder than words.

Dedicated to my Grandpa – I will always look up to you!

The Loss of The Lady Elgin

by Patricia Wendland (Asheville, NC)

> Then a fierce squall struck 'Loch Achray'
> and bowed her down to her watery way.

> – John Masefield

Growing up not far from the shore of Lake Michigan meant warm, wonderful summers at the beach for my brother and me. How welcome those days after long Wisconsin winters of snow, sleet and icy temperatures. Those were pleasant summers of building sandcastles, or just letting shore waves roll over us as the tide came in late in the afternoon. Yet, those refreshing summer waves could also turn to danger. Often, we fell asleep to the mournful drone of the foghorn. We learned about rip tides and the danger of venturing too far into the water. Yes, rip tides, for Lake Michigan is approximately 118 miles wide and 321 miles long. It is also subject to sudden squalls as many commercial fishing companies, yacht owners and travelers aboard ships can testify.

As my growing years added up, I came to enjoy sea stories. The first one, at the age of twelve, was one that I came back to as an adult – *Two Years Before the Mast* by Richard Henry Dana. In high school and in college, the novels of Joseph Conrad (Józef Teodor Konrad Korzeniowski) and those of Herman Melville intrigued me. Then one day, a member of St. John the Evangelist Parish asked me to research the tragic loss of The Lady Elgin on Lake Michigan more than a hundred years before. For me and the other members of St. John the Evangelist Parish, that tragedy held special meaning. Many of those who lost their lives on that September day in 1860 were members of the parish. This is their story.

On the first day of September that year, danger for The Lady Elgin still lay hundreds of miles and seven days away, her fate linked to the schooner Augusta as she lay at anchor near Port Huron, Michigan. At 4:00 p.m., her captain, Darius Mallot, gave orders to set sail. She carried a great a quantity of lumber causing her to ride low in the water and making navigating difficult. Charted on a course destined for a collision with The Lady Elgin, the disaster would claim the lives of over four hundred passengers. It would go down in Great Lakes maritime history as one of its most tragic events.

It was not just the Augusta and her strong captain who disliked the newer steamships that played a part in the fate of The Lady Elgin. The passions of politics, the whims of weather and the defective manner of carrying lights aboard ships also carried forward the tragedy. In that year preceding the Civil War, abolitionists in Wisconsin presented Governor Alexander Randall with a legislative resolution to secede from the Union if it did not soon abolish slavery. The governor then sent out agents to query the state militia units for support. When he learned that Captain Garret Barry's 70-member Union Guard would not support the resolution but remain loyal to the Union, the governor gave orders to seize the unit's guns.

Determined to finance his unit's guns, Captain Barry proposed a fundraising excursion to Chicago, the proceeds to go toward the purchase of eighty guns at two dollars apiece. The Lady Elgin was enlisted for this trip and the date set for the evening of September 6. Built in Buffalo, New York, The Lady Elgin was a 231-foot, 800-ton side-wheeler with square stern and one deck. Named after the wife of Lord Elgin, Governor General of Canada, The Lady Elgin carried Canadian traffic and mail for five years along the northern shores of the Great Lakes. Hubbard, Spencer and Company then bought The Lady Elgin and established service between Chicago and Bayfield, Wisconsin.

Under the experienced hand of Captain Jack Wilson, The Lady Elgin was to leave Milwaukee on the evening of September 6. She arrived late, however, and left Milwaukee after midnight. On board were Captain Barry and members of the Irish Union Guards in full uniform. On board were also members of militia units and the German Black and Green Yaegers. Many Milwaukeeans, eager for a fun trip to Chicago, were on board – husbands and wives and children, as well as many young folk. There would be singing and dancing for Milwaukee's City Band and the Light Drum Corps would provide music for the trip. It was to be a happy outing; many passengers having sacrificed to save money for the excursion. At 1:00 a.m., the evening of September 7, The Lady Elgin left

Milwaukee on what was destined to be her last trip.

After a night of merrymaking, daylight found The Lady Elgin docked in the Chicago River at La Salle and Clark Streets. Passengers spent the day sightseeing in the city. In the evening, they enjoyed a banquet and looked forward to another night of music and dancing on the return trip. After taking on additional passengers, The Lady Elgin moved out from Chicago at 11:30 p.m. Fog had set in. An ominous wind blew out of the northeast.

During this time, the schooner Augusta had been plying her way south by east. Both vessels neared Waukegan, Illinois, around 2:00 am. By then, the wind had reached gale strength and rain was falling. Lookouts on both vessels had seen the other's lights about a half mile away but could not determine each other's course. Shortly before the collision, with the waves running heavy, Captain Wilson shouted to the Augusta, "Hard a port!" The warning and maneuvers came too late. The Augusta struck the port side of The Lady Elgin forward of the wheelhouse tearing away a section of the hull. The vessel began to fill rapidly. Captain Wilson gave orders to head the ship toward the shore, but water rushing into the hold extinguished the fires under the boilers and left her the drifting helplessly.

Captain Wilson issued orders to some of the crew to lower away in one of the boats to assess the damage and plug the hole with mattresses. The crew, however, had difficulty maneuvering in the turbulent water and decided to head for shore. In a desperate attempt to raise the hole above water level, Wilson ordered the cattle used as ballast be driven overboard and the cargo moved to starboard. The passengers then became panic stricken for there were only three lifeboats on board and the room where lifejackets were stored was inaccessible. In frantic efforts to save themselves, passengers tore off doors to use as rafts. Captain Wilson, realizing that many lives would be lost with the sinking of the ship, gave orders to his crew to chop free sections of the deck to serve as rafts.

Twenty minutes later and six miles from the Winnetka shoreline, The Lady Elgin sank in 300 feet of water. Many passengers disappeared in the vortex of the sinking ship. Surmounting waves overcame some who had managed to escape in lifeboats. Captains Wilson and Barry, along with a load of passengers aboard a large section of the deck, attempted to make for the shore, but the rough waters broke the overburdened raft. Many aboard were lost. Even those passengers who had managed to reach shore in boats were not all saved. Huge breakers dragged them back into the lake.

Meanwhile, the Augusta sailed on. Captain Mallot, thinking his ship had merely "nudged" The Lady Elgin, was aware neither of the damage his ship had caused nor of the horrible plight that had befallen her passengers. The tragedy was not without its heroes and miracles of survival, though. When the first boat from The Lady Elgin reached shore about 6:00 a.m., news of the disaster spread rapidly. Residents of the area flocked to the shore to help in rescue attempts. One young man especially showed outstanding courage. He was Edward Spenser, a student at Northwestern College. With a line of rope tied to his waist, he swam out into the breakers sixteen times and rescued seventeen people, returning once with a husband and wife. Lying exhausted and panting on the shore, Spenser kept repeating, "Did I do my best?" Captain Wilson lost his life attempting to save two mothers and their children. Struck by some of the wreckage, high waves swept him into the lake. Captain Barry drowned within a few hundred feet from the shore. J.B. Rodee, a member of the Union Guards, however, saved his life by floating to shore on a snare drum.

When news of the disaster reached Milwaukee, wails of open mourning filled the third ward, the area hardest hit by the loss of lives. At the Milwaukee and Chicago Railroad Station, people awaited news of relatives and friends. When the noon train arrived from Chicago, they besieged one of the survivors, Timothy O'Brien, with questions about their loved ones. The full extent of the disaster soon spread, leaving few households untouched by the tragedy. Three hundred members of the Cathedral of Saint John the Evangelist were among the dead.

The days following the loss of The Lady Elgin saw seventeen of the victims buried. Milwaukee was a city in mourning. Flags rimmed with crepe flew at half-mast and the bells of churches and fire stations tolled for more than an hour. Businesses closed and the day proclaimed one of prayer. Mourners filled the cathedral while more than 800 stood outside.

For eight weeks following the tragedy, patrols combed the beaches on the lookout for bodies. Now and then came the dismal cry, "Another one!" Bodies of victims washed ashore as far away as Michigan, Indiana, and Sheboygan, Wisconsin. On September 16, searchers found Captain Wilson's body and identified it by his watch and the documents in his pocket. Captain Barry's body washed ashore in Indiana on November 12. The remains of one third of those who lost their lives that day were never found.

Since that day in 1860, Saint John Cathedral has commemorated the loss of The Lady Elgin each September 7 with a memorial mass. The tragic loss of human life will always evoke sympathy in gentle hearts, acts of heroism inspire and amaze. History is the vehicle that brings them to "life" again as Emily Dickinson once mused: "I wonder why a letter to me seems like immortality."

In Book One of *The Aeneid*, Aeneas, upon seeing the battles surrounding the fall of Troy depicted on the wall of the temple in Carthage observes: "There are tears for those woes and mortal sufferings touch the soul."

A Message in a Jar,
or
Discovering Common Roots and the Strength Given to Us by Ancestors

by Monika Wojdecka-Janiszewska (Poznań, Poland)

"Family is like the branches of a tree.
We all grow in different directions; yet, our roots connect us."
(Anna H. Niemczynow – "Her Portrait")

It was an October afternoon, still quite warm and sunny, but carrying the foreboding of the sad and dreary days of November that we annually experience in Poland. At that time, we usually tidy up the graves of our loved ones in preparation for All the Saints' Day, when everyone – in refection and contemplation – lights candles for their deceased family members. So, my father and I went to clean up our family graves at the cemetery. We removed the autumn leaves, old, burned-out candle holders, and cleaned the tombstones.

All of a sudden, standing in front of one of the graves, my attention was drawn to a glass jar next to a vase placed there by someone else. It seemed to have been deliberately left behind. With curiosity, I picked it up and noticed that there was a message inside. With a slight sense of unease, but also excitement, I opened the lid. The message hidden there was written in three languages: Polish, German and English. It was signed by a person unknown to me, who introduced herself as Martina, a distant relative living in Germany (her complete address provided). In the message, she wrote that her family search for ancestors had led her to my great-grandmother Katarzyna, and that she had contacted a photographer who volunteered to help her create a global database of graves, suggesting, at the same time, that she should leave such a message on the grave. Attached to the letter was a drawn family tree, which indicated that her (Martina's) great-grandmother and my great-grandmother were sisters. There was also a small photo of her great-grandfather Stanisław.

This discovery deeply moved me. Could it be that I have just found someone who was also searching for a connection to past generations? I returned home full of home and curiosity, and, a few days later, I went to visit my father's sister, Aunt Maria, who, among all of us, cherished the memory of our family's ancestors the most. Aunt Maria not only confirmed the information about Martina's great-grandfather, but she also showed me a photo of him and his family – wife and children. It was also amazing that the image I was looking at was a complete version of the fragment that was left in the jar! I wrote a letter to Martina, and thus our correspondence began – by now full of stories about the fate of our families, which, over the years, both have intertwined and gone in different directions.

A year later Martina, with her daughter Celina, came to visit me in Poznań. The meeting was extraordinary! We walked around the city, and we also visited the grave, which – as incredible as it is – still exists, that of our mutual great-great-grandmother Agnieszka! At that moment, I strongly felt that genealogy was more than just knowledge of the past – it was a living connection between us, a bridge between former generations and the present ones.

Finding a distant cousin not only brought me joy, but also a sense that our lives are part of something bigger. The stories of our ancestors, their collective experiences create the fabric that weaves all of us together. Their life choices, both good and bad, shape who we are and where we are. Genealogy was previously just a collection of names and dates on tombstones for me; today it is the story of people I do not want to be forgotten, because it is a story about ourselves, about our roots, about what makes us who we are.

When we discover common roots with other people – even very distant relatives – something incredibly valuable suddenly emerges: a sense of community. Somewhere, sometimes on the other side of a border or ocean, someone or everyone carries a piece of the same story, the same blood. Sometimes these roots provide answers to questions we have carried within us for years – about character, tendencies, family fates, about heritage.

After Martina's visit and departure, the emotions and elation kept me awake for several days. Both of us are women, just like our great-great-grandmother who lived over a century ago. I thought about how the world in which Agnieszka lived has changed, and how we live now. When I think of the life of our common ancestor, I see a strong, fierce, brave woman, but trapped in the realities of her time. She worked hard physically in the fields, often from dawn till dusk, carrying responsibilities on her shoulders that are hard to imagine today. She often had to move with her children in search of seasonal work. She could not write because she had no opportunity to learn, and she had no choice but sign documents with three crosses. Her world was limited to daily toil and family duties. If dreams appeared in her mind, they had to give way to necessities.

I then wrote to Martina: "Our common great-great-grandmother would be proud of us, of what we have achieved, of how we can live now!" We have free access to knowledge, we can develop our passions, change career paths, travel around the world and express ourselves in countless forms. We have the right to speak, to access education and enjoy all sorts of technologies that make everyday life easier. Laundry no longer takes all day by the river, and cooking does not require hours of tedious work at the stove. Life has become simpler, but also richer, because we have the opportunity and time to seek fulfillment and self-realization.

These changes are the result of generations of women who have fought for a better tomorrow and gradually pushed boundaries. Our great-great-grandmother Agnieszka, even though she herself had no education, passed on to subsequent generations the strength and perseverance to change the world. It is thanks to her that we can walk our own path today.

The message in a jar left on the grave of my ancestor led to a meeting that transcends time and space. Shared roots give us a sense of belonging, purpose and perspective. And perhaps that is why discovering them is so moving, because it reminds us that life is continuity, not just a moment.

Translated from Polish by Henryk Hoffmann

It Is Never Too Late
or
Dum Spiras, Spera!

by Philip Wright (Pennsburg, PA)

Society has always pushed for growth and development in nice, clean, orderly milestones. Graduate, get a degree, get a job, get married with a kid by the time you are thirty, get a nicer job, etcetera etcetera. Life is many things such as tenacious, miraculous, unrelenting, but it can hardly ever be considered "clean." Sometimes, all it takes are several rainy days to bring you back to remind you that not everyone grows and blooms in the same way.

I graduated from college with a degree in political science when I was twenty-one. Fresh out of school, I applied to law school to try and further myself to get that "dream job" everyone hunts for. After being waitlisted, I got a job to build some experience and was optimistically looking forward to (quoting my former English teacher here) "reaching that apple pie dream of a white picket fence, a little missy, a dog and 2.5 kids." Life decided that was not going to happen. Ten years later, I was back to square one living back at my parent's farmhouse helping my mother and my ailing father in what would end up being his last years of life while working multiple jobs to keep myself barely afloat. Meanwhile my brother was across the ocean working his dream job in Sweden and absolutely thriving in his own way. I was constantly worried that I was failing, and felt like I was falling behind everyone and stagnating. This continued until my father was taken to the hospital due to his slipping health.

The days following my father's passing were a blur. Simultaneously everything and nothing needed to be done. Picking up the pieces that he left behind became a job in and of itself, and I fell into a state of limbo not sure exactly what I was doing. Life would then show its head and work in its own funny way. Two days after his funeral this state was shaken up when I got chosen for a federal jury duty in a multibillion-dollar lawsuit between corporations and had to spend the better part of three weeks in

Philadelphia for the trial. During the case I was hit in the face with what I wanted to do with my life and the reminder of the school that I got wait-listed for ten years prior. As I was surrounded by the legal profession and had the privilege to speak with the federal judge and his clerks. As the trial came to a close, the judge pulled me aside and asked me when the last time I applied to law school was, and that nothing was standing in my way from trying again.

The experience brought a need to reflect on everything that I had been doing up to that point. How much of my own life I put on hold for other people, and how comparing myself to other's successes only served to hamper my ability to flourish. This drove me to start focusing not on how much later I was reaching my goals, but instead on what steps I could take in my current situation to move closer to what I hoped to achieve.

I am now writing this having finished my first year in law school finally starting on that path that I tried to get on a decade ago; however, all the experiences that I have faced throughout those ten years have given me insight that I would not have had at my disposal back then and I am able to help see things from a different perspective than those of my peers. There is no such thing as "where you should be," only where you are and what you do with the circumstances you are currently in. Do not compare yourself to the growth of other people. Growing up on the farm taught me that every plant is unique, even among the same crop. Some grow quickly and produce a lot of fruits, others won't grow until later in the season when the rest of those vines have already dried and withered. Take your life in the strides that it gives you to the best of your ability. Thus, if I may paraphrase the famous Latin aphorism, used as the motto of South Carolina (and turn the first-person singular indicative form into second person singular imperative), REMEMBER:

"Dum spiras, spera!"

The Badger
by Michal J. Zablocki (Nowa Iwiczna, Poland)

Working in film production had fascinated me since childhood—there was something mysterious about it. The secret behind the technology and techniques used to create that magical final result—the film on the screen. I instinctively knew it had to be the product of the hard work of many people from various professions, some more talented than others, using special tools and materials, applying creativity, improvisation skills, and relying on countless other factors that, as a kid, I couldn't even begin to imagine.

After earning a degree in economics, I steadily pursued a path into film crews—and I made it! The story below is true and offers a glimpse into the slightly absurd realities of working in film during the era of real socialism in Poland. It was a time when everything was in short supply, and filmmaking was, on the one hand, a thrilling adventure in building a fairy-tale world, and, on the other hand, a serious challenge in an age without the internet, mobile phones, or computers.

The head of the "Silesia" Film Unit, Jan Wlodarczyk—a well-known and seasoned production manager—was the one under whose wing I began my career in the film industry, working as an assistant production manager on a feature film. Later, he supported my progress when I became a production manager myself. One day, he made me a phone call that turned out to be a kind of challenge.

This was around the middle of 1981, shortly after we wrapped up production on the film *Wielka majówka* (*The Great May Day Out*), which was also made within the same Film Unit.

"Michal, I've got a series for you," Włodarczyk said. "And it's a serious one – nine hours long, shot on location, but with some set pieces in studio halls. The title is *Popielec* (*Ash Wednesday*). Of course, the office will be at the Wrocław Film Studio. Come over for a meeting. I'll introduce you to the director. Excited?"

Yes, I was excited. I figured I'd have my tried-and-true crew, a permanent office at the studio, and the assurance that the so-called producer—basically the script office under the name "Silesia" Film Unit—would make sure the funding promised by public Polish Television actually came through. And if any hiccups did come up, they'd offer full support (by phone, naturally) ... or at the very least, stay out of the way (which, to be fair, they had a solid track record of doing). Most likely, we wouldn't see each other again until much later, under pleasant circumstances—say, at the final internal screening where the film would be officially rubber-stamped.

From where I stood, the production risk seemed pretty minimal, and the fees listed in the contract nothing to sneeze at. Plus, I'd never done a series before as the sole production manager.

So, I said yes without hesitation. I headed over to the "Silesia" HQ, which—like all the other state-run film units—was docked at 61 Puławska Street in Warsaw, under the command of Ernest Bryll.

At the Unit's office, I met the director, Ryszard Ber—a friendly, short, older gentleman, chain smoker and a devoted fan of tea brewed from double-used express bags. His young wife, Lidia—whom I recognized from the studio hallways—was set to be my assistant production manager, one of those so-called "second unit" folks. Behind the camera would be Łódź-based cinematographer Zdzisław Kaczmarek, whom I remembered from earlier Wroclaw shoots as a wisecracking cameraman always ready with a snarky remark about whatever film chaos was unfolding at the time.

The production designer was handpicked by "Silesia": that job went to the one and only Tadeusz Kosarewicz, a seasoned pro I knew well—who absolutely hated leaving Wrocław and had a personal vendetta against working anywhere outside his usual production design workshop at the studio.

When it came to the rest of the crew, I had a pretty free hand. I suggested more and more people to the director—technicians, assistants—and thankfully, he went along with all of them. The whole thing was to be shot on 16 mm film, in color, of course. We quickly put together the budget, location folders, and the shooting schedule.

The series was based on *Popielec* (*Ash Wednesday*), a novel by Włodzimierz Kłaczyński—a former village vet turned writer, who, since 1970, had been cranking out short stories with notable success. In *Popielec*, he captured rural life in south-eastern Poland during the German occupation and just after liberation with the kind of gritty realism only someone who'd actually lived it could muster.

When I arrived at the "Silesia" office, all the scripts for the series were—surprisingly—already finished. Ryszard Ber, along with the well-known writer Wiesław Myśliwski, had put together thick stacks of pages for each episode. I picked them up and, wanting to make life easier for the crew and cast, decided to mass-produce them on a good old duplicating machine in handy A5 booklet format.

I bought a copy of Kłaczyński's novel to compare, and I noticed right away that the style was vaguely reminiscent of our Nobel Prize-laureate Reymont's *Chłopi* (*The Peasants*)—only more ... intense. Instead of poetic nature descriptions or patriotic chest-puffing, we got raw, earthy scenes filled with blood-and-guts characters of all kinds: Ukrainians, Jews, Roma, Russians. Hardly any of the main characters resembled the wholesome, salt-of-the-earth farmer from classic Polish literature. No one was peacefully plowing fields in an idyllic countryside. Quite the opposite—these folks lived life at full volume, driven by whatever temperament they'd been blessed or cursed with.

There were bold—let's say literary—sex scenes. And no shortage of unfiltered hunting episodes—sometimes for enemy German occupiers, sometimes for actual woodland creatures you could shoot, roast and eat right there.

The shooting schedule included a batch of autumnal, on-location scenes at the end of 1981 in the Krosno region. All the scenes inside peasant cottages—rebuilt as sets in the Wrocław Studio—were slated for winter. And in spring 1982, we'd head back outside. This meant we had a real shot at capturing multiple seasons on film—always a nice bonus.

To stay as true as possible to the novel's setting, we had to find a truly forgotten village—something convincingly backward to stand in for *Bledna*, the fictional heart of the story. Miraculously, we found the perfect place almost immediately, thanks to the author's own suggestions. The village of Wesoła was nestled in a valley with lousy access roads, no TV signal and an atmosphere where time had flat-out stopped—which, of course, was a dream come true for our set designers. Only a few minor tweaks were needed.

The villagers of Wesoła not only welcomed the shoot with open arms, they eagerly volunteered as extras and helped with props and access to barns, courtyards and homes. They even pointed out which cottages would be best to, well ... burn down for the fire scenes.

The number one issue that we faced—at least for me and the directing team—was the casting. The story called for a colorful bunch with equally colorful names and nicknames (like Half-Gentleman, Wykukal, Nozder, Bator, Beblok, Waluś and Siwek, to name a few). Director Ber insisted we needed "types"—actors with strong personalities and real on-screen presence. The lead was a young peasant named Juzuś Garstka, and in the background loomed a massive crowd of over 120 roles to cast, which, frankly, gave me a mild panic attack.

Luckily for us, there was no shortage of actors itching to rack up a few—or even a few dozen—shooting days out in the middle of nowhere, far from the hustle and hum of modern life. Bit by bit, we assembled a cast so ambitious that even today, the series is considered a cult classic.

Sure, a few actors grumbled. Some pointed out that actors had been boycotting TVP since 1980 and wouldn't set foot in a propaganda outlet. "What will our theater friends say?" they asked. We explained that this wasn't some run-of-the-mill TV show—we were making a film, a proper production, almost a year in the making. And let's face it, who knew what Poland would even look like by the time we finished? The themes of *Popielec* were timeless—Shakespearean, even. In short: this was shaping up to be a major artistic event.

We managed to recruit the crème de la crème of character actors... The core cast was made up mostly of actors from Warsaw and Kraków—many of them seasoned film veterans.

For the first time in his career, young Tomasz Dedek played a leading role (as Garstka). And of course, it wouldn't be complete without the master of supporting roles—Leon Niemczyk—who appeared in one of the final episodes. Niemczyk's career had kicked off with Roman Polanski's *Nóż w wodzie* (*Knife in the Water*), where he was, incidentally, the only actor whose voice wasn't dubbed in post.

In short—what followed (and did, indeed, happen!) was a kind of nationwide actor mobilization to Hotel Rzeszów. We rented out nearly the entire place. From there, every day, the crew would set out to the village of Wesoła—a commute that took about an hour and a half one way, on a good day.

While reading the book and scripts, one particular issue started gnawing at me ... animal scenes.

Here's the thing: in one scene, wolves were supposed to tear a dog apart in its pen. In a cart race, a horse was meant to drop dead from a heart attack. Poachers were supposed to trap a young deer in a snare and hang it upside down by the legs. Not to mention all the other animals in the script: cows, horses, chickens, geese, frogs, pike, leeches and various insects.

But what really made my head spin was Scene 59, planned for Part II, episode titled "The Hladik Homestead." The scene was lifted almost word-for-word from the novel. Here are some key excerpts:
"Shot 117 – 3 meters

A large, dirty animal was moving through the potato field. Its striped head flickered in and out of view, sometimes stopping, sometimes speeding up. It was big and heavy.

Shot 118 – 2 meters

Hladik felt around behind him, found an axe, shoved it into Jasiek's hands, and grabbed a pitchfork for himself.

HLADIK: A badger.
Shot 119 – 1 meter

The badger headed back toward the forest. Its movements were hesitant.

Shot 120 – 4 meters

The Hladiks stared at the badger.

JASIEK: He's not afraid.
HLADIK: Someone must've dug out his burrow and scared him off.

Hladik shoved Jasiek forward.

HLADIK: After him!

Shot 121 – 7 meters

The badger didn't even speed up, just trudged along. Hladik caught up, jabbed it with the pitchfork, pinning it to the ground. The animal struggled with loud, wheezing grunts, snapping at his legs.

HLADIK: Hit him in the snout!

Jasiek swung the axe. It was a hard blow, but he only clipped the back of its neck. The badger kicked with its hind legs. Jasiek struck again. The animal twitched, its legs stretching and curling.

Shot 122 – 12 meters

Stefek walked slowly toward them, tripping now and then over potato mounds with his boot tips and heels. Hladik and Jasiek stood there, out of breath.

HLADIK: What God creates, He won't undo.
JASIEK: We're not seriously going to eat the badger, are we?
HLADIK: Why not? There's three kilos of fat on him. People with TB ask for badger fat at the pharmacy. It's medicine. The clever ones sell dog fat instead and no one's the wiser.

Hladik grabbed one of the badger's clawed paws and barked at Stefek.

HLADIK: Grab the other one.

They each took a paw and dragged the badger through the green brush and potato plants."

I immediately checked and found that the Polish badger isn't under any special protection. In fact, in areas where capercaillies, black grouse or pheasants are found, badgers can be hunted year-round—since they're known to raid nests and do real damage to those rare bird populations.

It became clear to me that we needed a live badger—not a stuffed stand-in—but a real, living, breathing animal that we'd have to "murder" on camera in cold blood. The director wasn't going to let this go. If it was in the script, it was going on film. No room for negotiation.

So, I called the Ministry of Agriculture and Food Economy to discreetly inquire about a formal permit for catching a badger. I was told I needed to submit a written request with a detailed description and justification ... and then wait for a response.

Meanwhile, I figured I should learn more about this charming little striped creature—who, at the time, still seemed rather cute to me. I dug up an entry in the PWN Nature Encyclopedia. It was pretty bare-bones:

"Badger (*Meles meles*), mammal, member of the weasel family ... body length 90 cm including a 16 cm tail; habitat: hilly groves and large forests, more common in the eastern part of the country. Forages at dusk and at night, feeds mainly on insects and larvae, also eats worms, frogs, bird eggs, berries, and mushrooms; digs its burrows in hilly terrain."

Further information in the "Hunting" section covered mating season and the time of year badgers give birth (February to April). Another name for a badger: *jaźwiec* (in old Polish). The tip of its tail is called a *kiść*.

The matter of sourcing a badger for the film absorbed me to the point that I decided to begin a methodical operation—no time to waste. I headed over to the zoo—conveniently located right across from the film studio. I must remind the reader here that before World War II, Wrocław was a German city known as Breslau.

The director, Antoni Gucwiński, was always happy to help filmmakers. As is well known, he co-hosted the TV show With a Camera Among Animals with his wife, and he could "sell" the image of even the most exotic creature. I already knew him—he'd occasionally served as a film consultant.

Mr. Antoni listened to me and asked:

— Do you know anything about badger behavior?
— No...
— Then please take a walk over to its cage, way in the back of the garden, in that old German section—and then come back to me.

I made my way to a concrete base surrounded by thick, tall iron bars, over which a dense mesh had been stretched. A rusted little plaque read: BADGER. Behind the bars, in a small dirt enclosure, was a smooth tree trunk, completely stripped of bark. And that was it.

Not a trace of an animal.
I stood there for five minutes, saw no burrow or hiding place, and returned to the director's office.
— So? — Gucwiński asked. — I'm making coffee.
— There's nothing there... — I replied.
— You're mistaken. It is there! Underground. It's nocturnal—it feeds at night and sleeps during the day in its burrow.
— And how do you know it's not dead?
Gucwiński gave me a pitying look:
— Sir, every evening the caretaker leaves it a chunk of meat. If it's gone in the morning, that means it was eaten. Simple.
This didn't exactly calm my nerves.
— If it's such a little miner — I asked — aren't you afraid it might escape through a tunnel?
Gucwiński burst out laughing. Offering me coffee, he sat down and looked me straight in the eye:
— Mr. Michał, before the war—as you know—this was a zoo too. And there was a badger in that cage. Of course, not *this* badger. This one came from an exchange. The Germans were excellent naturalists. They worked with precision. That's not just a regular cage—it's a concrete bucket filled with dirt. That badger has no chance of digging his way out!
I made a casual remark that a school field trip also had no chance of seeing a live badger during visiting hours. The director agreed and added:

— True. But I'm the only one with a badger. No one else! There used to be one in Kraków, but it died. Right now, I have the most animal species of any zoo in Poland. I get calls every day asking for exchanges.

I asked if he would consider lending the badger to our film. I showed him the relevant part of the script. He read it quickly ... and declined. But as I was leaving, he added:

— There are badgers in the Rzeszów forests, where you will be filming. Talk to the poachers. But I'm warning you—it's a dangerous animal. It's got teeth—so-called "side jaws"—as sharp as a shark's. It can bite with a pressure of 100 kilograms per square centimeter. It can split a chicken, a fox, or a rabbit in half. If you come across one on a forest path, I suggest you run. Fast. It can lunge at you and ... bite off your manhood in one snap.

I turned a little pale.

Seeing my expression, the director patted me on the shoulder and—walking me to the door—said:

— Relax. A badger can run 30 kilometers per hour, but only for a short while. It tires quickly. It hunts earthworms and baby birds mostly out of laziness—they're easy to catch. But it loves sneaking into henhouses.

And then he added:

— If, by some miracle, you do catch a badger—intact, not torn up— I'd be happy to buy it from you. And I'll pay well.

After a moment, he added:

— But in my opinion, you won't catch one. And you won't film that scene. That got my back up.

— We'll manage. Once we're on location. We've handled worse problems than this. Gucwiński smiled, waved goodbye, and called over his shoulder:

— But if it doesn't work out—drop by again. Maybe we'll figure something out ...?

On our crew, we had a prop master named Jerzy Matysiak—a short guy with a huge personality, a former jockey (in my opinion, booted from the racetrack for fixing races), affectionately nicknamed *Koń* (which means "Horse"). He was absolutely indispensable in the art department, especially when it came to handling farm animals (horses in particular), wagons, carts, stables, and the like.

But beyond that, Koń was a born filmmaker—he had a knack for saving the day on set. He'd pull off the wildest ideas the creators threw at him, building something from nothing, rigging up special effects with little more than string and a hammer. Honestly, MacGyver could've learned a thing or two from him.

That's why he was a favorite among several directors, serving as their "creative assistant" and it didn't take long before Ryszard Ber became one of his fans, too. Everyone called him Koń—his real name was practically forgotten. Only people he didn't like ever heard him say, "For some folks, I'm just Koń. But to you, I'm Mr. Horse."

Looking back, I'm convinced Koń saved the production of *Popielec*. I adored him for how effective he was.

It wasn't with the cinematographer or the set designers but with Koń that I discussed all the animal scenes from the script. As for the "dead" horse and cow scenes—Koń wasn't worried. He knew exactly how to "lay them down" without hurting them. He even solved the issue with the deer later on location. A forester brought us a live deer, and Koń offered it a glass of vodka. When it passed out, he tied it by the legs and hung it upside down from a tree for a quick shot (yep, that footage made it into the final film). Once untied, the deer sobered up and wandered off into the woods. That scene was very important—it showed how primitive snares worked. (A wire loop on the ground would tighten around the leg, trigger a lever, and fling the animal upward with a flexible tree branch.) In the final scene of the series, the main character—Juzuś Garstka—falls into an identical trap and can't escape.

As for the badger—Koń had no ideas.

And then dir. Ber added fuel to the fire:

— Well, Michał, if you manage to catch a badger—I'll buy you the best bottle of whisky you want.

— Make it a Chivas — I said, quick on the draw. — But if I fail, I'm buying.

Deal!

I remembered one of my other mentors, Tadeusz Drewno, who always said: "There are no matters that can't be handled, there are only shitty production managers."

So off we went to Rzeszow, full crew in tow.

Once we settled into our hotel rooms, which had been converted into offices, prop storage and various workspaces, we kicked off the first autumn shoot. I passed along a message to the crew to spread the word to locals on set: I was looking to hire a real-deal poacher.

Didn't take long. A tall fellow in a gray suit showed up at my office door offering his services. Let's call him K1—since I genuinely can't remember his name.

— I know where there's a badger — he said straight up, grinning from ear to ear. — And I know how to catch it. Got an hour?

I did.

We took a taxi about 40 km out of town, then went into the woods until we reached a small, empty forest cabin—more like a shepherd's hut than an actual house—sitting on a hilltop clearing.

— The badger's under the floor — K1 announced. — I heard it scratching around at night.

We walked around the cabin. I counted several holes in the ground, like oversized molehills.

— Those are the badger's ventilation shafts! — K1 informed me.

— Yeah, I know ... — I muttered, still fresh off my zoo education.

— Are you sure there's really a badger here? — I asked, skeptical.

— Have you seen it?

— I heard it. Two nights ago. If you stay here with me tonight, you'll hear it too! It's here.

— Okay ... but how exactly do we catch it? — I asked, baiting him.

— Do you have a pyrotechnician on your crew?

— Yeah. He got in from Łódź yesterday.

— You see those five burrow holes? We'll drop smoke bombs into four of them and stretch a strong net over the fifth. The badger'll bolt like he's on fire—right into the net. Guaranteed! Ha! Then we give him a knock on the head, and he's yours.

— So? You staying? I've got a kettle and some tea...

I did a quick internal inventory. We'd need our "pyro guy" with his gear, a metal net, maybe a baseball bat. We could transport the badger in a small van, used for props.

But what if those holes weren't badger burrows? What if they were just from moles? And what about the production office? Wardrobe was buzzing, the makeup department was rolling, the plan for the first day of shooting was ready, Wehrmacht vehicles were booked, rooms were waiting for lead actors ... Okay. No shower tonight. I'm staying.

I wrote a quick note for the production team, via the secretariat: "Urgent matter. Back tomorrow." Then I sent the taxi driver off with instructions to come back at 7 a.m. the next day.

The night passed quietly—too quietly. ... We barely spoke,

listening hard for any sound beneath the floorboards. We smoked a pack of extra strong cigarettes and sipped sugarless black tea. I half-dozed through the night, one ear tuned to the forest, birds and all. But under the floor—nothing.

When I said goodbye to K1, he looked like a kicked dog.
— I'm sorry. He's here—I swear! I don't know what's going on. I'm staying. If he shows up, I'll let you know.

I left my phone number and returned to civilization—dirty, sleep-deprived and grumpy.   I never told anyone what went down. K1 never called in the following days.

The shoot was hitting its stride just as the political atmosphere in Poland grew increasingly tense. Solidarity strikes, and on TV, there was talk of cracking down on "agitators." When we got back to Wroclaw in November 1981—without ever having filmed Scene 59—I was still relatively calm about my bet with the director. I knew we had another shot at filming the badger scene in spring, in the same region.

Kosarewicz and his team were prepping the set interiors at the Wrocław Film Studio, including the Hladik cottage. And then came that cursed day—December 13th.

We heard it on the radio and TV: Martial law had been declared.

It threw our entire production into chaos. Phones were shut down nationwide for weeks.   A military curfew was introduced—no public movement between 10 p.m. and 6 a.m. Rationing of basic food products was expanded to include things like toilet paper, which you could only get by trading in a kilogram of wastepaper. And so on ...

But the worst part? No communication.

We lost contact with our out-of-town crew and most of our lead actors. The Wrocław team—called the "creative-auxiliary unit" in film slang—kept showing up at the studio every day, asking what we'd do next. Meanwhile, the set construction crew kept working in the halls, and by the end of December, we had all the interiors ready for shooting.

There was no choice but to try and make the best of it. Luckily, trains were still running.

The irreplaceable Rysia, Assistant director, our queen of the shooting schedule, put together a studio plan for the next month based on actors' availability, not locations (which were already built). Our team sent messengers with permits and letters all over

Poland—to actors' homes. Each courier's job was to get a clear yes or no from the addressee and bring it back to the production office.

The saving grace? Most of the actors outside Wrocław—mainly from Warsaw and Gdańsk—had plenty of time on their hands. Theaters were shut down, and the media were broadcasting only military propaganda under the "Military Council for National Salvation."

I brought the director and cinematographer back for an extended stay. And guess what? It worked. Once we had an actor on site, we filmed all their scenes from different episodes in one go. In one scene, they'd say "good morning," in the next, "goodbye."

In fact—our daily productivity skyrocketed. There were no distractions, no temptations, and no way to do anything other than shoot the damn movie.

In the scene where the badger was eaten (yes, that scene really was in the script), its innards were faked using regular meat, which Hladik (Tomasz Zaliwski) cooked in a pan. Hanging on the wall of the set was a real badger pelt—borrowed from the same local museum I'd gotten a stuffed giraffe from the year before for the film *The Great May Day Out.*

I had time to wonder what badgers actually do during the winter, so I did a bit of reading. Turns out—just like other wild animals living in Poland (bears, ground squirrels, moles, marmots and hamsters)—badgers hibernate. But when there's even a brief winter thaw, they wake up, step out of their burrow, grab a bite to eat and something to drink and then go back to sleep. They cleverly block parts of their burrow and ventilation shafts to keep the cold out. During these few months of sleep, they live off their body fat— losing up to a third of their weight.

Eventually, the harsh restrictions of martial law began to ease. The regime had initially terrified the public by brutally crushing "illegal" demonstrations and strikes, but at the same time, they began lifting the most oppressive travel bans. Phone service was slowly restored. Yes, calls were monitored—and so was the mail—but no one paid much attention to that anymore. We survived the worst of it under what were, ironically, almost greenhouse-like conditions.

By April, we were back out on location—same places as before—back at Hotel Rzeszów and back to shooting in Wesoła. We shot portions of the badger hunt scene—reverse angles, ready for later editing—with the appropriate dialogue ("Hit him in the snout!"

etc.) featuring Jasiek (actor Skupień) and Hladik (Zaliwski), but sadly ... without Stefek (who was in the script) and—most tragically—without the badger ...

The actors waved their murder tools around in front of the camera. Ber still held out hope that I'd come through and we'd get two final inserts: the badger running through the grass and the scene where it gets pinned to the ground with a pitchfork and axe.

My pride couldn't take a loss, so I started the hunt again—reaching out to subject-matter experts: foresters, gamekeepers, local farmers in Wesoła and so on. I held dozens of conversations.

Of course, I tried not to let other responsibilities slip—but at some point, I started noticing that parts of the crew—especially the lighting guys and drivers—were beginning to think I was completely out of my mind. And I'm pretty sure that when I turned my back, they were twirling fingers at their temples.

That's when another poacher showed up at the hotel—initially anonymous. Let's call him K2. He seemed a little more reasonable than the first guy ... or so I thought at the time.

They sent him straight to me. He looked a bit hungover, with dark circles under his eyes, dressed in a camo jacket and army boots. And right away, he filled me with hope:

— There's a badger under the oak. Not far from here. Wanna see?

I did.

We drove out, and I saw the entrance to the burrow tucked beneath the roots of an old, sprawling oak. Nearby were the remains of a chicken and a whole mess of bloodied feathers.

— Heh-heh — fresh signs. He snatched the chicken and dragged it into the den.

I walked around the oak, looking for a ventilation shaft. Found nothing.

— So how do we lure him out? — I asked.

He shot back with "Do you have a pyrotechnician or something?" Funny how every single one of these guys immediately had a plan that involved our pyrotechnician.

And yes—by some miracle—we managed once again to bring our guy from the Łódź Film Studio back onto the team in spring of '82. (That studio had the only pyrotechnics department in Poland at the time—a total monopoly.) He came with all the necessary gear, housed in a separate, specially outfitted truck. It took all kinds of permits, usage logs, safety plans and red tape to make it happen.

— I've got him! — I said.

— Perfect. We'll tempt the badger out tomorrow evening with some fresh meat. And your guy can plant a charge—whatever you've got—under a plank at the burrow's entrance. As soon as the badger steps out—BOOM—he'll go flying. Then we'll smack him on the head and …

— Hold up. We? Who's we exactly?

K2 was prepared. He laid out exactly how we should position ourselves in a nearby tree, three meters off the ground, with as few people as possible: he himself and the pyrotechnician with a remote trigger system—preferably with two failsafes. And maybe I, the production manager, if I really wanted to be there. When he started spouting off part numbers for fuses and wiring, I began to suspect he was ex-military—someone who used to hunt with live rounds. K2 offered to build a simple blind at a safe distance from the action and set it up quietly during the day. I kind of liked the idea. I let the pyro guy and his driver in on the plan. They refused outright.

— An explosion? No way!

The next day, I went to the agreed meeting point with K2. I was already feeling pretty defeated—but I underestimated the motivational power of money. K2 was still game.

— Don't worry, boss. I've got everything we need. I've got my own dynamite. Let's do it tomorrow. Just bring a vehicle so we can take the badger back.

A day passed. I came back—with sacks, a blanket, and a net for the animal. It never occurred to me that if the dazed badger woke up, it could bite us and escape.

K2 had already installed a fairly sturdy pseudo-hunting stand in a nearby tree—basically a platform with one side wall, about 20 meters from the oak. He'd hidden a thick wooden board near the burrow entrance, with sticks of dynamite underneath. He unspooled a long cable to the detonator. He'd even brought meat.

We were counting on the badger being in deep hibernation—hoping our movements and sounds wouldn't spook it into running.

— What do you think? — I asked K2. — Will the badger come out for the bait?

— Of course! — he grinned. — Remember, badgers don't need much light to go looking for food at night. Their hearing and smell are top-notch. If he's hungry—and this time of year, he will be—

then we've got him for sure.

As dusk fell, we sat on the lookout platform, wrapped in blankets, staring at the burrow entrance. What we didn't anticipate: a forest at night can be pitch black. You couldn't see a thing. At all. We had to rely entirely on sound.

At one point, just as I was nodding off and seeing spots in front of my eyes, K2 shouted something—and then …

WHAM!

A blinding flash. A thunderous explosion.

Our platform cracked—we fell to the ground.

Double shock—for my eardrums and a few other body parts. K2 scrambled up with a flashlight; I crawled after him. Then we saw the damage.

The blast was no joke—it blew out a chunk of the oak's root system, leaving a crater ten times the size of the original hole. The meat had flown off into the leaves. There was no badger. K2 had detonated the charge for no good reason, though he later tried to justify it.

If I'd had a tail, I would've tucked it between my legs in shame.

After a few days of recovering from that disaster, I started collecting intel from local foresters—who had seen a badger, when and where. I heard some pretty intense stories: hunting dogs mauled to death, fences around chicken coops chewed right through. One French tourist tried to kill a badger with a stick—hoping to harvest its famously "medicinal" fat. That (obviously failed) attempt cost him three fingers on his right hand and part of his calf. There were tales of brutal hunts with gaffs and axes, full-on chases ending with the animal so torn apart that it was impossible to skin it in any usable pieces. One badger had apparently gotten caught in a snare—and to escape, chewed off its own leg and limped back into the forest.

Meanwhile, Ber started poking at me again.

— So, when are you buying me that whisky we bet on?

I was losing it—getting feverish with frustration. At night, I dreamed of herds of badgers running in circles around me. Their leader would rear up on his hind legs and give me this smug look, like, "Coo-coo! I'm right here, buddy!" Even during the day, looking out the production office window, I started seeing things. I knew that no other animal could be convincingly made up to look like a badger—and forget about using any nonexistent CGI. This wasn't Hollywood. I started to accept the crushing realization that I'd taken on an impossible task.

I kept my composure, mostly—but I was getting jumpy. I snapped at "surprises" on set. Thankfully, my closest team handled the giant film-machine of logistics, scheduling, and crew wrangling like pros. Filming moved forward despite the usual technical mishaps and the increasingly impossible scheduling of actors.

Days passed ... and suddenly, a light appeared at the end of my badger-shaped tunnel.

The hotel reception told me that some guy had been calling at random times, urgently trying to reach me about something "of great importance," but refused to leave a number. It turned out to be K1— and he finally got through.

He was thrilled.

He told me the badger had returned to the forest cabin. He'd seen it with his own eyes—rampaging around the property at night—and heard thumping under the floorboards. This was our golden opportunity to finally carry out the original plan: smoke him out.

— Let's go, teddy bear — I thought.

More good news landed on my desk shortly after: a letter from the Ministry of Agriculture. We had official permission to capture one (1) badger. One.

I managed to talk our film pyrotechnician into joining Operation Cabin. And once he found out it didn't involve napalm, machine guns or actual explosives—just smoke bombs—he surprisingly agreed. (Naturally, after threatening me with extra daily rates and overtime pay.)

I didn't care anymore. I was going all in. This was going to be our final shot. One last chance. And this time—we were going to get that damn badger.

If there was ever going to be an end to my madness—which, at that point, was clearly a form of psychosis bordering on mild schizophrenia—then the climax of this whole hunt for one poor, solitary animal was finally about to reach its grand finale.

The moment had come: four holes in the ground around the forest cabin were plugged with smoke bombs, ready to go, and a double-layered net had been secured over the fifth. Earlier, to prove he wasn't just making things up, K1 had shown me the badger's latrine—a little pit dug specifically for droppings. (I had no idea badgers were such hygienic creatures—they remove all waste from the burrow and bury it outside.) He also pointed out the distinctive tracks of the badger's front paws: five clawed toes in a neat little fan shape.

Once we lit the smoke bombs, we successfully filled the entire clearing with choking, eye-burning fog. Coughing our lungs out, we stood at the ready by the net. The weather, for once, was on our side—no wind. The thick smoke from the burning bombs rose upward, even seeping out of two other holes we hadn't known existed. After a few minutes, the canisters burned out, and a column of smoke drifted into the sky.

Half an hour passed.

It became painfully clear: the badger had completely ignored our efforts. He hadn't exited where we'd laid the trap—known in hunting slang as a "blind." We exchanged the usual repertoire of manly profanity.

What happened?

Had the badger died down there, suffocating?

Did he have an escape plan—tunnel B?

Had he simply burrowed into a deeper corridor of his labyrinth?

Our theorizing was cut short by a sound—soft at first, then growing louder: the unmistakable wail of a siren. From a fire truck.

Unfortunately, it was headed straight for us.

A big red fire truck rolled onto the clearing. Several men stepped out.

After a quick inspection—and me nobly taking the blame—I was issued a 500-zlotys fine for "creating a fire hazard."

And that ... was the humiliating end of the badger hunt.

* * *

After we wrapped the shoot in Podkarpacie, the core technical team returned to Wrocław. It was time for editing and sound design. The director spent his days holed up in his favorite editing room at the Łódź Film Studio. We kept in touch by phone.

I dragged myself back to the zoo. Director Gucwiński greeted me warmly, with just a hint of satisfaction in his voice:

— So? Didn't I tell you it wouldn't work out? I had a feeling you'd come back ...   — You also mentioned you had an idea ...

— I said, gloomily. — What did you mean?   —
Exactly. You're still missing the badger-in-the-grass shot and the one where he takes a hit to the snout, right?

— Right.

— Well, let me tell you up front—he won't be doing any running here ... but as for the other shot, I think we can handle it without much trouble. —

Really? — I asked, a flicker of hope in my voice.

— I trust you'll name me as a consultant again, like last time. Okay? Got your cameraman handy? Listen, I mean—the grass here is just as green as it is under Rzeszów, right?

Gucwiński clearly loved rhetorical questions. I shut up and listened, as advised.

— We'll sedate my badger — Gucwiński continued — pull him out onto the grass, and you can position him however you want for the camera. Just don't hurt him. You'll "kill" him cinematically, got it? But we'll need to coordinate closely. Let's say ... next week. I'll confirm.

I lit up. Back at the office, I immediately called the camera operator and asked him to come to Wrocław for a day or two. I booked the camera. Talked to Koń and his assistant. Sounded the alarm in makeup about fake blood. The only thing I didn't know was how the zoo director planned to actually get the badger out.

After the fact, I learned that the sedation process went relatively smoothly. The zookeepers had been feeding him meat laced with luminal—or some other heavy-duty tranquilizer normally reserved for much larger animals. When the badger didn't surface from his burrow for two days, the cage crew dug into the ground—nervously, not knowing how he'd react. They worked under the protection of colleagues armed with sticks and rakes.

At the bottom of the concrete enclosure, they found him: filthy, covered in mud. When they dragged him out to a small grassy clearing, I was already there with a mini-crew.

The badger—completely knocked out and literally limp—was hosed down with water. Our makeup artist, the ever-dependable, was clearly horrified when asked to towel him dry. He gave me a pleading look, but eventually pulled himself together—and soon the badger was camera-ready.

The props team propped him up from behind using a forked board to raise his stubby head. They wedged a small stick into his mouth to show off his teeth. He looked, honestly, like a circus seal balancing a ball.

The plan was to film it in 16 mm with reverse roll: starting with the axe near his mouth, then quickly jerking it upward. When projected in standard playback, it would appear as a believable blow—perfectly synced with the line "Hit him in the snout!"

The makeup team painted the axe handle and the badger's mouth bright red with Max Factor. The prop guy handled the axe. Camera rolled. We did three takes.

I called the shoot a wrap and phoned the director with the good news. The negative was sent to the lab.

Once copied, the footage was spliced into its proper spot. The last missing shot needed to complete the scene was handled by our client—Telewizja Polska, which found a few seconds of footage in the Tele-Ar archive showing a badger running through the grass ... in Australia. The grass there was a bit yellowish, but it was a reasonable compromise. We figured no one watching on a small TV would notice the difference.

Rysiek Ber and I agreed to call off our whisky bet. I hadn't caught the badger physically—but the original, key dramatic shot still made it into the series.

The music was composed by Jerzy Maksymiuk, who also conducted the acclaimed Sinfonia Varsovia. Maksymiuk wove motifs from the Carpathian folk tradition seamlessly into his score.

To this day, I still consider the series' musical leitmotif—played during the opening credits of each episode—to be one of its greatest triumphs.

The final screening at the "Silesia" Film Unit went astonishingly smoothly. Team director Ernest Bryll declared it an excellent series, and that TVP would have no reason to object to anything. How wrong he was—we would find out just a few weeks later.

The approval screening of *Popielec* at TVP headquarters on Woronicza Street had been scheduled far in advance, toward the end of 1982. Aside from the director, I was the only one from the crew in attendance. The cinematographer, sound editors and lead editor didn't show up. Screenings of light-sensitive film were done "off two reels," meaning the projector ran the picture while a synced magnetic tape deck played the final sound mix. This "dual-reel" system allowed for post-screening fixes before final mastering.

We screened two hour-long episodes early in the morning with representatives from the programming department. Director Ber and I sat in the back row, watching for the audience's reactions. There were some disapproving hisses and murmured comments during the more emotionally charged scenes. But the real red flags came during the hallway chat between a few women editors between screenings.

Back in the theater, Ber was visibly nervous, pacing. He looked like he'd seen a ghost.

At the time, you could still smoke in the halls at TVP. Ber lit up his first cigarette just as we overheard a loud exchange between two editors, who didn't seem to care that we were standing right there:

— You know what, Maria? I'm honestly shocked. I thought we were going to air this during prime time, but what I've seen today gives me chills. This is not for young audiences!

— Well, we're certainly not airing it after ten p.m. ...

— We'll have to prepare an introductory segment or something. Did you see those sex scenes? And those poor animals—such cruelty! I wonder what the execs will say ...

At that point, Ber jumped up and ran off. I thought maybe he was headed to the restroom. A few minutes later, they called us back for the next episode. I went in alone —reluctantly. The screening started without waiting for the latecomers. After about 20 minutes, Ber slipped back into the room and sat beside me. He was clearly shaken, but managed to keep his hands from trembling.

And then—Episode 4. The badger scene. I was dying to see how the editors would react. To my surprise—absolutely nothing happened. Because the shot of the badger getting hit in the snout? Wasn't there.

There was a brief splice pop, and the sound went out of sync for a few seconds. Then everything returned to normal.

After the screening, outside the building, Ber confessed. During the break, he'd gone into the projection booth. With help from the projectionist, he found the badger shot on the preview reel and ... cut it out with scissors. They patched the splice with a bit of Scotch tape. Apparently, nobody in the audience noticed they'd missed anything.

***

That's where my badger saga ends.

After the screening, I still held out hope that the director might add the missing shot back into the master print. But that never happened.

TVP officially accepted the film—but then shelved it for two more years.

Maybe it would've stayed on the shelf even longer ... but someone at the network had the good sense to submit the series to the Teleconfronto Festival in Italy, where it returned with a special distinction: "For its original, rhetoric-free portrayal of Polish village life during the Nazi occupation."

Still, after its first TV broadcast, a heated debate erupted in the press:
Was it okay to show Polish peasants in such a raw, non-idealized way? Viewers wrote letters to the network demanding the show be pulled from the air—for its unfiltered social scenes and earthy dialogue. All serial became a cultural flashpoint, splitting critics into two camps. Some accused the creators of cynicism and cruelty. Others praised the directing as bold and modern, the cinematography as beautiful and the performances as mature and powerful.

Post scriptum

Years later, with some distance from my mad chase after the elusive badger, I realized I needed to add a word of caution— especially for younger filmmakers.

Do not, under any circumstances, try to imitate what I did.

Never. Ever.
It deserves only condemnation.

Granted, the Polish Hunting Law Act wasn't passed until 1995— fifteen years after the events described here—but nature conservation in Poland has a long and noble tradition. And we broke just about every rule and principle of ethical hunting. Today, such acts of animal cruelty can carry a prison sentence of up to five years.

Many of my other actions at the time were equally far from legally sound—or even from basic common sense. Not to mention what could politely be called economic misuse of resources. I have no defense—except that I just really wanted to catch a live badger.

So, all I can do is apologize to the Reader and present this tale as a historical document of one young man's psychological detour—a 30-year-old in the Poland of the 1980s, doing whatever it took ... in the name of cinema.

Final Remarks

Now that all the pieces are already in, printed and available to the readers, the contents of the book can be analyzed more comprehensively and accurately. As mentioned in the Introduction, one of the major assets of the collection is the diversity of the pieces in several aspects or areas, starting with their form, which ranges from a short story or an essay to a poem or a conversation. Some of the compositions are purposefully inconsistent in form; they start as a story and, with the authors' emotions rising, they turn into a discourse resembling a play. Most of the essays are straightforward and realistic; but, there is one compound contribution that consists of a short story and a poem, both rather metaphysical but logically connected and their unconventional nature satisfactorily explained.

The most obvious area of the compilation's diversity is the geographical location of the authors, the information about which is unambiguously provided in parentheses next to the authors' names. While the majority of the contributors reside either in the United States (on the East Coast, in Virginia, North Carolina, Pennsylvania, New York or Maine) and Poland (primarily in Poznań, where my roots are, but also in Warsaw and other cities or towns), there are also several pieces sent to me from Germany (even though only one of the authors was born there) and one from Austria (from an author born in Poland). Thus, it is rather clear that not in all of the cases, the current residence is synonymous with the author's nationality/ethnicity. Because one of the frequent themes is emigration/immigration (along with its challenges and advantages) or simply relocation (temporary or permanent) – usually in search of one's ideal place to live – it is quite common that the authors do not reside in a country where they were born. There is one particularly interesting case, that of a man born in the USA and presently residing in Poland, which happens to be a situation opposite to mine (much more common, needless to say).

Traveling to countless places all over the world is addressed by several authors, in a couple of cases as the main topic, in others as a side motif, and, occasionally, in the description of circumstances of some personal experiences, sometimes romantic, sometimes traumatic and sometimes related to unexpected but serious health conditions. What is significant about most of those pieces is the perceptiveness of the authors' comments regarding the character, atmosphere and landscape of those places, sometimes remote and sometimes just around the corner, as well as their historical, cultural and religious background and/or the people living there.

What was to be expected, there are two essays entirely involved in natural disasters, one recent, triggered by the current events, taking place in a town and its area, and one, in a relatively remote past (in 1860), affecting a steamboat, but both involving quite numerous casualties. Both of the stories testify to their authors' sensitivity, even though only one of them happened to be a witness of the tragic occurrence.

Discussed in the book are human relations of different kinds, between parents and children (from both points of view), grandparents and grandchildren (from the perspective of the young ones), between siblings, spouses and friends, and even between a girlfriend and a boyfriend. The theme of widowhood (mostly in the context of the void resulting from the loss of a spouse and different ways of dealing with it) is honestly and convincingly elaborated on by four authors, all female about the same age and all losing their husbands at roughly the same stage of married life. Those stories, on the one hand, corroborate the well-known statistics regarding men's life expectancy being shorter than women's and, on the other, illustrate women's mental toughness (contrary to general beliefs), which, however, does not diminish their tendency to be more caring, devoted and emotional. Animals are the main theme of two stories; however, human relations and human nature are still at the forefront of their authors' focus and motivation.

There are three engaging essays focused on professional careers, all written by relatively young gentlemen. Each treatise, however, is much more than just a series of advice about choosing and/or pursuing a career of one's dream. The three authors provide an abundance of crucial circumstances and justified motivations – all leading to some ingenious philosophical ideas and speculations that cover life in a comprehensive, objective and extremely mature way, and address matters far beyond those related merely to a job, however impressive or appealing it may appear.

Several themes refer to the arts in a broad sense of the word. There are two pieces addressing the process of music appreciation, one focused on classical music and one on popular. Artistic creativity is discussed in two entries, one in the context of any artistic expression (but musical in particular) and one focused on painting. Filmmaking, professional and amateur, is the subject matter of two different essays, one related to unexpected complications caused by the scheme of trying to capture a wild animal on film and one concentrated on the idea of teaching teenagers how to make films and promoting their productions at a festival created specifically for that purpose.

At least two of the articles in the collection do a great job reminding us that people in our lives are not only those that we have had the pleasure of meeting in person because they are our relatives, friends, acquaintances or associates, but also many perfect strangers, people we may have desired to meet but never have and seldom do because they are out of our league. They are celebrities, famous artists and intellectuals whose creations – especially in the form of literature, film and music – are indispensable and omnipresent parts of our lives. Some of them come and go; others, like Elvis (in one of our stories), stay with us forever.

Since the whole project puts people in the center of attention, it was to be expected that birth and death would become frequent elements of the stories. And, yes, they did. There are two essays primarily focused on the birth of a child and a few concentrated, not entirely though, on the death of someone very close to the authors. While the former is rightly described as an amazing miracle or reward, a life-changing event in the lives of the parents, the latter is consistently associated with an enormously painful loss, a tragedy that is hard or even impossible to be prepared for, and affecting the survivors' lives for a long time. In either situation, the impact on the author (and other people) is extraordinary – testifying to or reminding us about the axiom that birth and death encapsulate the fundamental cycle of human existence, marking the beginning and end of an individual's journey. However, regardless of whether a given story is focused on someone that has passed away or a living person, the journey is usually quite complex. All the journeys, when put together, brim with expected, unpredictable and completely accidental turns, minor and vital decisions, and partial or absolute resolutions – either dependent on or unrelated to the previous circumstances and developments. As a result, they offer an abundance of ideas for philosophical deliberations and discussions.

Betsy and I consider ourselves serious cinephiles. Over thirty-five years or so, together, we have been watching artistic films from all around the world, from Charlie Chaplin's to Fred Zinnemann's to Quentin Tarantino's, from Jean Renoir's to Federico Fellini's to Akira Kurosawa's. We believe that we have seen almost everything in terms of cinema artform that is worth watching, with the possible exceptions mostly related to recent years – a period in which we, like most people of our age, do not find many masterpieces appealing to our tastes. Consequently, out of boredom at the pre-bedtime hours, we have switched to watching some TV series, not dramas (enough of that in our own lives), not slapstick (we never liked it), but well-written mysteries with some elements of humor, made in many different parts of the world, the USA, the United Kingdom, France, Italy, Germany, Sweden and a few other countries. Recently, we have been especially fond of the English miniseries *The Chelsea Detective* (2002; starring Adrian Scarborough, Vanessa Emme, Sophie Stone, Lucy Phelps and Peter Bankolé), because its crime puzzles are realistic and complicated enough but not too foggy for the viewer to lose interest, and because the main characters, four coppers in charge of the murder investigations (two men and two women), are captivating individuals, not only smart enough to figure out who-done-it and loyal and helpful to each other, but, more importantly, genuinely human beings, enormously caring, understanding and honorably addressing problems of others and their own.

However, the reason why I mention this series in the context of our book project is its unusual formula (more typical in a morality tale than in a detective story), according to which, at the end of each episode (or almost each), once the culprit gets arrested, all things fall into place. The supporting characters (each group different in every episode), conspicuously experiencing serious issues in their relationships with their dearest ones, not only are cleared of suspicion despite the lies they have been caught on telling (which made them suspects), but finally realize their own mistakes, in addition to accepting the wisdom behind the famous aphorism "Nobody's Perfect" (from Billy Wilder's *Some Like It Hot*, 1959) and making necessary amendments to find reconciliation and peace with others. Admittedly, such multi-level uplifting resolutions may appear somewhat naïve, stretched or unrealistic, hardly to be expected in real life or extremely artistic films, but, considering the idealistic premise of our project, they are arguably worth mentioning here – as something all of us should strive to accomplish no matter how difficult it may seem.

To conclude the whole project with one more philosophical quotation, or, as a matter of fact, a quotation within a quotation, I have decided to reach out to Larry McMurtry's novel *Duane's Depressed* (1999), the third part of the author's Thalia/Duane pentalogy (started with *The Last Picture Show*, 1966), and share the protagonist's thoughts at the autumn stage of his life:

The distant horizon, which had been clear and sharp at sunrise, was already hazy from heat. He had the Thoreau book with him and looked through it idly now and then, but could not really get up enough momentum to read it straight through. There was one sentence he liked so much that he had underlined it and stuck a little piece of paper in the   book to mark the place. "I went into the woods because I wished to live deliberately, to front only the essential facts of life," the sentence read, "and see if I could not learn what   it had to teach, and not, when I came to die, discover that I had not lived."

Duane read the sentence over and over again, forty or fifty times; it was that sentence that explained exactly what he himself was trying to do—explained it so clearly that he didn't really want to read the rest of *Walden*. He had parked his pickup, left his   family; and settled in the cabin to attempt to learn about life and not feel that he was just plodding through it. [pp. 308-309]

When I wrote the Introduction to share with the potential contributors, I had a lot of hope related to the content of the book and the number of people participating. I have to admit that the reason why, at that time, I put the adjective 'tentative' in parentheses next to the numeral '28' in the subtitle was a result of my belief that the expectation of including twenty-eight pieces in the collection was optimistic on my part and rather presumptuous. But, as it has turned out, the ultimate number is … thirty-three, just a little bit better. Thus, what has happened in the end exceeds my initial expectations.

I have read carefully every piece submitted to me for the project, and, as a result, I have learned a great deal not only about the authors (even those that I had believed I knew very well) and their lives, but also about life in general. It is not presumptuous on my part to expect that a lesson of a similar character and comparable proportions will be learned by anyone who happens the read this volume from cover to cover.

HH

Bibliography

Auster, Paul. *The Brooklyn Follies.* New York: Henry Holt and Company, 2006.

Auster, Paul. *Oracle Night.* New York: Henry Holt and Company, 2003.

Hoffmann, Henryk. *Ironies, Coincidences and Absurdities in My Ordinary Life on Both Sides of the Atlantic.* Springfield, OH: Higher Ground Books and Media, 2019.

Janis, Byron, with Maria Cooper Janis. *Chopin and Beyond: My Extraordinary Life in Music and the Paranormal.* Hoboken, NJ: John Wiley & Sons, 2010.

McMurtry, Larry. *Duane's Depressed.* New York: Simon & Schuster, 1999.

Thoreau, Henry David. *Walden; or Life in the Woods.* Layton, UT: Gibbs Smith, (1854) 2017.

Other titles from Higher Ground Books & Media:

Ironies, Coincidences and Absurdities in My Ordinary Life on Both Sides of the Atlantic by Henryk Hoffmann

It's Only a Game by Darrel Johnson

Our Journey of Faith by Miranda Thornsberry

Single, Sober, & Serious by Rebecca Benston

One Day in May by Joanne Piccari Coleman

Bloom by Robin Stone

Of Love and Weight Loss by Marjorie Joseph

The Bottom of This by Tramaine Hannah

Shameless Persistence by Sandra Bretting

Soul Solutions by Terri Kozlowski

The Children's Bread by Terra Kern

Through the Sliver of a Frosted Window by Robin Melet

Music and the Holy Spirit by Stephen Shepherd

The Real Prison Diaries by Judy Frisby

Full Gospel by Jerry C. Crossley

Add these titles to your collection today!

http://www.highergroundbooksandmedia.com

***

Need Bulk Copies?

If you would like to order bulk copies of this book or any other title at Higher Ground Books & Media, please contact us at highergroundbooksandmedia@gmail.com.

We offer discounts for purchases of 10 or more copies. Excellent for small groups, book clubs, classrooms, etc.

Get in touch today and get a set of great stories for your students or group members.

Share Your Story with the World

At Higher Ground Books & Media, we believe every story has the power to heal, inspire, and change lives. Whether you're ready to publish your first book or seeking support to refine your message, our author services are designed to help you every step of the way.

We offer editing, ghostwriting, publishing, and platform development to help you bring your message to life and reach the readers who need it most.

Let's work together to help others heal, use their gifts, and grow in faith—one book at a time.

📖 *Learn more at HigherGroundBooksandMedia.com*

www.ingramcontent.com/pod-product-compliance
Lightning Source LLC
La Vergne TN
LVHW051042080426
835508LV00019B/1664